53rd Annual Meeting of the Association for Computational Linguistics and 7th International Joint Conference on Natural Language Processing of the Asian Federation of Natural Language Processing

(ACL-IJCNLP 2015)

System Demonstrations

Beijing, China
26 – 31 July 2015

ISBN: 978-1-5108-0847-8

Printed from e-media with permission by:

Curran Associates, Inc.
57 Morehouse Lane
Red Hook, NY 12571

Some format issues inherent in the e-media version may also appear in this print version.

Printed by Curran Associates, Inc. (2015)

For permission requests, please contact the Association for Computational Linguistics at the address below.

Association for Computational Linguistics
209 N. Eighth Street
Stroudsburg, Pennsylvania 18360

Phone: 1-570-476-8006
Fax: 1-570-476-0860

acl@aclweb.org

Additional copies of this publication are available from:

Curran Associates, Inc.
57 Morehouse Lane
Red Hook, NY 12571 USA
Phone: 845-758-0400
Fax: 845-758-2634
Email: curran@proceedings.com
Web: www.proceedings.com

ACL-IJCNLP 2015

The 53rd Annual Meeting of the Association for Computational Linguistics and The 7th International Joint Conference on Natural Language Processing

Proceedings of System Demonstrations

July 26-31, 2015
Beijing, China

Preface

Welcome to the proceedings of the system demonstrations session. This volume contains the papers of the system demonstrations presented at the 53rd Annual Meeting of the Association for Computational Linguistics and the 7th International Joint Conference on Natural Language Processing, on July 26-31, 2015 in Beijing, China.

The system demonstrations program offers the presentation of early research prototypes as well as interesting mature systems. We received 62 submissions, of which 25 were selected for inclusion in the program (acceptance rate of 40.32%) after review by three members of the program committee.

We would like to thank the members of the program committee for their timely help in reviewing the submissions.

System Demonstration Co-Chairs
Hsin-Hsi Chen
Katja Markert

Organizers

Co-Chairs:

Hsin-Hsi Chen, National Taiwan University (Taiwan)
Katja Markert, University of Hanover (Germany) and University of Leeds (UK)

Program Committee:

Johan Bos, University of Groningen (Netherlands)
Miriam Butt, University of Konstanz (Germany)
Wenliang Chen, Soochow University, Suzhou (China)
Gao Cong, Nanyang Technological University (Singapore)
Katja Filippova, Google Inc.
E. Dario Gutierrez, University of Berkeley (USA)
Yufang Hou, University of Heidelberg (Germany)
Hen-Hsen Huang, National Taiwan University (Taiwan)
Wai Lam, The Chinese University of Hong Kong (HK)
Gary Geunbae Lee, POSTECH (Korea)
Maria Liakata, University of Warwick (UK)
Chuan-Jie Lin, National Taiwan Ocean University (Taiwan)
Annie Louis, University of Edinburgh (UK)
Saif Mohammad, National Research Council Canada (Canada)
Roberto Navigli, Sapienza University of Rome (Italy)
Vincent Ng, University of Texas at Dallas (USA)
Malvina Nissim, University of Groningen (Nederlands)
Naoaki Okayaki, Tohoku University (Japan)
Jong Park, KAIST (Korea)
Barbara Plank, the University of Copenhagen (Denmark)
Andrei Popescu-Belis, Idiap Research Institute (Switzerland)
Antonio Reyes, Instituto Superior de Intérpretes y Traductores (Mexico)
Arndt Riester, University of Stuttgart (Germany)
Stefan Riezler, Heidelberg University (Germany)
Satoshi Sekine, New York University (USA)
Ekaterina Shutova, University of Cambridge (UK)
Stefan Siersdorfer, Leibniz-University Hannover (Germany)
Lucia Specia, Sheffield University (UK)
Efstathios Stamatatos, University of the Aegean (Greece)
Hiroya Takamura, Tokyo Institute of Technology (Japan)
Richard Tzong-Han Tsai, National Central University (Taiwan)
Yuen-Hsien Tseng, National Taiwan Normal University (Taiwan)
Yannick Versley, University of Heidelberg (Germany)
Liang-Chih Yu, Yuan Ze University (Taiwan)
Wei Zhang, Institute for Infocomm Research (Singapore)
Heike Zinsmeister, University of Hamburg (Germany)

Table of Contents

Conference Program

Monday, July 27th, 2015

18:00–21:00

A System Demonstration of a Framework for Computer Assisted Pronunciation Training
Renlong Ai and Feiyu Xu

IMI — A Multilingual Semantic Annotation Environment
Francis Bond, Luís Morgado da Costa and Tuan Anh Lê

In-tool Learning for Selective Manual Annotation in Large Corpora
Erik-Lân Do Dinh, Richard Eckart de Castilho and Iryna Gurevych

KeLP: a Kernel-based Learning Platform for Natural Language Processing
Simone Filice, Giuseppe Castellucci, Danilo Croce and Roberto Basili

Multi-modal Visualization and Search for Text and Prosody Annotations
Markus Gärtner, Katrin Schweitzer, Kerstin Eckart and Jonas Kuhn

NEED4Tweet: A Twitterbot for Tweets Named Entity Extraction and Disambiguation
Mena Habib and Maurice van Keulen

Visual Error Analysis for Entity Linking
Benjamin Heinzerling and Michael Strube

A Web-based Collaborative Evaluation Tool for Automatically Learned Relation Extraction Patterns
Leonhard Hennig, Hong Li, Sebastian Krause, Feiyu Xu and Hans Uszkoreit

A Dual-Layer Semantic Role Labeling System
Lun-Wei Ku, Shafqat Mumtaz Virk and Yann-Huei Lee

A system for fine-grained aspect-based sentiment analysis of Chinese
Janna Lipenkova

Plug Latent Structures and Play Coreference Resolution
Sebastian Martschat, Patrick Claus and Michael Strube

Monday, July 27th, 2015 (continued)

SCHNÄPPER: A Web Toolkit for Exploratory Relation Extraction
Thilo Michael and Alan Akbik

OMWEdit - The Integrated Open Multilingual Wordnet Editing System
Luís Morgado da Costa and Francis Bond

SACRY: Syntax-based Automatic Crossword puzzle Resolution sYstem
Alessandro Moschitti, Massimo Nicosia and Gianni Barlacchi

LEXenstein: A Framework for Lexical Simplification
Gustavo Paetzold and Lucia Specia

Sharing annotations better: RESTful Open Annotation
Sampo Pyysalo, Jorge Campos, Juan Miguel Cejuela, Filip Ginter, Kai Hakala, Chen Li, Pontus Stenetorp and Lars Juhl Jensen

A Data Sharing and Annotation Service Infrastructure
Stelios Piperidis, Dimitrios Galanis, Juli Bakagianni and Sokratis Sofianopoulos

JoBimViz: A Web-based Visualization for Graph-based Distributional Semantic Models
Eugen Ruppert, Manuel Kaufmann, Martin Riedl and Chris Biemann

End-to-end Argument Generation System in Debating
Misa Sato, Kohsuke Yanai, Toshinori Miyoshi, Toshihiko Yanase, Makoto Iwayama, Qinghua Sun and Yoshiki Niwa

Multi-level Translation Quality Prediction with QuEst++
Lucia Specia, Gustavo Paetzold and Carolina Scarton

WA-Continuum: Visualising Word Alignments across Multiple Parallel Sentences Simultaneously
David Steele and Lucia Specia

A Domain-independent Rule-based Framework for Event Extraction
Marco A. Valenzuela-Escárcega, Gus Hahn-Powell, Mihai Surdeanu and Thomas Hicks

Storybase: Towards Building a Knowledge Base for News Events
Zhaohui Wu, Chen Liang and C. Lee Giles

WriteAhead: Mining Grammar Patterns in Corpora for Assisted Writing
Tzu-Hsi Yen, Jian-Cheng Wu, Jim Chang, Joanne Boisson and Jason Chang

Monday, July 27th, 2015 (continued)

A System Demonstration of a Framework for Computer Assisted Pronunciation Training

Renlong Ai, Feiyu Xu
German Research Center for Artificial Intelligence, Language Technology Lab
Alt-Moabit 91c, 10559 Berlin, Germany
{renlong.ai, feiyu}@dfki.de

Abstract

In this paper, we demonstrate a system implementation of a framework for computer assisted pronunciation training for second language learner (L2). This framework supports an iterative improvement of the automatic pronunciation error recognition and classification by allowing integration of annotated error data. The annotated error data is acquired via an annotation tool for linguists. This paper will give a detailed description of the annotation tool and explains the error types. Furthermore, it will present the automatic error recognition method and the methods for automatic visual and audio feedback. This system demonstrates a novel approach to interactive and individualized learning for pronunciation training.

1 Introduction

Second language (L2) acquisition is a much greater challenge for human cognition than first language (L1) acquisition during the critical period. Especially by older children and adults, L2 is usually not acquired solely through imitation in daily communication but by dedicated language education. The teaching of second and further languages normally combines transmission of knowledge with practicing of skills. One major hurdle is the interference of L1 proficiency with L2.

Modern language learning courses are no longer exclusively based on books or face-to-face lectures. A clear trend is web-based, interactive, multimedia and personalized learning. Learners want to be flexible as to times and places for learning: home, trains, vacation, etc. Both face-to-face teaching and 7/24 personal online language learning services are very expensive. There is a growing economic pressure to employ computer-assisted methods for improving language learning in quality, efficiency and scalability. The current philosophy of Computer Assisted Language Learning (CALL) puts a strong emphasis on learner-centered materials that enable learners to work on their own. CALL tries to support two important features in language learning: interactive learning and individualized learning.

Natural language processing (NLP) technologies play a growing important role for CALL (Hubbard, 2009). They can help to identify errors in student input and provide feedback so that the learners can be aware of them (Heift, 2013; Nagata, 1993). Furthermore, they can help to build models of the achieved proficiency of the learners and provide materials and tasks appropriate.

In this paper, we demonstrate an implementation of a framework of computer assisted pronunciation training for L2. The current version, which is a further development of the Sprinter system (Ai et al., 2014), automatically recognises and classifies the pronunciation errors of learners and provides visual and audio feedback with respect to the error types. The framework contains two subsystems: 1) the annotation tool which provides linguists an easy environment for annotating pronunciation errors in learners' speech data; 2) the speech verification tool which identifies learners' prosody and pronunciation errors and helps to correct them.

The remainder of the paper is as follows: Section 2 describes the system architecture; Section 3 and 4 explain how each subsystem works; Section 5 evaluates the speech verification tool; A brief conclusion and future plan is mentioned at last in Section 6.

2 System Description

Figure 1 depicts the framework and the interaction between the annotation tool and the speech verification tool. As presented below, the speech ver-

Proceedings of ACL-IJCNLP 2015 System Demonstrations, pages 1–6,
Beijing, China, July 26-31, 2015. ©2015 ACL and AFNLP

ification tool is initialised with a language model trained with audio data from 10 learners. In case that learners' audio data can be collected and annotated in the online system, the error database can be updated on the fly and the language model can be updated dynamically, hence speech verification will improve itself iteratively until enough pronunciation errors are gathered and no annotation will be needed. Comparing to existing methods on

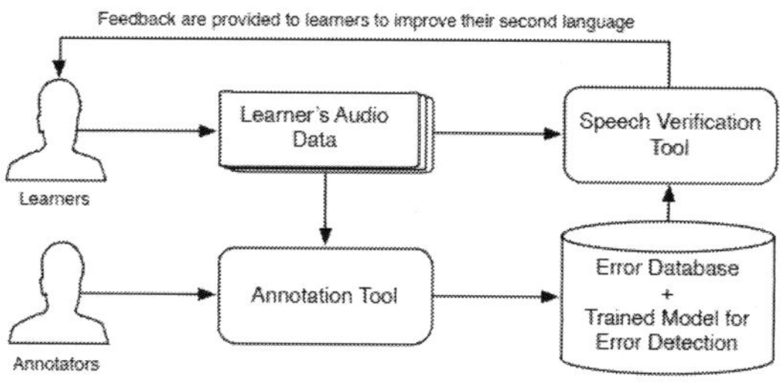

Figure 1: Overall Framework Architecture

pronunciation error detection, including building classifiers with Linear Discriminant Analysis or Decision Tree (Truong et al., 2004), or using Support Vector Machine (SVM) classifier based on applying transformation on Mel Frequency Cepstral coefficients (MFCC) of learners' audio data (Picard et al., 2010; Ananthakrishnan et al., 2011), our HMM classifier has the advantage that it is trained from finely annotated L2 speech error data, hence can recognise error types that are specifically defined in the annotations. Moreover, the results not only show the differences between gold standard and learner data, but also contain information of corrective feedback. Comparing to a general Goodness of Pronunciation (GOP) score or simply showing differences in waveform, our feedback pinpoints different types of error down to phoneme level and show learners how to pronounce them correctly via various means. The same annotating-training-verifying process can be adapted to all languages as far as our open source components support them, thus, with almost no extra efforts. Since people with the same L1 background tend to make the same pronunciation errors while learning a second language (Witt, 2012), we choose a specific L1-L2 pair in our experiment, namely, Germans who learn English.

3 Annotation Tool

To provide annotators an easy and efficient interface, we have further developed MAT (Ai and

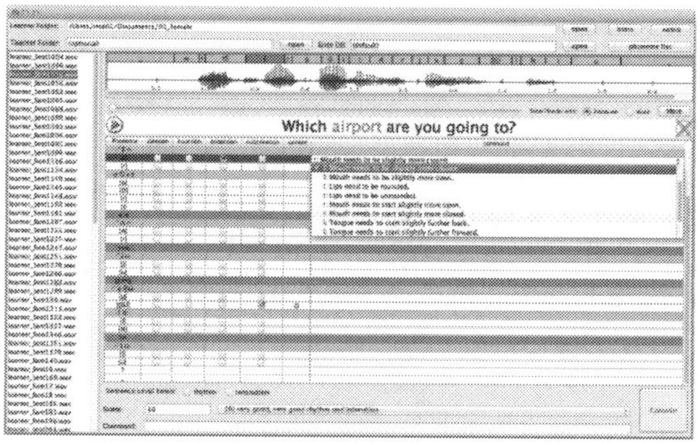

Figure 2: Screenshot of the Annotation Tool

Charfuelan, 2014), with which pronunciation errors can be annotated via simple mouse clicks and single phoneme inputs from keyboard. During the annotation, errors are automatically stored in an error database, which then updates the speech verification tool. We also add checking mechanisms to validate the annotations and ask annotators to deal with conflicts.

3.1 Target Pronunciation Errors

Four types of phoneme-level pronunciation errors can be annotated in the ways as shown in Figure 2. They are:

- Deletion: A phoneme is removed from learner's utterance, e.g. to omit /g/ in "England". Annotators only need to check the checkbox in column *deletion*.
- Insertion: A phoneme is inserted after another one, e.g. learner tries to pronounce a silent letter, like 'b' in "dumb". In this case the annotator should check *insertion* and type the inserted phoneme in column *spoken*.
- Substitution: A phoneme is replaced by another one, e.g. replacing /z/ with /s/ in "was". The annotator should check *substitution* and type the actually pronounced phoneme in *spoken*.
- Distortion: A phoneme is not pronounced fully correct, yet is not so wrong that it becomes another phoneme, e.g. pronouncing /u/ with tongue slightly backward. In this case the annotator should also select a hint from the drop down list in *hint* column to indicate how the error phoneme can be corrected.

3.2 Annotations

As depicted in Figure 2, annotations can be conducted easily and directly with this tool. If an annotator finds a pronunciation error, he/she can simply check the checkbox at line: phoneme and column: error type from the table, and provide extra information of the actually spoken phoneme and also hints of how to pronounce correctly. To make the annotation more convenient and efficient, several functions are built in the tool:

- Phoneme sequences are generated via MARY phonemizer. Phonemes are listed in the first column of the table and also in the header of the waveform panel. Clicking on a phoneme in the header will highlight the row of the corresponding phoneme in the table, and vice versa. The word, which the clicked phoneme belongs to, is also highlighted in the middle panel where the sentence is shown. Syllables in words are also retrieved from text analysis and displayed in the first column.
- Phoneme boundaries are recognized via forced alignment performed with HTK. Annotators can play any single phoneme, syllable or word by double-clicking them in the first column, or play any part of the sentence by choosing a range in the waveform panel with mouse and hit space on keyboard. In this way annotators can focus on error phonemes without bothering to listen to the whole sentence.
- There is already a list of hints on articulation provided. If a correction cannot be found in the list, annotators can click *hints* button and add the correction to the list.

After the annotation for a single audio file is done, the annotator clicks *Commit* to submit the annotations. The *Commit* function will check the annotation additionally:

- If *insertion* is marked, the inserted phoneme should be also written in *spoken*.
- If *substitution* is marked, the phoneme, which the original phoneme is substituted to, should also be written in *spoken*.
- If *distortion* is marked, a comment should be provided by annotators to indicate in which way this phoneme is distorted.
- Only one kind of error can be annotated per phoneme.

If the annotations are valid, the pronunciation errors and their diphone or triphone informations

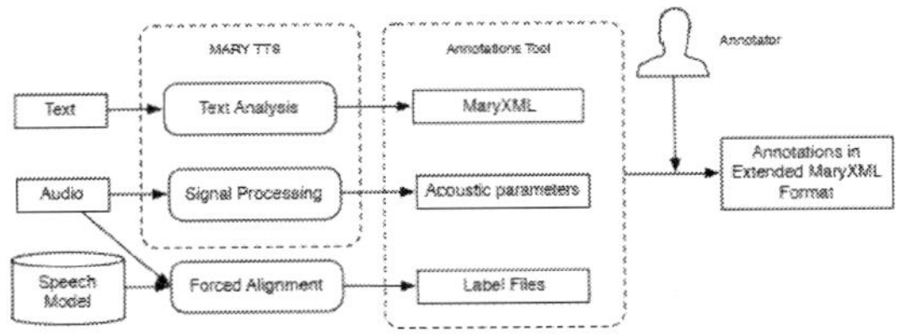

Figure 3: Components in annotation tool

are stored in an error database, which is later used in training the language model for error detection and also in feedback generation.

4 Speech Verification Tool

The speech verification tool identifies the pronunciation errors in learners' speech and provides feedback on correction, and also analyze the differences in pitch and duration between gold standard and learners' speech and display them in comprehensive ways. The goal is to help learners speak second language error-free and with rhythm and intonation like native speakers.

4.1 Pronunciation Error Detection

Pronunciation error detection is realized by performing phoneme recognition with HTK and comparing the correct and recognized phoneme sequence. Errors can be retrieved from the differences between the sequences. The sentence read by learner is processed by MARY phonemizer to generate the correct phoneme sequence. Possible pronunciation errors are then fetched from the error database based on the phonemes and their diphone and triphone information in the sequences. A grammar for phoneme recognition is then composed from the errors and the phoneme sequence.

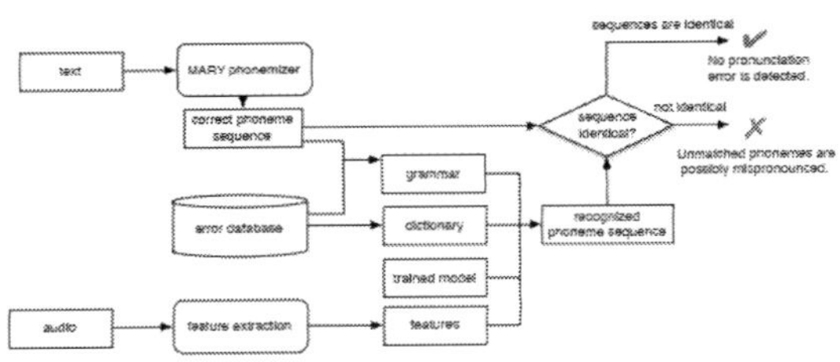

Figure 4: Workflow of Pronunciation Error Detection

Errors are handled differently as they appear in the grammar:

- Deletion means a phoneme can be optional in the grammar.

- Insertion means an extra phoneme, i.e. the inserted one, can be optional in the grammar.
- Substitution means multiple phonemes can appear at this position: the correct one and the substituted ones.
- Distortion also means multiple phonemes can appear at the same position: the correct and their distorted alias, which are represented with phoneme plus number. For example, the phoneme /ɑ/ can be distorted in two ways: either tongue is placed backward or tongue starts too forward. Since /ɑ/ is represented as /A/ in MARY, its two distorted versions are /A1/ and /A2/.

If a given sentence with its MARY phoneme sequence is:

I'll	be	in	London	for	the	whole	year.
A l	b i	I n	l V n d @ n	f O r	D @	h @U l	j I r

A grammar with following content

(sil A l b (i |i1) I n l (V |A |O) n {d} @ n f (O |O2) r (D |z) @ h @U l j (I |I1) {(r |A)} sil)

will be generated, because the following pronunciation errors have been learned:

1. /i/ in *be* can be distorted.
2. /ʌ/ in *London* can be substituted with /ɑ/ or /ɔ/.
3. /d/ in *London* can be removed by learners while pronouncing.
4. /ɔː/ in *for* can be distorted.
5. /ð/ in *the* can be replaced with /z/.
6. /iː/ in *year* can be distorted.
7. /ə/ in *year* can be substituted with /ɑ/, and can also be deleted by learners.

If the predefined errors appear in learners' speech, they will be identified by comparing the different phonemes in the correct phoneme sequence generated with MARY phonemizer and the recognized sequence with HTK. Moreover, corrective feedback can also be created by fetching the hint, which annotators provide, from the error database. E.g. if /A1/ instead of /A/ is recognized for word *are*, we can provide the hint for this distorted /ɑ/: *Tongue needs to be slightly further forward.*

4.2 Prosody Differences

Prosody differences between gold standard and learners' speech are calculated and shown to learners, not only visually, but also with audio feedback. The prosody from gold standard is applied to learners' speech, so learners can hear their own voice with native prosody, in this way it might be easier for them to mimic the gold standard prosody (Flege, 1995).

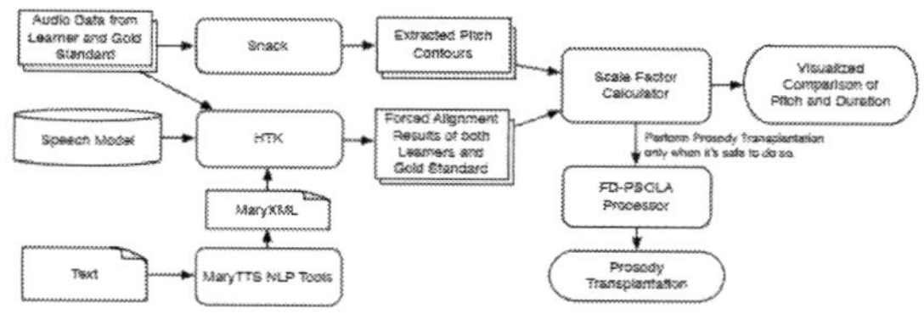

Figure 5: Workflow of Prosody Comparison and Transplantation

Duration differences can be calculated directly from the results of forced alignment. To gain more accurate alignment, the language model is trained with gold standard data and a selected set of learners' data. Before displaying the differences to learners as in Figure 6, the durations in learners' speech are normalized so that only words with large duration differences are shown.

Pitch differences are calculated with Snack Sound Toolkit[1]. Dynamic time warping is applied to the gold standard against speech data from learners, so that differences in pitch can be shown per phoneme synchronously. Due to the fact that each person has a distinct baseline in pitch, differences in pitch value are not considered as differences, we show only differences in pitch variation.

We use FD-PSOLA combined with DTW (Latsch and Netto, 2011) to perform prosody transplantation and generate audio feedback that learners can perceive. Despite the high performance of the method, there are still cases that prosody transplantation yields faulty results, e.g. the synthesized speech sounds very artificial or there are significant gaps between words or even phonemes. Therefore a scale factor calculator runs before the transplantation to determine if it makes sense to transplant the prosody, and will only do it and provide it as feedback when the scale factors do not exceed the threshold.

4.3 User Interface

Figure 6 shows a screenshot of the speech verification tool. Learners can choose sentences they want to practice from the list in the left, and

[1] http://www.speech.kth.se/snack/

click *Record* and speak to the microphone. After the audio is recorded, they can click *Check* to display the verification results. Pronunciation errors are marked in the first panel with colors other than green. Red, pink, yellow and purple are used for substitution, distortion, deletion and insertion. The second panel shows the differences in pitches, significant and medium differences are rendered with red and yellow. The panel below shows the differences in durations. Hints of correction or improvement are shown as text if learners click on the colored phonemes or words. If prosody transplantation is feasible, the button *Transplanted* is enabled and will play audio with learners' voice and transplanted gold standard prosody upon click.

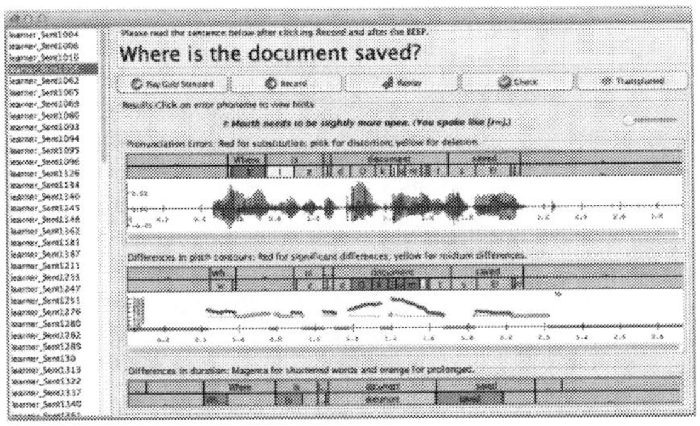

Figure 6: Screenshot of the Speech Verification Tool

5 Evaluation

Experiments are conducted both objectively and subjectively, in order to evaluate the performance of error detection and also how our feedback can help learners improve their second language skills

5.1 Objective Evaluation

To train the language model for pronunciation error detection, we let 1506 sentences read by native Britons. Given these sentences, 96 sentences are carefully selected, which cover almost all typical pronunciation errors made by Germans who learn English, and have been read by 10 Germans at different English skill levels. To evaluate our error detection system, we let 4 additional German people read these 96 sentences. The recordings were sent to both annotators and the error detection system. The results from error detection are transformed to MARYXML format and compared with the annotations.

	true positive	false positive	false negative	total	recall	precision
deletion	46	0	4	50	92%	100%
insertion	17	0	1	18	94.4%	100%
substitution	1264	14	2	1266	99.8%	98.9%
distortion	745	102	26	771	96.6%	88.0%
total	2072	116	33	2105	98.4%	94.6%

Table 1: A statistic of the error detection result. True positive: actually detected errors; false positive: correct pronounced phonemes detected as errors; false negative: errors not detected.

The results show a very high precision in recognizing *deletion* and *insertion*. The recalls are also very good considering that there are new deletion phenomena in testers' speech that are not involved in old training data. Although a large amount of substitution errors appear in the test data, they have been detected accurately. This proves that training a language model considering specific L1 background is important for correct error recognition. For example in our case, most typical substitution errors made by Germans are well trained, like pronouncing /ð/ like /z/ in *the*, or /z/ like /s/ in *was*.

Detecting distortion errors seems a more difficult task for the system. Although a good recall is achieved, the precision is not satisfying. In CALL, this is perhaps not helpful because learners will be discouraged if they make correct pronunciation but are told wrong by the system. More speech data is required for training the model. Our annotators are experienced linguists but they may still holds different criterion on judging distortion. Having more linguists working on the annotation should also help to improve the accuracy of error detection.

5.2 Subjective Evaluation

To evaluate whether and how our feedback can help learners improve their second language, we designed a progressive experiment. 4 learners are chosen to read 30 sentences from the list. They can listen to gold standard as many times as they need, and record the speech when they are ready. If there are pronunciation errors or prosody differences, they can view hints or listen to gold standard, and then try again. If there are still prosody differences, they can then hear the transplanted speech, as many times as they need, and then try to record again. Insertions and deletions are easily corrected by learners once they have been pointed out. We examined the substitution errors that were not corrected, and found most of them are be-

	insertion	deletion	substitution	distortion	total
detected errors	13	4	467	220	704
corrected errors	13	4	429	116	562

Table 2: Amount of detected and corrected pronunciation errors from test speech data.

tween phoneme /æ/ and /e/, and also /əʊ/ and /ɔ/. The differences between the phoneme pairs were not easily perceived by learners, and they need to be taught systematically how to pronounce these phonemes. It was difficult for learners to correct distortions. Besides providing tutorial on how to pronounce error phonemes correctly, our system also needs to be modified so that it doesn't handle distortion so strictly.

	differences in count of phonemes (pitch) or words (duration)	correct after viewing hints	corrected after listening to prosody transplantation
pitch	474	343	438
duration	205	135	177

Table 3: Amount of detected and corrected prosody differences from test speech data.

The results on prosody differences show that most of these differences can be perceived and adjusted by learners, if they are given enough information. Almost all the remaining differences are from long sentences. Learners couldn't pay attention to all differences in one attempt. We believe that learners should be able to read all sentences in native intonation and rhythm if they try another several times.

6 Conclusion

In this paper we presents a framework for computer assisted pronunciation training. Its annotation tool substantially simplifies the acquisition of speech error data, while its speech verification tool automatically detects pronunciation errors and prosody differences in learners' speech and provide corrective feedback. Objective and subjective evaluations show that the system not only performs accurately in error detection but also helps learners realize and correct their errors.

In the future, we attempt to integrate more feedback content such as video tutorial or articulation animation for teaching pronunciation.

7 Acknowledgment

This research was partially supported by the German Federal Ministry of Education and Research (BMBF) through the projects Deependance (01IW11003) and ALL SIDES (01IW14002).

References

Renlong Ai and Marcela Charfuelan. 2014. Mat: a tool for l2 pronunciation errors annotation. In *Proceedings of the 9th International Conference on Language Resources and Evaluation (LREC-2014)*. European Language Resources Association.

Renlong Ai, Marcela Charfuelan, Walter Kasper, Tina Klwer, Hans Uszkoreit, Feiyu Xu, Sandra Gasber, and Philip Gienandt. 2014. Sprinter: Language technologies for interactive and multimedia language learning. In *Proceedings of the 9th International Conference on Language Resources and Evaluation (LREC-2014)*. European Language Resources Association.

Gopal Ananthakrishnan, Preben Wik, Olov Engwall, and Sherif Abdou. 2011. Using an ensemble of classifiers for mispronunciation feedback. In *SLaTE*, pages 49–52.

James E Flege. 1995. Second language speech learning: Theory, findings, and problems. *Speech Perception and Linguistic Experience: Theoretical and Methodological Issues*, pages 233–273.

Trude Heift. 2013. Learner control and error correction in icall: Browsers, peekers, and adamants. *Calico Journal*, 19(2):295–313.

Philip Hubbard. 2009. *Computer Assisted Language Learning: Critical Concepts in Linguistics*, volume I-IV. London & New York: Routledge.

V. L. Latsch and S. L. Netto. 2011. Pitch-synchronous time alignment of speech signals for prosody transplantation. In *IEEE International Symposium on Circuits and Systems (ISCAS)*, Rio de Janeiro, Brazil.

Noriko Nagata. 1993. Intelligent computer feedback for second language instruction. *The Modern Language Journal*, 77(3):330–339.

Sébastien Picard, Gopal Ananthakrishnan, Preben Wik, Olov Engwall, and Sherif Abdou. 2010. Detection of specific mispronunciations using audiovisual features. In *AVSP*, pages 7–2.

Khiet Truong, Ambra Neri, Catia Cucchiarini, and Helmer Strik. 2004. Automatic pronunciation error detection: an acoustic-phonetic approach. In *InSTIL/ICALL Symposium 2004*.

S. M. Witt. 2012. Automatic error detection in pronunciation training: where we are and where we need to go. In *International Symposium on Automatic Detection of Errors in Pronunciation Training*, Stockholm, Sweden.

IMI — A Multilingual Semantic Annotation Environment

Francis Bond, Luís Morgado da Costa and Tuấn Anh Lê
Linguistics and Multilingual Studies
Nanyang Technological University, Singapore
{bond@ieee.org, luis.passos.morgado@gmail.com, tuananh.ke@gmail.com}

Abstract

Semantic annotated parallel corpora, though rare, play an increasingly important role in natural language processing. These corpora provide valuable data for computational tasks like sense-based machine translation and word sense disambiguation, but also to contrastive linguistics and translation studies. In this paper we present the ongoing development of a web-based corpus semantic annotation environment that uses the Open Multilingual Wordnet (Bond and Foster, 2013) as a sense inventory. The system includes interfaces to help coordinating the annotation project and a corpus browsing interface designed specifically to meet the needs of a semantically annotated corpus. The tool was designed to build the NTU-Multilingual Corpus (Tan and Bond, 2012). For the past six years, our tools have been tested and developed in parallel with the semantic annotation of a portion of this corpus in Chinese, English, Japanese and Indonesian. The annotation system is released under an open source license (MIT).

1 Introduction

Plain text parallel corpora are relatively widely available and widely used in NLP, such as machine translation system development (Koehn, 2005, e.g.,). In contrast, there are very few parallel sense tagged corpora due to the expense of tagging the corpora and creating the sense inventories in multiple languages. The one exception is the translations of English SemCor (Landes et al., 1998) for Italian (Bentivogli and Pianta, 2005), Romanian (Lupu et al., 2005) and Japanese (Bond et al., 2012). Even for this corpus, not all of the original English texts have been translated and tagged, and not all words are tagged in the translated text (typically only those with a corresponding English sense).

In this paper we present IMI, a web-based multilingual semantic annotation system designed for the task of sense annotation. The main goals of its design were to decrease the cost of production of these resources by optimizing the speed of tagging, and to facilitate the management of this kind of project. To accomplish this, we aimed at developing a simple and intuitive web-based system that allows parallel tagging by many users at a time, optimized for speed by requiring minimum input from the annotators.

We centered our development around the annotation of the NTU-Multilingual Corpus (NTU-MC: Tan and Bond, 2012). The NTU-MC is an open multilingual parallel corpus originally designed to include many layers of syntactic and semantic annotation. We selected a portion of this corpus based on 7,093 sentences of English, totaling 22,762 sentences of Chinese, Japanese and Indonesian parallel text. A series of undergraduate linguistics students were trained on the tool and annotated the corpus over several years. They also offered extensive qualitative and quantitative feedback on the usage of our system.

The remainder of this paper is arranged as follows. In Section 2 we introduce related work. Section 3 describes the main functionality of our system then we finish with Section 4, which summarizes and discusses our current and future work.

2 Related Work

In this section we introduce the corpus (NTU-MC), the sense inventory (OMW), and a brief overview of currently available tools.

Proceedings of ACL-IJCNLP 2015 System Demonstrations, pages 7–12,
Beijing, China, July 26-31, 2015.

2.1 The NTU-Multilingual Corpus (NTU-MC)

The NTU-MC (Tan and Bond, 2012) has data available for eight languages from seven language families (Arabic, Chinese, English, Indonesian, Japanese, Korean, Vietnamese and Thai), distributed across four domains (story, essay, news, and tourism). The corpus started off with monolingual part-of-speech (POS) annotation and cross-lingual linking of sentences. We are extending it to include monolingual sense annotation and cross-lingual word and concept alignments (Bond et al., 2013). Out of the available languages, Chinese, English, Japanese and Indonesian were chosen for further processing and annotation (due to the availability of lexical and human resources). As part of the annotation, we are also expanding the sense and concept inventory of the wordnets: Princeton Wordnet (PWN: Fellbaum, 1998), the Japanese Wordnet (Isahara et al., 2008), the Chinese Open Wordnet (Wang and Bond, 2013) and the Wordnet Bahasa (Nurril Hirfana *et al.* 2011) through the Open Multingual Wordnet (Bond and Foster, 2013).

2.2 The Open Multilingual Wordnet

The task of semantic annotating a corpus involves the manual (and often automated) disambiguation of words using lexical semantic resources – selecting, for each word, the best match in a pool of available concepts. Among this type of resources, the PWN has, perhaps, attained the greatest visibility. As a resource, a wordnet is simply a huge net of concepts, senses and definitions linked through many different types of relations. Because of popularity and confirmed utility, many projects have developed wordnets for different languages.

The Open Multilingual Wordent (OMW) (Bond and Foster, 2013) is an open source multilingual resource that combines many individual open-source wordnet projects, along with data extracted from Wiktionary and the Unicode Common Locale Data Repository. It contains over 2 million senses distributed over more than 150 languages, linked through PWN. Browsing can be done monolingual or multilingually, and it incorporates a full-fledged wordnet editing system which our system uses (OMWEdit: da Costa and Bond, 2015).

2.3 Other Available Systems

There are many text annotation tools available for research (e.g., Stenetorp et al., 2012). However, sense annotation has some features that differ from most common annotation tasks (such as NE or POS annotation). In particular, the number of tags, and the information associated with each tag is very large. Sense tagging for English using the PWN, for example, when unrestricted, defaults at over a hundred thousand possible tags to chose from: even constrained by the lemma, there may be over 40 tags and the set of tags will very from lemma to lemma.

There are only a few annotation tools designed specifically for sense annotation. We were able to find the following: the tools to tag the Hinoki Corpus (Bond et al., 2008), for Japanese, and the Sense Annotation Tool for the American National Corpus (SATANiC: Passonneau et al., 2009), for English. Both of these tools were developed to be used in a monolingual environment, and have not been released.

The only open source tool that we could find was Chooser (Koeva et al., 2008), a multi-task annotation tool that was used to tag the Bulgarian Sense Tagged Corpus (Koeva et al., 2006). This tool is open source, language independent and is capable of integrating a wordnet as a sense inventory. Unfortunately, it was not designed to be a web-service which means it is difficult to coordinate the work of multiple users.

3 System Overview and Architecture

Given the scenario of available systems, we decided we had enough motivation to start the development of a new Semantic Annotation Environment (IMI).

Because a large part of sense-tagging is adding new senses to the inventory, we integrated IMI with the existing tools for editing and displaying the Open Multilingual Wordnet. This integration was done mainly through the development of a single web-based environment, with a common login, and API communications between interfaces. We also designed a custom mode to display OMW results in a condensed way.Sharing a common login system allows our annotators to access the OMW wordnet editing mode (right hand of Figure 1) so that, when needed, annotators can add new senses and concepts to fit the data in the corpus.

Our system is written in Python and uses SQLite

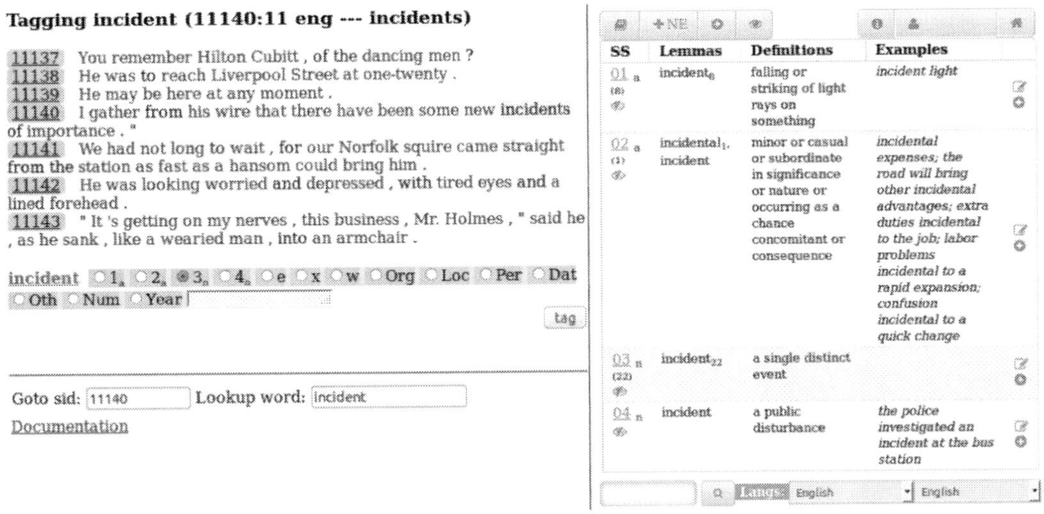

Figure 1: Sequential/Textual Tagger Interface

to store the data. It is tested on Firefox, Chrome and Safari browsers. In the remainder of this section we discuss its main functionality.[1]

3.1 The Annotation Interfaces

The sequential/textual tagger (Figure 1) was designed for concept-by-concept sequential tagging. It shows a short context around the sentence currently being tagged. Clicking a word generates an automated query in the OMW frame (on the right of Figure 1).

As it is costly to remember the set of senses for each word, we normally tag with a lexical/targeted tagger (Figure 2 displays only the left side of this tagging interface, as the OMW frame is identical to that of Figure 1). Querying the OMW with this tagger is very similar to the description above. The main difference of this interface is that it focuses on a single lexical unit across the corpus. In the example provided in Figure 2, every occurrence of the lemma ***wire*** is tagged at the same time. For frequent words, the number of results displayed can be restricted. In this interface, only the sentence where the word occurs is provided as context, but a larger context can also be accessed by clicking on the sentence ID. Since the concept inventory is the same for the full list of words to be tagged, time is saved by keeping the concepts fresh in the annotator's mind, and quality is ensured by comparing different usages of different senses at the same time.

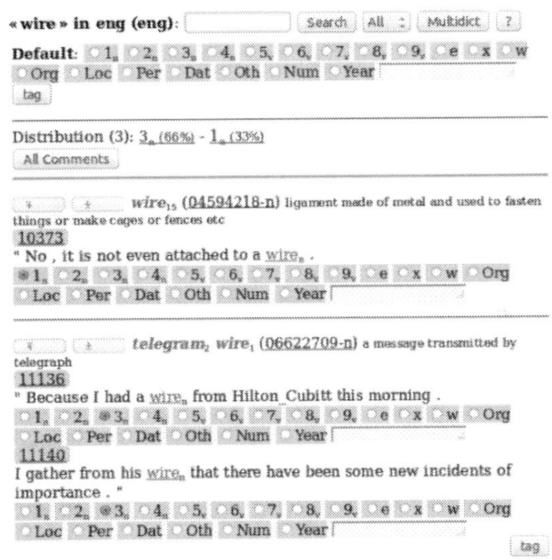

Figure 2: Targeted/Lexical Tagger

In both tagging interfaces, a tag is selected among an array of radio buttons displayed next to the words being tagged. Besides the numerical options that match the results retrieved by the OMW, the interface also allows tagging with a set of meta tags for named entities and to flag other issues. We use a similar set to that of Bond et al. (2013). With every tag, a comment field is provided as an optional field, where annotators can leave notes or describe errors.

[1]The annotation interface software and corpora are available from the NTU-MC page: `<http://compling.hss.ntu.edu.sg/ntumc/>`.

Missing senses are one of the major problems during the semantic annotation. We overcome this by integrating the wordnet editing interface provided by the OMW. Depending on the annotation task at hands, the annotation of a corpus can be done in parallel with the expansion of the respective wordnet's concept and sense inventory.

A third tagging interface (not shown) allows also the direct manipulation of the corpus structure. Its major features include creating, deleting and editing sentences, words and concepts. It is too generalized to be used as an efficient tagger, but it is useful to correct POS tags, tokenization errors and occasional spelling mistakes. It can also be used to correct or create complex concept structures of multi-word expressions, that could not be automatically identified.

The minimal input required by our interfaces (in the typical case, just clicking a radio button), especially the lexical tagger, ensures time isn't wasted with complex interfaces. It also guarantees that through the automated linking of the databases, we avoid typos and similar noise in the produced data. An earlier version allowed annotators to tag directly with synset IDs, but it turned out that it was very common for the ID to be mangled in some way, so we now only allow entering a synset through the linking to the OMW.

3.2 Annotation Agreement

IMI also includes a tool to measure inter-annotator agreement (Figure 3). Up to four annotations can be compared, for any section of the corpus. The tool also calculates the majority tag (MajTag). Average agreements scores are then computed between annotators and between annotators and the majority tag. Results are displayed by sentence and for the selected portion (e.g. the entire corpus). Agreement with the MajTag is color coded for each annotation so that the annotators can quickly spot disagreements. The interface provides quick access to database editing for all taggers, and to the OMW editing tools. The elected MajTag can also be automatically propagated as the final tag for every instance.

For some texts up to three annotators have been used, with one being a research assistant and two being students in a semantics class. These students only had a half hour of training, and used the sequential tagger to tag around 250 concepts each. The average inter-annotator agreement was 67.5%. Tagging speed was around 60 concepts/hour (self reported time). Note that roughly 25% of the potential concepts were pre-marked as `x`: entries such as preposition *in*, which should only be tagged on the very rare cases it is an adjective (*This is very in this year* or noun (*I live in Lafayette, IN*). Because the students were minimally trained (and not all highly motivated) we expected a low agreement. If two out of three annotators agreed then the words were tagged with the majority tag. Where all three annotators disagreed the students were required to discuss and re-tag those entries, and submit a report on them. An expert (the first author) then read (and marked) all the reports and fixed any tags where he disagreed with their proposed solution. Adjudicating and marking the reports takes about 30 minutes each, with some difficult to fix problems left for later. As a result of this process, all words have been seen by multiple annotators, and all hard ones by an expert (and our students have a much better understanding of the issues in representing word meaning using a fixed sense inventory)

For most texts, we only have enough funding to pay for a single annotator. **Targetted** tagging (annotating by word type) is known to be more accurate (Langone et al., 2004; Bond et al., 2008) and we use this for the single annotator. We expect to catch errors when we compare the annotations across languages: the annotation of the translation can serve as another annotator (although of course not all concepts match across languages).

3.3 Journaling

We take advantage of the relational database and use SQL triggers to keep track of every committed change, time-stamping and recording the annotator on every commit (true for both scripted and human manipulated data). The system requires going through a login system before granting access to the tools, hence permitting a detailed yet automatic journaling system. A detailed and tractable history of the annotation is available to control both the work-flow and check the quality of annotation. We can export the data into a variety of formats, such as RDF compatible XML and plain text triples.

3.4 Corpus Search Interface

Snapshots of the corpus are made available through an online corpus look up (Figure 4: available here: `<http://compling.hss.ntu.edu.sg/ntumc/cgi-bin/showcorpus.cgi>`). This search tool can query the corpus by concept key,

(SID:11140) **I gather from his wire that there have been some new incidents of importance."**

cid	lemma	A	B	C	D	MajTag	Comments
0	gather	00945125-v	00945125-v	00158804-v	00945125-v	00945125-v	
1	wire	06622709-n	06622709-n	None	06622709-n	06622709-n	
2	there	00109461-r	00109461-r	None	w	00109461-r	
3	have	x	x	x	x	x	**A:** auxiliary verb
4	be	02749904-v	x	None	02603699-v	?	
5	some	02267308-a	02267308-a	None	02267308-a	02267308-a	
6	new	00112601-r	02070491-a	None	00112601-r	00112601-r	
7	incident	07307477-n	07307477-n	01856929-a	07307477-n	07307477-n	
8	importance	05168261-n	05168261-n	05168261-n	05168261-n	05168261-n	
9	i	77000015-n	77000015-n	None	None	77000015-n	
10	his	77000050-n	77000050-n	None	None	77000050-n	
11	that	77000079-a	77000079-a	None	None	77000079-a	

	B	C	D	M
A	0.833	0.167	0.583	0.917
B		0.167	0.500	0.833
C			0.167	0.167
D				0.583

Figure 3: Inter-annotator Agreement Reports

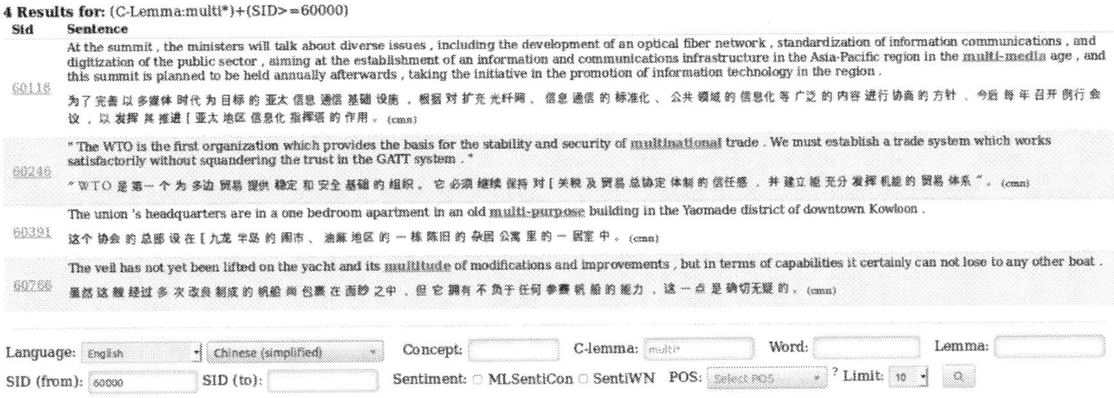

Figure 4: Corpus Search Interface (results for the regular expression '`multi*`' as concept lemma, using sentence ids to restrict the search to the Kyoto News Corpus, in bitext mode for Mandarin Chinese)

concept lemma, word, lemma, sentence id and POS, as well as any combination of these fields. Mousing over a word shows its lemma, pos, sense and annotators' comments (if any), clicking on a word pops up more information about the lemma, pos and sense (such as definitions) that can be clicked for even more information. Further, it is possible to see aligned sentences (for as many languages as selected), and color coded sentiment scores using two freely available sentiment lexicons, the SentiWordNet (Baccianella et al., 2010) and the ML-SentiCon (Cruz et al., 2014) (individually or intersected). Further improvements will allow highlighting cross-lingual word and concept alignments (inspired by Nara: Song and Bond, 2009).

4 Summary and Future Work

We have described the main interfaces and functionality of IMI. It has undergone almost six years of development, and is now a mature annotation platform. The improvement of its interfaces and functionality have not only greatly boosted the speed of the NTU-MC annotation, but has also greatly facilitated its coordination - making it easier to maintain both consistency and quality of the corpus.

In the near future we intend to:

- refine the cross-lingual word and concept alignment tool (not shown here)
- develop a reporting interface, where the project coordinators can easily review the history of changes committed to the corpus database
- add a simple corpus import tool for adding new texts in different languages
- further develop the corpus search interface, to allow highlighting cross-lingual word and concept links
- implement more automated consistency checks (e.g. match lemmas of words with

the lemmas of concepts, verify that concept lemmas are still senses of the concept used to tag a word, etc.)

- improve graphical coherence, as different parts of the toolkit have originally been developed separately, as a whole, our system currently lacks graphical coherence

We hope that the open release of our system can motivate other projects to embrace semantic annotation projects, especially projects that are less oriented towards development of systems. We would like every wordnet to be accompanied by a sense-tagged corpus!

Acknowledgments

This research was supported in part by the MOE Tier 2 grant *That's what you meant: a Rich Representation for Manipulation of Meaning* (MOE ARC41/13). We would also like to thank our annotators for their hard work and patience during this system's development.

References

Stefano Baccianella, Andrea Esuli, and Fabrizio Sebastiani. 2010. Sentiwordnet 3.0: An enhanced lexical resource for sentiment analysis and opinion mining. In Nicoletta Calzolari (Conference Chair), Khalid Choukri, Bente Maegaard, Joseph Mariani, Jan Odijk, Stelios Piperidis, Mike Rosner, and Daniel Tapias, editors, *Proceedings of the Seventh International Conference on Language Resources and Evaluation (LREC'10)*. European Language Resources Association (ELRA), Valletta, Malta.

Luisa Bentivogli and Emanuele Pianta. 2005. Exploiting parallel texts in the creation of multilingual semantically annotated resources: the multisemcor corpus. *Natural Language Engineering*, 11(3):247–261.

Francis Bond, Timothy Baldwin, Richard Fothergill, and Kiyotaka Uchimoto. 2012. Japanese SemCor: A sense-tagged corpus of Japanese. In *Proceedings of the 6th Global WordNet Conference (GWC 2012)*, pages 56–63. Matsue.

Francis Bond and Ryan Foster. 2013. Linking and extending an open multilingual wordnet. In *51st Annual Meeting of the Association for Computational Linguistics: ACL-2013*, pages 1352–1362. Sofia. URL `http://aclweb.org/anthology/P13-1133`.

Francis Bond, Sanae Fujita, and Takaaki Tanaka. 2008. The Hinoki syntactic and semantic treebank of Japanese. *Language Resources and Evaluation*, 42(2):243–251. URL `http://dx.doi.org/10.1007/s10579-008-9062-z`, (Re-issue of DOI 10.1007/s10579-007-9036-6 as Springer lost the Japanese text).

Francis Bond, Shan Wang, Eshley Huini Gao, Hazel Shuwen Mok, and Jeanette Yiwen Tan. 2013. Developing parallel sense-tagged corpora with wordnets. In *Proceedings of the 7th Linguistic Annotation Workshop and Interoperability with Discourse (LAW 2013)*, pages 149–158. Sofia. URL `http://www.aclweb.org/anthology/W13-2319`.

Fermín L Cruz, José A Troyano, Beatriz Pontes, and F Javier Ortega. 2014. Building layered, multilingual sentiment lexicons at synset and lemma levels. *Expert Systems with Applications*, 41(13):5984–5994.

Luís Morgado da Costa and Francis Bond. 2015. OMWEdit - the integrated open multilingual wordnet editing system. In *ACL-2015 System Demonstrations*. (this volume).

Christine Fellbaum, editor. 1998. *WordNet: An Electronic Lexical Database*. MIT Press.

Hitoshi Isahara, Francis Bond, Kiyotaka Uchimoto, Masao Utiyama, and Kyoko Kanzaki. 2008. Development of the Japanese WordNet. In *Sixth International conference on Language Resources and Evaluation (LREC 2008)*. Marrakech.

Philipp Koehn. 2005. Europarl: A parallel corpus for statistical machine translation. In *MT Summit X*.

Svetla Koeva, Sv Leseva, and Maria Todorova. 2006. Bulgarian sense tagged corpus. In *Proceedings of the 5th SALTMIL Workshop on Minority Languages: Strategies for Developing Machine Translation for Minority Languages, Genoa, Italy*, pages 79–87.

Svetla Koeva, Borislav Rizov, and Svetlozara Leseva. 2008. Chooser: a multi-task annotation tool. In *LREC*.

Shari Landes, Claudia Leacock, and Christiane Fellbaum. 1998. Building semantic concordances. In Fellbaum (1998), chapter 8, pages 199–216.

Helen Langone, Benjamin R. Haskell, and George A. Miller. 2004. Annotating wordnet. In *Workshop On Frontiers In Corpus Annotation*, pages 63–69. ACL, Boston.

Monica Lupu, Diana Trandabat, and Maria Husarciuc. 2005. A Romanian semcor aligned to the English and Italian multisemcor. In *Proceedings 1st ROMANCE FrameNet Workshop at EUROLAN 2005 Summer School*, pages 20–27. EUROLAN, Cluj-Napoca, Romania.

Nurril Hirfana Mohamed Noor, Suerya Sapuan, and Francis Bond. 2011. Creating the open Wordnet Bahasa. In *Proceedings of the 25th Pacific Asia Conference on Language, Information and Computation (PACLIC 25)*, pages 258–267. Singapore.

Rebecca J Passonneau, Ansaf Salleb-Aouissi, and Nancy Ide. 2009. Making sense of word sense variation. In *Proceedings of the Workshop on Semantic Evaluations: Recent Achievements and Future Directions*, pages 2–9. Association for Computational Linguistics.

Sanghoun Song and Francis Bond. 2009. Online search interface for the Sejong Korean-Japanese bilingual corps and auto-interpolation of phrase alignment. In *Proceedings of the Third Linguistic Annotation Workshop (LAW III)*, pages 146–149. Singapore.

Pontus Stenetorp, Sampo Pyysalo, Goran Topić, Tomoko Ohta, Sophia Ananiadou, and Jun'ichi Tsujii. 2012. brat: a web-based tool for NLP-assisted text annotation. In *Proceedings of the Demonstrations Session at EACL 2012*.

Liling Tan and Francis Bond. 2012. Building and annotating the linguistically diverse NTU-MC (NTU-multilingual corpus). *International Journal of Asian Language Processing*, 22(4):161–174.

Shan Wang and Francis Bond. 2013. Building the Chinese Open Wordnet (COW): Starting from core synsets. In *Proceedings of the 11th Workshop on Asian Language Resources, a Workshop at IJCNLP-2013*, pages 10–18. Nagoya.

In-tool Learning for Selective Manual Annotation in Large Corpora

Erik-Lân Do Dinh[†], **Richard Eckart de Castilho**[†], **Iryna Gurevych**[†‡]
[†]Ubiquitous Knowledge Processing Lab (UKP-TUDA)
Department of Computer Science, Technische Universität Darmstadt
[‡]Ubiquitous Knowledge Processing Lab (UKP-DIPF)
German Institute for Educational Research and Educational Information
http://www.ukp.tu-darmstadt.de

Abstract

We present a novel approach to the selective annotation of large corpora through the use of machine learning. Linguistic search engines used to locate potential instances of an infrequent phenomenon do not support ranking the search results. This favors the use of high-precision queries that return only a few results over broader queries that have a higher recall. Our approach introduces a classifier used to rank the search results and thus helping the annotator focus on those results with the highest potential of being an instance of the phenomenon in question, even in low-precision queries. The classifier is trained in an *in-tool* fashion, except for preprocessing relying only on the manual annotations done by the users in the querying tool itself. To implement this approach, we build upon CSniper[1], a web-based multi-user search and annotation tool.

1 Introduction

With the rapidly growing body of digitally available language data, it becomes possible to investigate phenomena of the language system that manifest themselves infrequently in corpus data, e.g. non-canonical constructions. To pinpoint occurrences of such phenomena and to annotate them requires a new kind of annotation tool, since manual, sequential annotation is not feasible anymore for large amounts of texts.

An *annotation-by-query* approach to identify such phenomena in large corpora is implemented in the recently published open-source tool CSniper (Eckart de Castilho et al., 2012).

To enable a selective manual annotation process, a linguistic search engine is used, allowing the creation of queries which single out potential instances of the phenomenon in question. Those potential instances are then displayed to the user, who annotates each one as being an instance of the phenomenon or not. This process of searching and annotating can be performed by multiple users concurrently; the annotations are stored for each user separately. In a subsequent evaluation step, a user can review the annotations of all users, e.g. to discard a query if it yields unsatisfying results. Finally, the annotations of multiple users can be merged into a gold standard.

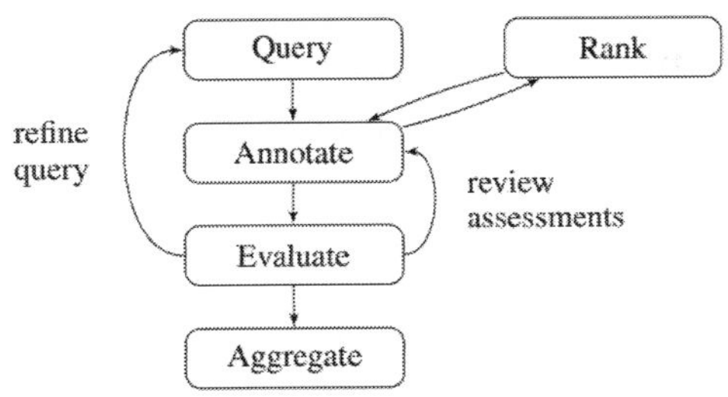

Figure 1: *Annotation-by-query* workflow extended with a ranking step.

This approach relieves the annotator from having to read through the corpus from the beginning to the end to look for instances of a phenomenon. However, the search may yield many results that may superficially appear to be an instance of the desired phenomenon, but due to ambiguities or due to a broadly defined query only a small subset may be actual instances. This still leaves the annotator with the tedious task of clicking through the search results to mark the true instances.

[1]https://dkpro.github.io/dkpro-csniper

Proceedings of ACL-IJCNLP 2015 System Demonstrations, pages 13–18,
Beijing, China, July 26-31, 2015.

To reduce the time and effort required, we present an extension of the *annotation-by-query* approach (Figure 1) that introduces a ranking of the query results (Section 2) by means of machine learning; we order the results by confidence of the used classifier. To obtain a model for the classifier, we employ an *in-tool* learning approach, where we learn from the annotations that are made by users in the tool itself. This makes our ranking approach useful for highly specific tasks, since no pre-trained models are needed.

Finally we demonstrate the viability of our concept by the example task of finding non-canonical constructions in Section 3.

2 Ranking linguistic query results

Our approach employs machine learning to facilitate — but not to completely replace — the manual annotation of query results. A query expresses the intention of the user to find a specific linguistic phenomenon (*information need*). An information retrieval search engine would provide the user with a list of results that are ranked according to their relevance, fulfilling the information need. However, linguistic search engines such as CQP (Evert and Hardie, 2011) — which is used by CSniper — are basically pattern-matching engines, operating on different lexical or morpho-syntactic features like part-of-speech (POS) tags and lemmata and do not have a concept of relevance. Thus, if the query provided by the user overgeneralizes, relevant results are hidden among many irrelevant ones, ultimately failing to satisfy the user's information need.

To tackle this problem, we use the annotations already created by users on the search results to train a classifier. Unannotated query results are then fed to the classifier whose output values are then used as relevance ratings by which the results are ranked. The classifier producing the ranking can be invoked by the user at any time; it can be configured in certain characteristics, e.g. the annotations of which users should be used as training data, or how many of the selected users have to agree on an annotation for it to be included.

2.1 Workflow and ranking process in CSniper

Currently, we train the classifier on features derived from the constituency parse tree, which makes it useful for tasks such as locating sentences containing infrequent ambiguous grammatical constructions (cf. Section 3). Since parsing the query results is too time-intensive to be done during runtime, we parsed the corpora in advance and stored the parse trees in a database. To train the classifier, we employed SVM-light-tk (Moschitti, 2006; Joachims, 1999), a support vector machine implementation which uses a tree kernel to integrate all sub-trees of the parse tree as features.

Consider the following typical scenario incorporating the ranking: A user constructs a query based on various features, such as POS tags or lemmata, which are used to search for matching sentences, e.g.

"It" [lemma="be"] [pos="AT0"]?
[pos="NN."]*[2]

The result is a list of sentences presented in a *keywords-in-context* (KWIC) view, along with an annotation field (Figure 2).

Then the user starts to annotate these sentences as *Correct* or *Wrong*, depending whether they truly represent instances of the phenomenon in question. Clicking on the *Rank results* button (Figure 2) invokes our ranking process: The SVM-light-tk classifier is trained using the parse trees of the sentences which the user previously annotated. The resulting model is then used to classify the remaining sentences in the query results. We rank the sentences according to the output value of the decision function of the classifier (which we interpret as a relevance/confidence rating) and transiently label a sentence as either *(Correct)* (output value > 0) or *(Wrong)* (output value ≤ 0). The results in the KWIC view are then reordered according to the rank, showing the highest-ranking result first. Repeatedly annotating those highest-ranking results and re-ranking allows for quickly annotating instances of the phenomenon, while also improving the classifier accuracy at the same time.

2.2 *Find* mode

After annotating instances based on simple queries and ML-supported ranked queries, we considered the natural next step to be searching automatically for the phenomenon in question utilizing machine learning, using arbitrary sentences from the corpus as input for the classifier instead of only the results returned by a query. Such an automatic search could address two concerns: 1) it removes

[2] It-cleft example query: "It", followed by a form of "to be", an optional determiner and a common noun.

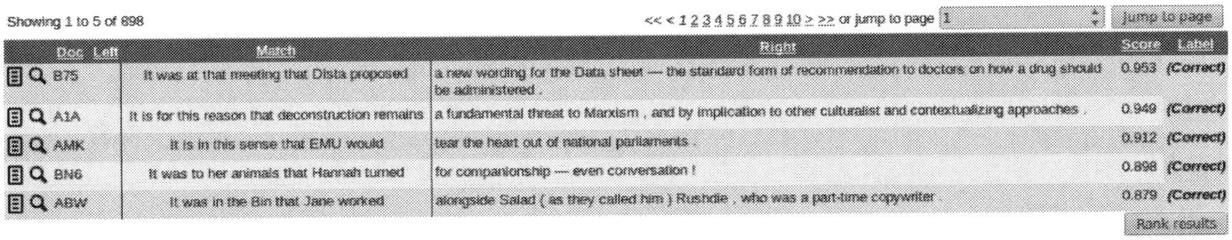

Figure 2: A screenshot showing the results table after the ranking process, with sentences sorted by confidence of the classifier (*Score*). The results are shown in a *keywords-in-context* (KWIC) view, separating left context, query match and right context (within a range of one sentence). Clicking on *(Correct)* changes the label to *Correct*.

the need for the user to design new queries, allowing users less experienced in the query language to annotate more effectively side-by-side with advanced users; 2) it could optimally generalize over all the queries that users have already made and potentially locate instances that had not been found by individual high-precision queries.

To support this, we implemented the *Find* mode, to locate instances of a phenomenon while abstracting from the queries. In this mode, the SVM is first trained from all previously (manually) labeled instances for a given phenomenon, without taking the queries into account that were used to find those instances. Then the corpus is partitioned into smaller parts containing a predefined amount of sentences (we used 500). One of these partitions is chosen at random, and the sentences therein are ranked using the SVM. This step is repeated, until a previously defined number of sentences have been classified as *Correct*. Those sentences are then shown to the user, who now can either confirm a sentence as containing the phenomenon or label it *Wrong* otherwise.

2.3 Related work

Existing annotation tools include automation functionality for annotation tasks, ranging from rule-based tagging to more complex, machine-learning-based approaches.

Such functionalities can be found in the annotation software WordFreak (Morton and LaCivita, 2003), where a plug-in architecture allows for a variety of different taggers and classifiers to be integrated, for example part-of-speech taggers or coreference resolution engines. Those require pretrained models, which limits the applicability of the automation capabilities of WordFreak to tasks for which such models are actually available. In addition to assigning annotations a single label, WordFreak allows plugins to rank labels for each annotation based on the confidence of the used classifier. Note that this is different to our ranking approach, where we instead perform a ranking of the search results which shall be annotated.

Another tool incorporating machine learning is WebAnno (Yimam et al., 2014), which implements features such as custom labels and annotation types. In addition, WebAnno supports automatic annotation similar to our approach, also employing machine learning to build models from the data annotated by users. Those models are then used to annotate the remainder of the documents. To accomplish this, WebAnno uses a split-pane view, showing automatic suggestions in one pane and manually entered annotations in another. The user can accept a suggested annotation, which is transferred to the manual pane. Lacking the search capability, WebAnno lists automatic annotations in the running corpus text, which makes it unsuited for selective annotation in large corpora. The approach that we implemented on top of CSniper instead ranks the search results for a given query by confidence of the classifier.

Yet another form of in-tool learning is *active learning*, as is implemented, e.g., in Dualist (Settles, 2011). In an active learning scenario the system aims to efficiently train an accurate classifier (i.e. with as little training data as possible) and thus repeatedly asks the user to annotate instances from which it can learn the most. Such an approach can work well for reducing the amount of training data needed to produce a model which achieves high accuracy, as has been — amongst others — shown by Hachey et al. (2005). However, they also learn in their experiments that those highly informative instances are often harder to annotate and increase required time and effort of annotators. Our approach is different from active learning as our goal is not to improve the training efficiency of the classifier but rather to allow the user to interactively find and label as many true instances of a phenomenon as possible in a large corpus. Thus, the items presented to the user are not determined by the expected information gain for the classifier but rather by the *confidence* of the classifier, presenting the user with those instances first which are most likely to be occurrences of the phenomenon in question.

3 Case study: Finding non-canonical constructions

We demonstrate our novel approach on the task of locating *non-canonical constructions* (NCC) and conduct an intrinsic evaluation of the accuracy of the system augmented with machine learning output on the data annotated by expert linguists. The linguists annotated sentences for occurrences of certain NCC subtypes: *information-packaging constructions* (Huddleston and Pullum, 2002, pp. 1365ff.), which present information in a different way from their canonical counterparts without changing truth conditions; specifically *It-clefts* ("It was Peter who made lunch."), *NP-preposing* ("A treasure, he was searching."), and *PP-inversion* ("To his left lay the forest.") clauses.

For our experiments, we used the British National Corpus (2007), comprising 100 million words in multiple domains[3]. Constituency parsing was conducted using the factored variant of the Stanford Parser (Klein and Manning, 2003), incorporated into a UIMA pipeline using DKPro Core (Eckart de Castilho and Gurevych, 2014).

As a baseline we use queries representing the experts' intuition about the realization of the NCCs in terms of POS tags and lemmata. We show that our system improves the precision of the query results even with little training data. Also we present run times for our ranking system under real-world conditions for different training set sizes. Further, we compare Krippendorff's α coefficient as an inter-annotator agreement measure among only annotators to the α which treats our system as one additional annotator.

We conducted the experiments based on the manually assigned labels of up to five annotators. If a sentence has been annotated by multiple users, we use the label that has been assigned by the majority; in case of a tie, we ignore the sentence. These so created gold standard annotations were used in an iterative cross-validation setting: for each query and the corresponding annotated sentences we ran nine cross-validation configurations, ranging from a $10/90$ split between training and testing data to a $90/10$ split, to investigate the reliability of the classifier as well as its ability to achieve usable results with little training data.

For *It-clefts*, we observe that elaborate queries already have a high precision, on which the SVM improves only marginally. The query

"It" /VCC[] [pos="NP0"]+ /RC[][4] (it17)

already yields a precision of 0.9598, which does not increase using our method (using 10% as training data, comparing the precision for the remaining 90%). However, while broader queries yield lower precision, the gain by using the SVM becomes significant (Table 1), as exemplified by the precision improvement from 0.4919 to 0.7782 for the following *It-cleft* query, even at a $10/90$ split.

"It" /VCC[] /NP[] /RC[][5] (it2)

For other inspected types of NCC, even elaborate queries yield a low baseline precision, which our approach can improve significantly. This effect can be observed for example in the following *NP-preposing* query, where precision can be improved from 0.3946 to 0.5871.

[pos="N."]{1,2} [pos="PNP" & word!="I"] [pos="V.*"]*[6] (np55)

We conducted a cursory, "real-world" test regarding the speed of the ranking system.[7] Training the SVM on differently sized subsets of the 449 sentences returned by a test query, we measured the time from clicking the *Rank results* button until the process was complete and the GUI had updated to reorder the sentences (i.e. including database queries, training, classifying, GUI update). The process times averaged over five "runs" for each training set size (20%, 50% and 90%) amount to 5 seconds, 7 seconds, and 14 seconds respectively. This leaves us with the preliminary impression that our system is fast enough for small to medium

[3]CSniper and the used SVM implementation are language independent, which allowed us to also run additional preliminary tests using German data.

[4]"It", verb clause, one or more proper nouns, relative clause. *VCC*, *NC*, and *RC* are macros we defined in CQP, see Table 2.

[5]"It", verb clause, noun phrase, relative clause.

[6]One to two nouns, personal pronoun other than "I", verb.

[7]System configuration: Intel i5 2,4 GHz, 2GB RAM, SSD 3GB/s, Linux in a VM

	it2	it17	it33	np34	np55	np76	pp42	pp99	pp103
Baseline	0.4919	0.9598	0.7076	0.4715	0.3946	0.4985	0.7893	0.4349	0.2365
SVM, 10/90	0.7782	0.9598	0.7572	0.5744	0.5871	0.5274	0.8152	0.8357	0.8469
SVM, 50/50	0.8517	0.9608	0.8954	0.6410	0.6872	0.6193	0.8657	0.8769	0.8720
SVM, 90/10	0.8634	0.9646	0.9261	0.6822	0.7723	0.6806	0.8865	0.8820	0.8796

Table 1: Precision for various NCC queries (*Baseline*) and for using the SVM with 10%, 50% and 90% training data.

sized training sets; as the last result suggests, for larger sets it would be desirable for our system to be faster overall. One way to achieve this is to pre-compute the feature vectors used in the training phase once — this could be done at the same time with the parsing of the sentences, i.e. at the setup time of the system.

Krippendorff's α, an inter-annotator agreement (IAA) measure which usually assumes values between 0 (no reliable agreement) and 1 (perfect agreement), amounts to 0.8207 averaged over all manually created *It-cleft* annotations. If we interpret the SVM as an additional annotator (α_{svm}), the IAA drops to 0.5903. At first glance this seems quite low, however upon closer inspection this can be explained by an overfitting of the classifier. This effect occurs for the already precise baseline queries, where in some cases less than 5% of the query results were labeled as *Wrong*. The same holds for *NP-preposing* (α: 0.6574, α_{svm}: 0.3835) and *PP-inversion* (α: 0.9410, α_{svm}: 0.6964). We interpret this as the classifier being successful in helping the annotators after a brief training phase identifying additional occurrences of particular variants of a phenomenon as covered by the queries, but not easily generalizing to variants substantially different from those covered by the queries.

4 Conclusion

With automatic ranking we introduced an extension to the *annotation-by-query* workflow which facilitates manual, selective annotation of large corpora. We explained the benefits of *in-tool* learning to this task and our extension of an open-source tool to incorporate this functionality. Finally, we showed the applicability of the concept and its implementation to the task of finding non-canonical constructions.

For future work, we plan to speed up the learning process (e.g. by saving feature vectors instead of re-calculating them), and also add the ability for users to configure the features used to train the classifier, e.g. incorporating lemmata or named entities instead of only using the parse tree. Integrating such configuration options in an easily understandable and user-friendly fashion may not be trivial but can help to generalize the approach to support additional kinds of sentence level annotation.

Acknowledgements

We would like to thank Pia Gerhard, Sabine Bartsch, Gert Webelhuth, and Janina Rado for annotating and testing. Furthermore we would like to thank Janina Rado for creating the CQP macros used in the tests.

This work has been supported by the German Federal Ministry of Education and Research (BMBF) under the promotional reference 01UG1416B (CEDIFOR), by the German Institute for Educational Research (DIPF) as part of the graduate program "Knowledge Discovery in Scientific Literature" (KDSL), and by the Volkswagen Foundation as part of the Lichtenberg-Professorship Program under grant No. I/82806.

References

Richard Eckart de Castilho and Iryna Gurevych. 2014. A broad-coverage collection of portable NLP components for building shareable analysis pipelines. In *Proceedings of the Workshop on OIAF4HLT at COLING 2014*, pages 1–11.

Richard Eckart de Castilho, Iryna Gurevych, and Sabine Bartsch. 2012. CSniper: Annotation-by-query for Non-canonical Constructions in Large Corpora. In *Proceedings of ACL 2012*, System Demonstrations, pages 85–90, Stroudsburg, PA, USA. ACL.

Stefan Evert and Andrew Hardie. 2011. Twenty-first century corpus workbench: Updating a query architecture for the new millennium. In *Proceedings of CL2011*, Birmingham, UK.

Shortcut	Expansion
VCC	([pos="VBB" | pos="VBD" | pos="VBZ"]* [lemma="be"]) | ([pos="V.*"]* [pos="VBG" | pos="VBI" | pos="VBN"]* [lemma="be"])
NP	[pos="AT0"]? []? [pos="AJ.*"]* [pos="N.*"]
RC	([pos="DTQ" | pos="PNQ" | pos="CJT"] /VCF[] []?) | ([pos="CJT"]? /NP[] /VCF[] []?) | ([pos="PR.*"]* [pos=".Q"] /NP[] /VCF[] []?)
VCF	[pos="V.?B" | pos="V.?D" | pos="V.?Z" | pos="VM0"] [pos="V.*"]*

Table 2: CQP macro expansions for self-defined macros. BNC uses the CLAWS5 tagset for POS tags (http://www.natcorp.ox.ac.uk/docs/c5spec.html).

Ben Hachey, Beatrice Alex, and Markus Becker. 2005. Investigating the Effects of Selective Sampling on the Annotation Task. In *Proceedings of CoNLL 2005*, pages 144–151, Stroudsburg, PA, USA. ACL.

Rodney D. Huddleston and Geoffrey K. Pullum. 2002. *The Cambridge Grammar of the English Language*. Cambridge University Press.

Thorsten Joachims. 1999. Making large-scale support vector machine learning practical. In Bernhard Schölkopf, Christopher J. C. Burges, and Alexander J. Smola, editors, *Advances in Kernel Methods*, pages 169–184. MIT Press, Cambridge, MA, USA.

Dan Klein and Christopher D. Manning. 2003. Accurate Unlexicalized Parsing. In *Proceedings of ACL 2003*, pages 423–430, Stroudsburg, PA, USA. ACL.

Thomas Morton and Jeremy LaCivita. 2003. WordFreak: An open tool for linguistic annotation. In *Proceedings of NAACL HLT 2003*, NAACL-Demonstrations, pages 17–18, Stroudsburg, PA, USA. ACL.

Alessandro Moschitti. 2006. Making Tree Kernels Practical for Natural Language Learning. In *Proceedings of EACL 2006*, pages 113–120, Trento, Italy.

Burr Settles. 2011. Closing the Loop: Fast, Interactive Semi-supervised Annotation with Queries on Features and Instances. In *Proceedings of EMNLP 2011*, pages 1467–1478, Stroudsburg, PA, USA. ACL.

The British National Corpus, version 3 (BNC XML Edition). 2007. Distributed by Oxford University Computing Services on behalf of the BNC Consortium. URL: http://www.natcorp.ox.ac.uk/.

Seid Muhie Yimam, Richard Eckart de Castilho, Iryna Gurevych, and Chris Biemann. 2014. Automatic Annotation Suggestions and Custom Annotation Layers in WebAnno. In *Proceedings of ACL 2014*, System Demonstrations, pages 91–96, Stroudsburg, PA, USA. ACL.

KeLP: a Kernel-based Learning Platform for Natural Language Processing

Simone Filice(†), **Giuseppe Castellucci**(‡), **Danilo Croce**(⋆), **Roberto Basili**(⋆)
(†) Dept. of Civil Engineering and Computer Science Engineering
(‡) Dept. of Electronic Engineering
(⋆) Dept. of Enterprise Engineering
University of Roma, Tor Vergata, Italy
{filice,croce,basili}@info.uniroma2.it; castellucci@ing.uniroma2.it

Abstract

Kernel-based learning algorithms have been shown to achieve state-of-the-art results in many Natural Language Processing (NLP) tasks. We present KELP, a Java framework that supports the implementation of both kernel-based learning algorithms and kernel functions over generic data representation, e.g. vectorial data or discrete structures. The framework has been designed to decouple kernel functions and learning algorithms: once a new kernel function has been implemented it can be adopted in all the available kernel-machine algorithms. The platform includes different Online and Batch Learning algorithms for Classification, Regression and Clustering, as well as several Kernel functions, ranging from vector-based to structural kernels. This paper will show the main aspects of the framework by applying it to different NLP tasks.

1 Introduction

Most of the existing Machine Learning (ML) platforms assume that instances are represented as vectors in a feature space, e.g. (Joachims, 1999; Hall et al., 2009; Chang and Lin, 2011), that must be defined beforehand. In Natural Language Processing (NLP) the definition of a feature space often requires a complex feature engineering phase. Let us consider any NLP task in which syntactic information is crucial, e.g. *Boundary Detection* in Semantic Role Labeling (Carreras and Màrquez, 2005). Understanding which syntactic patterns should be captured is non-trivial and usually the resulting feature vector model is a poor approximation. Instead, a more natural approach is operating directly with the parse tree of sentences. Kernel methods (Shawe-Taylor and Cristianini, 2004) provide an efficient and effective solution, allowing to represent data at a more abstract level, while their computation still looks at the informative properties of them. For instance, Tree Kernels (Collins and Duffy, 2001) take in input two syntactic parse trees, and compute a similarity measure by looking at the shared sub-structures.

In this paper, KELP, a Java kernel based learning platform is presented. It supports the implementation of Kernel-based learning algorithms, as well as kernel functions over generic data representations, e.g. vectorial data or discrete structures, such as trees and sequences. The framework has been designed to decouple data structures, kernel functions and learning algorithms in order to maximize the re-use of existing functionalities: as an example, a new kernel can be included inheriting existing algorithms and vice versa. KELP supports XML and JSON serialization of kernel functions and algorithms, enabling the agile definition of kernel-based learning systems without writing additional lines of code. KELP can effectively tackle a wide variety of learning problems. In particular, in this paper we will show how vectorial and structured data can be exploited by KELP in three NLP tasks: *Twitter Sentiment Analysis*, *Text Categorization* and *Question Classification*.

2 Framework Overview

KELP is a machine learning library completely written in Java. The Java language has been chosen in order to be compatible with many Java NLP/IR tools that are developed by the commu-

Proceedings of ACL-IJCNLP 2015 System Demonstrations, pages 19–24,
Beijing, China, July 26-31, 2015. ©2015 ACL and AFNLP

nity, such as Stanford CoreNLP[1], OpenNLP[2] or Lucene[3]. KELP is released as open source software under the Apache 2.0 license and the source code is available on github[4]. Furthermore it can be imported via Maven. A detailed documentation of KELP with helpful examples and use cases is available on the website of the Semantic Analytics Group[5] of the University of Roma, Tor Vergata.

In this Section, a closer look at the implementation of different kinds of data representations, kernel functions and kernel-based learning algorithms is provided.

2.1 Data Representations

KELP supports both vectorial and structured data to model learning instances. For example, `SparseVector` can host a Bag-of-Words model, while `DenseVector` can represent data derived from low dimensional embeddings. `TreeRepresentation` can model a parse tree and `SequenceRepresentation` can be adopted to represent sequences of characters or sequences of words. Moreover, the platform enables the definition of more complex forms of data such as pairs, which are useful in modeling those problems where instances can be naturally represented as pairs of texts, such as question and answer in Q/A re-ranking (Severyn and Moschitti, 2013), text and hypothesis in textual entailment (Zanzotto et al., 2009) or sentence pairs in paraphrasing detection (Filice et al., 2015).

2.2 Kernels

Many ML algorithms rely on the notion of similarity between examples. Kernel methods (Shawe-Taylor and Cristianini, 2004) leverage on the so-called kernel functions, which compute the similarity between instances in an implicit high-dimensional feature space without explicitly computing the coordinates of the data in that space. The kernel operation is often cheaper from a computational perspective and specific kernels have been defined for sequences, graphs, trees, texts, images, as well as vectors.

Kernels can be combined and composed to create richer similarity metrics, where information from different `Representations` can be exploited at the same time. This flexibility is completely supported by KELP, which is also easy to extend with new kernels. Among the currently available implementations of kernels, there are various standard kernels, such as `LinearKernel`, `PolynomialKernel` or `RbfKernel`. A large set of kernels specifically designed for NLP applications will be described in the following section.

2.2.1 Kernels for NLP

Many tasks in NLP cannot be properly tackled considering only a Bag-of-Words approach and require the exploration of deep syntactic aspects. In question classification the syntactic information is crucial has largely demonstrated in (Croce et al., 2011). In Textual Entailment Recognition or in Paraphrase Detection a pure lexical similarity between *text* and *hypothesis* cannot capture any difference between *Federer won against Nadal* and *Nadal won against Federer*. A manual definition of an artificial feature set accounting for syntax is a very expensive operation that requires a deep knowledge of the linguistic phenomena characterizing a specific task. Moreover, every task has specific patterns that must be considered, making a manual feature engineering an extremely complex and not portable operation. How can linguistic patterns characterizing a question be automatically discovered? How can linguistic rewriting rules in paraphrasing be learnt? How can semantic and syntactic relations in textual entailment be automatically captured? An elegant and efficient approach to solve NLP problems involving the usage of syntax is provided by tree kernels (Collins and Duffy, 2001). Instead of trying to design a synthetic feature space, tree kernels directly operate on the parse tree of sentences evaluating the tree fragments shared by two trees. This operation implicitly corresponds to a dot product in the feature space of all possible tree fragments. The dimensionality of such space is extremely large and operating directly on it is not viable.

Many tree kernels are implemented in KELP, and they differ by the type of tree fragment considered in the evaluation of the matching structures. In the `SubTreeKernel` (Collins and Duffy, 2001) valid fragments are subtrees (ST), i.e. any node of a tree along with all its descendants. A subset tree (SST) exploited by the `SubSetTreeKernel` is a more general structure since its leaves can be non-

[1] http://nlp.stanford.edu/software/corenlp.shtml
[2] https://opennlp.apache.org/
[3] http://lucene.apache.org/
[4] https://github.com/SAG-KeLP
[5] http://sag.art.uniroma2.it/demo-software/kelp/

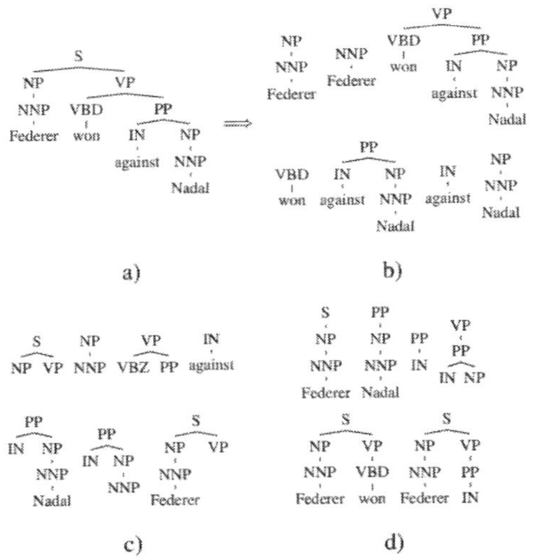

Figure 1: a) Constituent parse tree of the sentence *Federer won against Nadal.* b) some subtrees. c) some subset trees. d) some partial trees.

terminal symbols. The SSTs satisfy the constraint that grammatical rules cannot be broken. `PartialTreeKernel` (Moschitti, 2006) relaxes this constraint considering partial trees (PT), i.e. fragments generated by the application of partial production rules. Examples of different kinds of tree fragments are shown in Figure 1. The `SmoothedPartialTreeKernel` (SPTK) (Croce et al., 2011) allows to match those fragments that are not identical but that are semantically related, by relying on the similarity between lexical items, e.g. by applying a word similarity metric (e.g. WordNet or word embeddings similarities). The adopted implementation allows to easily extend the notion of similarity between nodes, enabling the implementation of more expressive kernels, as the Compositionally Smoothed Partial Tree Kernel (CSPTK) that embeds algebraic operators of Distributional Compositional Semantics (Annesi et al., 2014). Moreover, the `SequenceKernel` (Bunescu and Mooney, 2005) is included in the library, and it allows to compare two texts evaluating the number of common sub-sequences. This implicitly corresponds to operate on the space of all possible N-grams. Kernels operating over pairs, such as the `PreferenceKernel` (Shen and Joshi, 2003) for re-ranking, are also included in KELP.

2.3 Machine Learning Algorithms

In ML, a plethora of learning algorithms have been defined for different purposes, and many variations of the existing ones as well as completely new learning methods are often proposed. KELP provides a large number of learning algorithms[6] ranging from batch, e.g. Support Vector Machines (Vapnik, 1995), to online learning models, e.g. `PassiveAggressive` algorithms (Crammer et al., 2006), and from linear to kernel-based methods, for tackling classification, regression or clustering tasks. Moreover, algorithms can be composed in meta-learning schemas, like multi-class classification (e.g. `One-VS-One` and `One-VS-All`, (Rifkin and Klautau, 2004)) and multi-label classification, or can be combined in ensembles. A simple interface taxonomy allows to easily extend the platform with new custom learning algorithms. A complete support for tackling NLP tasks is thus provided. For example, in scenarios where the syntactic information is necessary for achieving good accuracy, `C-SVM` or ν`-SVM` (Chang and Lin, 2011) operating on trees with kernels can be effectively applied. When dealing with large datasets, many efficient learning algorithm can be adopted, like linear methods, e.g. `Pegasos` (Shalev-Shwartz et al., 2007) or `LibLinear`, (Fan et al., 2008), or like budgeted kernel-based algorithms, e.g. `RandomizedPerceptron` (Cesa-Bianchi and Gentile, 2006).

Listing 1: A JSON example.

```
{"algorithm" : "oneVsAll",
  "baseAlgorithm" : {
    "algorithm" : "binaryCSvmClassification",
    "c" : 10,
    "kernel" : {
      "kernelType" : "linearComb",
      "weights" : [1,1],
      "toCombine" : [
        {
          "kernelType" : "norm",
          "baseKernel" : {
            "kernelType" : "ptk",
            "mu" : 0.4,
            "lambda" : 0.4,
            "representation" : "parseTree"
          }
        },
        {
          "kernelType" : "linear",
          "representation" : "Bag-of-Words"
        }
      ]
    }
  }
}
```

2.4 A JSON example

Kernel functions and algorithms are serializable in JSON or XML. This is useful for instantiating a new algorithm without writing a single line of Java

[6]All the algorithms are completely re-implemented in Java and they do not wrap any external library

code, i.e. the algorithm description can be provided in JSON to an interpreter that will instantiate it. Listing 1 reports a JSON example of a kernel-based Support Vector Machine operating in a one-vs-all schema, where a kernel linear combination between a normalized Partial Tree Kernel and a linear kernel is adopted. As the listing shows kernels and algorithms can be easily composed and combined in order to create new training models.

3 Case Studies in NLP

In this Section, the functionalities and use of the learning platform are shown. We apply KELP to very different NLP tasks, i.e. *Sentiment Analysis in Twitter*, *Text Categorization* and *Question Classification*, providing examples of kernel-based and linear learning algorithms. Further examples are available on the KELP website[7] where it is shown how to instantiate each algorithm or kernel via JSON and how to add new algorithms, representations and kernels.

3.1 Sentiment Analysis in Twitter

The task of Sentiment Analysis in Twitter has been proposed in 2013 during the SemEval competition (Nakov et al., 2013). We built a classifier for the subtask B, i.e. the classification of a tweet with respect to the *positive*, *negative* and *neutral* classes. The contribution of different kernel functions is evaluated using the Support Vector Machine learning algorithm. As shown in Table 1, we apply linear (Lin), polynomial (Poly) and Gaussian (Rbf) kernels on two different data representations: a Bag-Of-Words model of tweets (BoW) and a distributional representation (WS). The last is obtained by linearly combining the distributional vectors corresponding to the words of a message; these vectors are obtained by applying a Skip-gram model (Mikolov et al., 2013) with the *word2vec* tool[8] over 20 million of tweets. The linear combination of the proposed kernel functions is also applied, e.g. Poly_{Bow}+Rbf_{WS}. The mean F1-measure of the *positive* and *negative* classes (pn)[9] as well as of all the classes (pnn) is shown in Table 1.

3.2 Text Categorization

In order to show the scalability of the platform, a second evaluation considers linear algorithms.

Kernel	MeanF1(pn)	MeanF1(pnn)
Lin_{BoW}	59.72	63.53
Poly_{BoW}	54.58	59.27
Lin_{WS}	60.79	63.94
Rbf_{WS}	61.68	65.05
Lin_{BoW}+Lin_{WS}	66.12	68.56
Poly_{BoW}+Rbf_{WS}	64.92	68.10

Table 1: Results of Sentiment Analysis

We selected the Text Categorization task on the RCV1 dataset (Lewis et al., 2004) with the setting that can be found on the LibLinear website[10]. In this version of the dataset, *CCAT* and *ECAT* are collapsed into a positive class, while *GCAT* and *MCAT* are the negative class, resulting in a dataset composed by $20,242$ examples. As shown in Table 2, we applied the LibLinear, Pegasos and Linear Passive-Aggressive implementations, computing the accuracy and the standard deviation with respect to a 5-fold cross validation strategy.

Task	Accuracy	Std
LibLinear	96.74%	0.0029
Pegasos	95.31%	0.0033
Passive Aggressive	96.60%	0.0024

Table 2: Text Categorization Accuracy

3.3 Question Classification

The third case study explores the application of Tree Kernels to Question Classification (QC), an inference task required in many Question Answering processes. In this problem, questions written in natural language are assigned to different classes. A QC system should select the correct class given an instance question. In this setting, Tree Kernels allow to directly model the examples in terms of their parse trees. The reference corpus is the UIUC dataset (Li and Roth, 2002), including 5,452 questions for training and 500 questions for test[11], organized in six coarse-grained classes, such as `HUMAN` or `LOCATION`. Again, Kernel-based SVM has been evaluated adopting the same setup of (Croce et al., 2011). A pure lexical model based on a linear kernel over a Bag-of-Words (BoW) is considered a baseline. The contribution of the syntactic information is demonstrated by the results achieved by the Partial Tree Kernel (PTK), the Smoothed Partial Tree Kernels (SPTK) and the Compositionally Smoothed Partial Tree Kernel (CSPTK), as shown in Table 3.

[7] `http://sag.art.uniroma2.it/demo-software/kelp/`

[8] `https://code.google.com/p/word2vec/`

[9] pn was the official metric of the SemEval competition.

[10] `http://www.csie.ntu.edu.tw/~cjlin/libsvmtools/datasets/`

[11] `http://cogcomp.cs.illinois.edu/Data/QA/QC/`

Kernel	Accuracy
BoW	87.2%
Poly_{BoW}	88.8%
PTK	91.6%
SPTK	94.6%
CSPTK	95.0%

Table 3: Question Classification Accuracy.

4 Related Work

Many software tools for computational linguistic research already exist. Tools like Stanford CoreNLP or OpenNLP provide a complete pipeline for performing linguistic tasks such as stemming, lemmatization, Part-of-Speech tagging or parsing. They are complementary to KELP: they can be used in the feature extraction phase, while KELP will care about the machine learning part. Regarding other machine learning platforms there are plenty of available possibilities, but for different reasons no one can provide something close to what the proposed library offers.

Weka (Hall et al., 2009) is a collection of machine learning algorithms for data mining tasks. The algorithms can either be applied directly to a dataset or called from Java. It contains various tools for different data mining activities: data pre-processing, classification, regression, clustering and visualization.

Mallet (McCallum, 2002) is more oriented to NLP applications. It is entirely in Java and includes feature extraction tools for converting text into vectors and statistical analysis tools for document classification, clustering, topic modeling, information extraction, and other machine learning applications to text. Regarding the kernel-based learning both Weka and Mallet leverage on LibSVM, and obviously inherit its limits.

LibSVM (Chang and Lin, 2011) is a machine learning platform focusing on Support Vector Machines. It is written in C++ language and it includes different SVM formulations: `C-svm`, `Nu-svm` and `OneClass-svm`, as well as a one-vs-one multi classification schema. It implements also regression support vector solvers. It has been ported in different languages, including Java. The batch learning part of KELP is strongly inspired by LibSVM formulations and implementations. LibSVM is mainly intended for plain users and does not provide any support for extendibility. It can operate only on sparse feature vectors via standard kernel functions. No structured representations are considered.

Another very popular Support Vector Machines (SVM) package is SvmLight (Joachims, 1999). It is entirely written in C language and its main feature is speed. It solves classification and regression problems, as well as ranking problems. Its efficiency is paid in terms of extensibility: C language does not allow a fast prototyping of new machine learning kernels or algorithms. Many times in research contexts fast prototyping is more important than performances: the proposed platform has been developed with extensibility in mind.

The most similar platform to ours is JKernelMachines (Picard et al., 2013). It is a Java based package focused on Kernel machines. Just like the proposed library, JKernelMachines is primary designed to deal with custom kernels that cannot be easily found in standard libraries. Standard SVM optimization algorithms are implemented, but also more sophisticated learning-based kernel combination methods such as Multiple Kernel Learning (MKL). However, many features covered by KELP are not offered by JKernelMachines, just like tree kernels, regression and clustering. Moreover, different architectural choices have been applied in KELP in order to support an easier composition and combination of representations, kernels as well as learning algorithms.

5 Conclusions

This paper presented KELP, a Java framework to support the application of Kernel-based learning methods with a particular attention to Language Learning tasks. The library implements a large variety of kernel functions used in NLP (such as Tree Kernels or Sequence Kernels) as well as many learning algorithms useful in classification, regression, novelty detection or clustering problems. KELP can be imported via Maven but its usage is not restricted to a Java-compliant environment as it allows to build complex kernel machine based systems, leveraging on JSON/XML interfaces to instantiate classifiers. The entire framework has been designed to support researchers in the development of new kernel functions or algorithms, providing a principled decoupling of the data structures in order to maximize the re-use of existing functionalities. The benefits of the proposed environment have been shown in three NLP tasks, where results in line with the state-of-the-art have been reached with the simple application of various kernel functions available in KELP.

References

Paolo Annesi, Danilo Croce, and Roberto Basili. 2014. Semantic compositionality in tree kernels. In *Proc. of CIKM 2014*, pages 1029–1038, New York, NY, USA. ACM.

Razvan C. Bunescu and Raymond J. Mooney. 2005. Subsequence kernels for relation extraction. In *NIPS*.

Xavier Carreras and Lluís Màrquez. 2005. Introduction to the conll-2005 shared task: Semantic role labeling. In *Proceedings of the Ninth Conference on Computational Natural Language Learning*, CONLL '05, pages 152–164, Stroudsburg, PA, USA. Association for Computational Linguistics.

Nicolò Cesa-Bianchi and Claudio Gentile. 2006. Tracking the best hyperplane with a simple budget perceptron. In *In Proc. of the 19th Annual Conference on Computational Learning Theory*, pages 483–498. Springer-Verlag.

Chih-Chung Chang and Chih-Jen Lin. 2011. LIBSVM: A library for support vector machines. *ACM Transactions on Intelligent Systems and Technology*, 2:27:1–27:27.

Michael Collins and Nigel Duffy. 2001. Convolution kernels for natural language. In *NIPS*.

Koby Crammer, Ofer Dekel, Joseph Keshet, Shai Shalev-Shwartz, and Yoram Singer. 2006. Online passive-aggressive algorithms. *JMLR*, 7:551–585, December.

Danilo Croce, Alessandro Moschitti, and Roberto Basili. 2011. Structured lexical similarity via convolution kernels on dependency trees. In *EMNLP*, Edinburgh.

Rong-En Fan, Kai-Wei Chang, Cho-Jui Hsieh, Xiang-Rui Wang, and Chih-Jen Lin. 2008. Liblinear: A library for large linear classification. *J. Mach. Learn. Res.*, 9:1871–1874, June.

Simone Filice, Giovanni Da San Martino, and Alessandro Moschitti. 2015. Structural representations for learning relations between pairs of texts. In *Proceedings of the 53rd Annual Meeting of the Association for Computational Linguistics*, Beijing, China, July. Association for Computational Linguistics.

Mark Hall, Eibe Frank, Geoffrey Holmes, Bernhard Pfahringer, Peter Reutemann, and Ian H. Witten. 2009. The weka data mining software: An update. *sigkdd explor.*, 11(1).

T. Joachims. 1999. Making large-scale SVM learning practical. In B. Schölkopf, C. Burges, and A. Smola, editors, *Advances in Kernel Methods - Support Vector Learning*, pages 169–184. MIT Press.

David D. Lewis, Yiming Yang, Tony G. Rose, and Fan Li. 2004. Rcv1: A new benchmark collection for text categorization research. *J. Mach. Learn. Res.*, 5:361–397, December.

X. Li and D. Roth. 2002. Learning question classifiers. In *Proceedings of ACL '02*, COLING '02, pages 1–7, Stroudsburg, PA, USA. Association for Computational Linguistics.

Andrew Kachites McCallum. 2002. Mallet: A machine learning for language toolkit. http://mallet.cs.umass.edu.

Tomas Mikolov, Kai Chen, Greg Corrado, and Jeffrey Dean. 2013. Efficient estimation of word representations in vector space. *arXiv preprint arXiv:1301.3781*.

Alessandro Moschitti. 2006. Efficient convolution kernels for dependency and constituent syntactic trees. In *ECML*, Berlin, Germany, September.

Preslav Nakov, Sara Rosenthal, Zornitsa Kozareva, Veselin Stoyanov, Alan Ritter, and Theresa Wilson. 2013. Semeval-2013 task 2: Sentiment analysis in twitter. In *Proceedings of SemEval 2013*, pages 312–320, Atlanta, USA. ACL.

David Picard, Nicolas Thome, and Matthieu Cord. 2013. Jkernelmachines: A simple framework for kernel machines. *Journal of Machine Learning Research*, 14:1417–1421.

Ryan Rifkin and Aldebaro Klautau. 2004. In defense of one-vs-all classification. *J. Mach. Learn. Res.*, 5:101–141, December.

Aliaksei Severyn and Alessandro Moschitti. 2013. Automatic feature engineering for answer selection and extraction. In *Proceedings of the 2013 Conference on EMNLP*, pages 458–467, Seattle, USA. ACL.

S. Shalev-Shwartz, Y. Singer, and N. Srebro. 2007. Pegasos: Primal estimated sub–gradient solver for SVM. In *Proc. of ICML*.

John Shawe-Taylor and Nello Cristianini. 2004. *Kernel Methods for Pattern Analysis*. Cambridge University Press.

Libin Shen and Aravind K. Joshi. 2003. An svm based voting algorithm with application to parse reranking. In *In Proc. of CoNLL 2003*, pages 9–16.

Vladimir N. Vapnik. 1995. *The Nature of Statistical Learning Theory*. Springer-Verlag New York, Inc., New York, NY, USA.

Fabio massimo Zanzotto, Marco Pennacchiotti, and Alessandro Moschitti. 2009. A machine learning approach to textual entailment recognition. *Nat. Lang. Eng.*, 15(4):551–582, October.

Multi-modal Visualization and Search for Text and Prosody Annotations

Markus Gärtner Katrin Schweitzer Kerstin Eckart Jonas Kuhn
Institute for Natural Language Processing
University of Stuttgart
{markus.gaertner,kati,eckartkn,kuhn}@ims.uni-stuttgart.de

Abstract

We present ICARUS for intonation, an interactive tool to browse and search automatically derived descriptions of fundamental frequency contours. It offers access to tonal features in combination with other annotation layers like part-of-speech, syntax or coreference and visualizes them in a highly customizable graphical interface with various playback functions. The built-in search allows multi-level queries, the construction of which can be done graphically or textually, and includes the ability to search F_0 contours based on various similarity measures.

1 Introduction

In this paper we present *ICARUS for intonation*, a new module for the query and visualization tool ICARUS by Gärtner et al. (2013). [1]

So far, ICARUS included modules for the handling of dependency treebanks (Gärtner et al., 2013) and coreference data (Gärtner et al., 2014), thus supporting typical annotation layers from the processing of written data. However, the graphical query builder and the intuitive example-based search could prove just as expedient for other types of data, such as speech corpora, transcribed and annotated for sub word features. This also allows combined research on speech and text data, e.g. the analysis of different tonal realizations of a certain syntactic structure.

ICARUS for intonation allows to import syllable-based prosodic features into ICARUS, which can then be visualized and queried either individually or in a combined search with e.g. syntactic features or coreference information. The latter targets several user groups: speech data experts can adjust fine-grained settings on pitch accent shapes in their queries and can easily add constraints on part-of-speech or syntax information, while an expert user of dependency treebanks can get a simple visualization of the intonation contour of a sentence.

Furthermore ICARUS focuses on automatic annotations to allow for search on large data sets. Thus ICARUS for intonation's main features for prosodic search are based on PaIntE, a parametric intonation model (Möhler, 1998; Möhler, 2001). So far, most data in intonation research is manually annotated, which is a very time consuming task: the time for annotating speech data is many times higher than the real time of the audio recording. For example the Tones and Break Indices (ToBI) system for American English (Beckman and Hirschberg, 1999) takes experienced annotators about 100-200 times the real time (Syrdal et al., 2001). While manual annotations for pitch accents and prosodic phrase boundaries can also be imported, our main goal with this module is to provide intonation researchers with a customizable tool to conduct thorough studies on very large sets of only automatically annotated speech data.

In Sections 2 and 3 we introduce the PaIntE model and describe the current input format for the data importer. Section 4 demonstrates several visualization functionalities, and Section 5 discusses the search facilities, including dependency and intonation as well as coreference and intonation queries. After discussing some related work in Section 6 we conclude in Section 7.

2 The PaIntE Model

The PaIntE model (Möhler, 1998; Möhler, 2001) approximates a peak in the F_0 contour by employing a model function operating on a 3-syllable

[1] ICARUS for intonation is written in Java and is therefore platform independent. It is open source (under GNU GPL) and we provide both sources and binaries for download on http://www.ims.uni-stuttgart.de/data/icarus.html

Proceedings of ACL-IJCNLP 2015 System Demonstrations, pages 25–30,
Beijing, China, July 26-31, 2015. ©2015 ACL and AFNLP

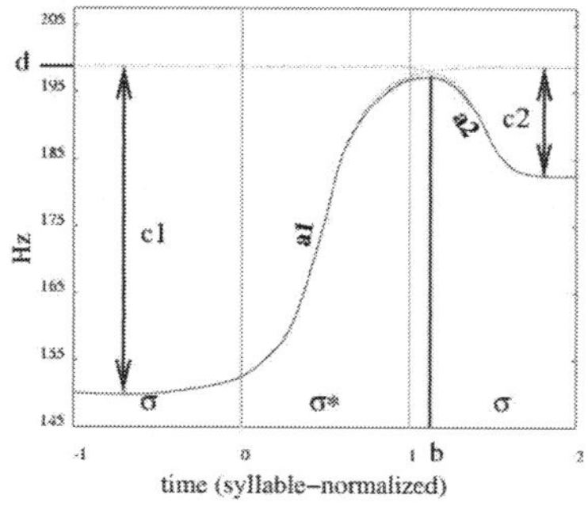

Figure 1: The PaIntE model function and its parameters. Figure adapted from (Möhler, 2001).

window. There are 6 free parameters in the function term which are set by the model so that the actual F_0 shape is fit best. They are linguistically meaningful: parameter b locates the peak within the 3-syllable window, parameter d encodes its absolute height. The remaining parameters specify the steepness and amplitude of the rise before, and the fall after the peak (parameters $a1$ and $a2$ for the steepness and $c1/c2$ for the amplitude).

Figure 1 illustrates the function. It displays the syllable for which the parametrization is carried out ($\sigma*$) and its immediate neighbors. The x-axis indicates time (normalized for syllable duration, the current syllable spans from 0 to 1) and the y-axis displays the fundamental frequency in Hertz. The PaIntE model has been used for the modeling of different languages, e.g. Norwegian, Italian, German and English (Cosi et al., 2002; Kelly and Schweitzer, in press; Schweitzer et al., 2015).

3 Data Representation

ICARUS for intonation ships with reader implementations for two very different formats. One is an extended version of the format used for the 2011 and 2012 CoNLL shared tasks (Pradhan et al., 2011; Pradhan et al., 2012) with a number of additional columns to accommodate features for the syllable level. This format stores all annotations corresponding to a word token in one line and packs syllable features into a list separated by pipe-characters ('|'). To address syllable centric data like the typical output of speech processing systems, a second flexible tabular format was specified where each line of text corresponds to a single syllable and a global header describes the content of all columns and how to read and map them to the internal data model of ICARUS.

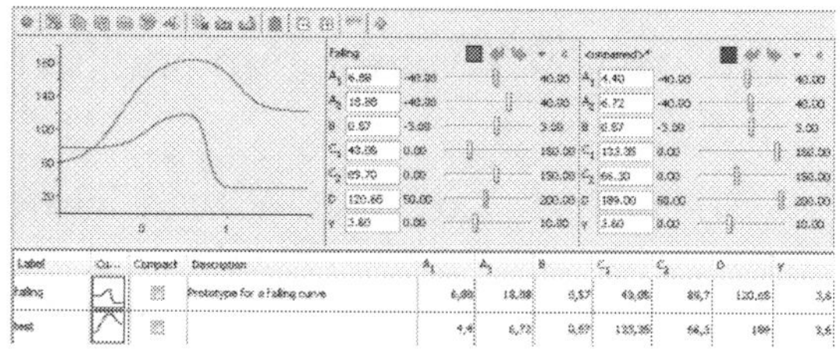

Figure 2: PaIntE Editor currently displaying 2 curves and their respective parameters. The lower section shows saved and named prototypes.

To enable audio playback functionality ICARUS for intonation requires access to the appropriate sound files. In both formats described above, special properties define the name of a sound file to be used for playback. Timestamp values on various levels (syllable, word, sentence or document) point to the respective section in the audio data, which currently is required to be in the Waveform Audio File Format (*.wav files).

4 Visualization

Since the ICARUS for intonation module is build on the data model used for corpora with coreference annotations in ICARUS, existing visualizations for coreference data can be used. However, they make no use of syllable level features and do not provide playback functionality. Therefore a couple of new visualizations have been implemented, adding visual information about PaIntE curves in several levels of granularity.

4.1 PaIntE Editor

To get familiar with the visualization of PaIntE parameters the PaIntE Editor (Figure 2) offers users with little or no knowledge about PaIntE a starting point to directly see the impact of changes to certain parameters. In this editor the user can define multiple PaIntE curves either from scratch or by importing them from real examples in a corpus. Changes to individual parameters can be applied via sliders or input fields and are displayed in real-time. Additionally a persistent storage of PaIntE curves is provided where the user can save parameter sets that are of interest to him along with a description and identifier, the latter of which can be used when searching (see Section 5).

4.2 Curve Preview

For all visualizations dealing with PaIntE curves ICARUS for intonation provides a compact "preview" on the sentence level (lower parts of Figures 3 and 4b). Instead of drawing the full curves for all syllables, only syllables in which a peak was found (based on the peak's timing encoded in the PaIntE parameter b) are displayed. The visualization of the curve then only uses the amplitudes of rise and fall and the absolute height of the peak ($c1$, $c2$ and d). Since the user can freely customize the filter window for the peak this curve preview offers a fast way to spot interesting parts of the F_0 contour when exploring data manually.

4.3 Document Outline

Figure 3 shows parts of the main entry point for manual exploration in ICARUS for intonation. Having selected a section of the corpus the user wishes to inspect (with sentences grouped into documents in the left section of the figure) he then gets a detailed outline of the contents of that document using one of several available presentation modes. The default visualization for data holding PaIntE annotations arranges the document's content one sentence per line, making use of the above mentioned curve preview to provide the user with a very compact overview of an entire document. For each sentence a detail panel can be unfolded which renders the complete PaIntE curves above the preview area. Several aspects of the visualization are highly customizable (like the number of words to show detailed curves for) and the user can select the content of the detail panel by moving a slider through the sentence.

An important feature of the Document Outline is the fine-grained playback functionality. The user is free to play a variety of sections of the sound data linked to the document currently being displayed. Speaker buttons at the left border play predefined parts of the sound data like sentences or the current content of a detail panel. By clicking on individual word or syllable labels in the detail panel the playback can be selected even finer.

4.4 Sentence Outline

When only single sentences are visualized, ICARUS for intonation displays a more detailed outline showing the PaIntE curves for all syllables in the sentence grouped by the surrounding words. In Figure 4b part of a sentence is visualized in this way (the screenshot also contains visual highlighting as its content is the result of a search).

In contrast to the more condensed document outline, this visualization offers a great deal more space for additional information on the syllable level to be displayed. As for playback functionality it offers granularity similar to the document outline, allowing the user to play the entire sentence or restrict it to individual words or syllables.

4.5 Label Patterns

Both formats currently read by ICARUS for intonation can contain more information on the syllable and word level than can be presented to the user without overloading the visualization. Therefore the two visualizations described above make heavy use of so called *label patterns* to produce the actual text displayed at various locations. A label pattern is a string describing a format according to which a certain text should be created. Expressions of the form "{<level>:<property>}" define where information extracted from the visualized data should be inserted. The <level> specifies the level of data to query ({syl, word, sent, doc} for the syllable, word, sentence and document levels). For example the default pattern "{word:form}\n{word:pos}", used in the Document Outline (see Section 4.3) to display the text for a sentence, extracts the surface form and part-of-speech tag for a word and places them below each other as shown in Figure 3. The user can freely define the default patterns for a number of locations as well as change the patterns used for the active visualization on the fly. Besides directly extracting data and displaying it as text, patterns offer additional options that define how to convert e.g. numerical values into strings or how to post process or aggregate generated texts. However, going into details of the pattern engine is beyond the scope of this paper.

5 Search

ICARUS for intonation augments both the coreference and dependency search facilities already available in ICARUS by adding access to various syllable features and implementing multiple specialized search constraints based on the PaIntE model. For example the user can search for predefined F_0 contours (rise, fall, rise-fall or unaccented) based on customizable criteria or use one of several similarity measures available, like Euclidean distance or cosine similarity.

Sets of PaIntE parameters can either be defined explicitly by listing all values or by referencing a previously saved prototype from the PaIntE Editor

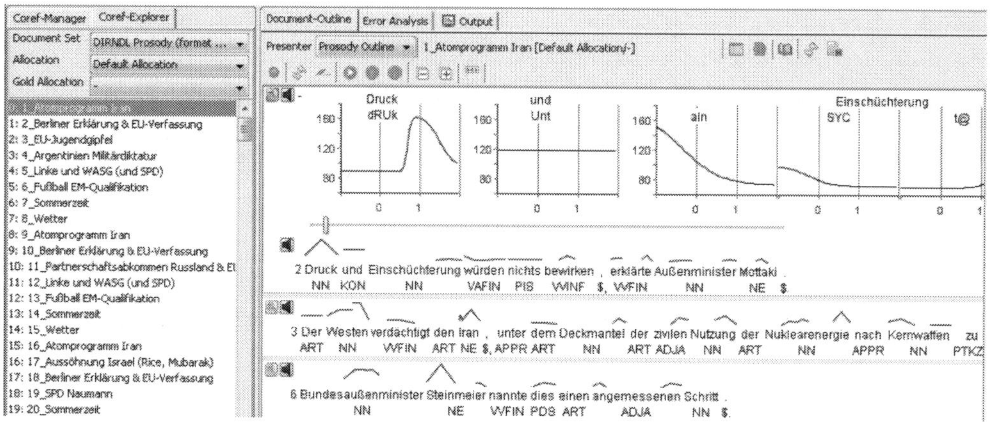

Figure 3: Visualization of the first few sentences in a document with preview curves painted above the raw text outline. The top sentence has its detail panel unfolded, showing PaIntE curves for all syllables of a selected number of words.

by name (see Section 4.1). The ICARUS search engine allows queries to be created either graphically (by creating nodes and attaching constraints to them) or textually via a simple query language (Gärtner et al., 2013).

The following two sections outline some example use cases that combine prosodic features with structural information on different layers for analysis and Section 5.3 shows some of the similarity measures used for searching. Example data in those sections is taken from the DIRNDL corpus (Eckart et al., 2012) with coreference information (Björkelund et al., 2014) and some added features.

5.1 Syntax and Intonation

As part of a recent study (Riester and Piontek, in press) adjective-noun sequences from the DIRNDL corpus have been analyzed based on their tonal realization. Of interest in this study concerning *relative givenness* (Wagner, 2006) were those adjective-noun sequences where the adjective was tonally more prominent than the adjacent noun. An example of how to find them is shown in Figure 4. The query (Figure 4a) will match adjectives (ADJA) adjacent to a following noun (NN) which must not have another dependent that is either a modifying noun or name (NE). The results are presented to the user using the detailed Sentence Outline (Figure 4b) from Section 4.4.

5.2 Coreference and Intonation

Besides finding exact matches in a data set the search engine in ICARUS can be used to analyze value distributions for an annotation. Using the query in Figure 5a the search engine is asked to look for mentions the size of up to 2 words that are not the root of a coreference chain. The special *grouping operator* <*> results in the creation of a frequency list (Figure 5b) over the Boolean *tonal prominence* property (which purely relies on the peak excursion with a customizable threshold) of the head word of each mention that was found based on the above constraints. By clicking on one of the entries in this list the user will then be presented with all the instances that contributed to the respective frequency for further exploration.

5.3 Similarity Search

The continuous nature of the PaIntE parameters makes using absolute values to search for curve forms very impractical. Therefore ICARUS for intonation provides a collection of similarity measures and other constraints that can be used to find syllables with PaIntE curves similar to a given prototype. Most of them are customizable by the user and investigation and refinement of the available similarity measures is subject of ongoing work.

Figure 6 shows an example of using cosine similarity to find instances in the data set that are similar to a defined prototype curve. In this case the first syllable of the accented word "Steinmeier" was found to be of interest and saved in the PaIntE editor with the identifier `prototype_stein`. The query `[painteAngle$"$prototype_stein"<="5.0"]` then looks for PaIntE curves which do not differ from the prototype by more than 5 degrees.

When using PaIntE curves as part of a search

(a) graphical query

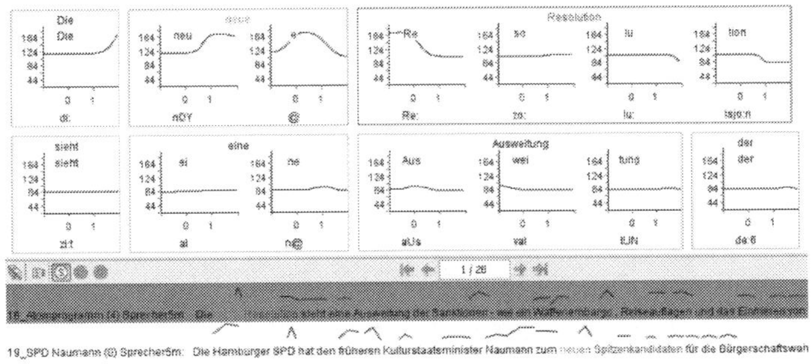

(b) result outline with highlighting

Figure 4: Example search query combining syntax and intonation constraints and an excerpt of the corresponding result outline.

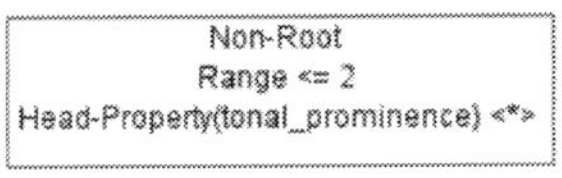

(a)

	Head-Property
false	453
true	125

(b)

Figure 5: Simple search combining coreference and intonation features. It is meant to investigate the distribution of "tonally prominent" mentions that are *given* (already introduced) in a discourse.

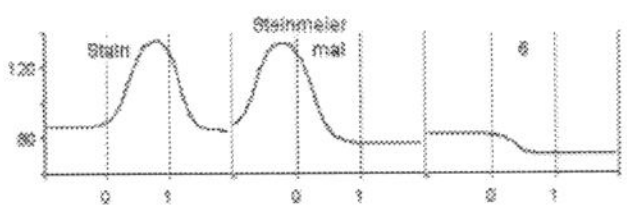

(a)

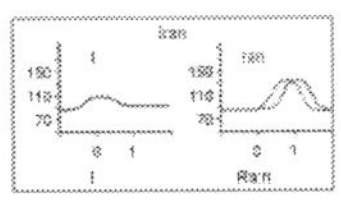

(b)

Figure 6: Prototype of a PaIntE curve as found in the data and an example result of a search using cosine similarity.

constraint the corresponding result visualization will render those curves when highlighting result instances as can be seen on the first peak (dashed blue curve) in Figures 6b. This provides the user with accurate information on how "visually close" a match is towards the used constraints.

6 Related Work

A number of well established tools exist for visualization of text corpora annotated with dependency or coreference, many of which have been discussed in other ICARUS related papers (Gärtner et al., 2013; Gärtner et al., 2014). In terms of search functionality those tools offer a broad range of complexity, ranging from string-searching on surface forms[2] up to queries on multi-level annotations (Zeldes et al., 2009; Pajas and Štěpánek, 2009). However, they do not support a dedicated search and visualization for prosodic syllable level annotations. Tools like ELAN (Wittenburg et al., 2006) provide an interface for adding (flat) annotations to multi-modal corpora, but focus on audio and video data. More importantly, ICARUS for intonation is so far the first tool using the PaIntE model for F_0 contour visualizations, a task previously worked around via general curve plotting tools like R[3] and also is first to provide a collection of search constraints dedicated to PaIntE curves.

Eckart et al. (2010) describe a database that serves as a generic query tool for multiple annotation layers. It allows to take annotations of tonal features into account and has also been tested with the DIRNDL corpus. However, this database has been designed as an expert system, e.g. for internal use in projects that create annotations. It does not provide any visualization or query functions besides basic SQL queries and no sound playback.

The focus on preprocessed or completely annotated data in ICARUS distinguishes it from typical tools in the domain of Spoken Document Retrieval (SDR) or Spoken Term Detection (STD). These use automatic speech recognition and information retrieval technologies in order to prepare and process audio data (Garofolo et al., 2000).

7 Conclusion

We presented ICARUS for intonation, a flexible visualization and search tool for multi-modal (text and speech) data. The tool augments existing visualization and search features of ICARUS to handle prosodic annotations and introduces a collec-

[2] http://code.google.com/p/whatswrong/

[3] http://www.r-project.org

tion of novel visualizations and search functionalities. In addition to the highly customizable visualizations it allows for a very fine-grained playback of speech data for displayed sections of a corpus directly from within the graphical user interface. The built-in search engine lets the user combine prosodic constraints with constraints of other annotation layers like syntax or coreference, thereby supporting complex search queries, and it features aggregated result views. Being based on the ICARUS platform's plugin-engine, the module can be extended to cover additional data formats.

Acknowledgments

This work was funded by the German Federal Ministry of Education and Research (BMBF) via CLARIN-D, No. 01UG1120F and the German Research Foundation (DFG) via the SFB 732, project INF.

References

Mary Beckman and Julia Hirschberg. 1999. The ToBI Annotation Conventions. `http://www.ling.ohio-state.edu/~tobi/ame_tobi/annotation_conventions.html`.

Anders Björkelund, Kerstin Eckart, Arndt Riester, Nadja Schauffler, and Katrin Schweitzer. 2014. The Extended DIRNDL Corpus as a Resource for Coreference and Bridging Resolution. In *LREC*.

P. Cosi, C. Avesani, F. Tesser, R. Gretter, and F. Pianesi. 2002. A modified "PaIntE" model for Italian TTS. In *Speech Synthesis, 2002. Proceedings of 2002 IEEE Workshop on*, pages 131 – 134.

Kerstin Eckart, Kurt Eberle, and Ulrich Heid. 2010. An Infrastructure for More Reliable Corpus Analysis. In *LREC: Workshop on Web Services and Processing Pipelines in HLT*, pages 8–14, Valletta.

Kerstin Eckart, Arndt Riester, and Katrin Schweitzer. 2012. A Discourse Information Radio News Database for Linguistic Analysis. In Christian Chiarcos, Sebastian Nordhoff, and Sebastian Hellmann, editors, *Linked Data in Linguistics*, pages 65–75. Springer, Heidelberg.

John S. Garofolo, Cedric G. P. Auzanne, and Ellen M. Voorhees. 2000. The TREC Spoken Document Retrieval Track: A Success Story. In *in Text Retrieval Conference (TREC) 8*, pages 16–19.

Markus Gärtner, Gregor Thiele, Wolfgang Seeker, Anders Björkelund, and Jonas Kuhn. 2013. ICARUS – An Extensible Graphical Search Tool for Dependency Treebanks. In *ACL: System Demonstrations*, pages 55–60, Sofia, Bulgaria.

Markus Gärtner, Anders Björkelund, Gregor Thiele, Wolfgang Seeker, and Jonas Kuhn. 2014. Visualization, Search, and Error Analysis for Coreference Annotations. In *ACL: System Demonstrations*, pages 7–12, Baltimore, Maryland.

Niamh Kelly and Katrin Schweitzer. in press. Examining Lexical Tonal Contrast in Norwegian Using Intonation Modelling. In *Proceedings of the 18th International Congress of Phonetic Sciences*, Glasgow, UK.

Gregor Möhler. 1998. Describing intonation with a parametric model. In *ICSLP*, volume 7, pages 2851–2854.

Gregor Möhler. 2001. Improvements of the PaIntE model for F_0 parametrization. Technical report, Institute of Natural Language Processing, University of Stuttgart. Draft version.

Petr Pajas and Jan Štěpánek. 2009. System for Querying Syntactically Annotated Corpora. In *ACL-IJCNLP: Software Demonstrations*, pages 33–36, Suntec, Singapore.

Sameer Pradhan, Lance Ramshaw, Mitchell Marcus, Martha Palmer, Ralph Weischedel, and Nianwen Xue. 2011. CoNLL-2011 Shared Task: Modeling Unrestricted Coreference in OntoNotes. In *CoNLL: Shared Task*, pages 1–27, Portland, Oregon, USA.

Sameer Pradhan, Alessandro Moschitti, Nianwen Xue, Olga Uryupina, and Yuchen Zhang. 2012. CoNLL-2012 Shared Task: Modeling Multilingual Unrestricted Coreference in OntoNotes. In *EMNLP-CoNLL: Shared Task*, pages 1–40, Jeju Island, Korea.

Arndt Riester and Jörn Piontek. in press. Anarchy in the NP. When new nouns get deaccented and given nouns don't. *Lingua*.

Katrin Schweitzer, Michael Walsh, Sasha Calhoun, Hinrich Schütze, Bernd Möbius, Antje Schweitzer, and Grzegorz Dogil. 2015. Exploring the relationship between intonation and the lexicon: Evidence for lexicalised storage of intonation. *Speech Communication*, 66(0):65–81.

Ann K. Syrdal, Julia Hirschberg, Julie McGory, and Mary Beckman. 2001. Automatic ToBI Prediction and Alignment to Speed Manual Labeling of Prosody. *Speech Commun.*, 33(1-2):135–151.

Michael Wagner. 2006. Givenness and Locality. In Masayuki Gibson and Jonathan Howell, editors, *Proceedings of SALT XVI*, pages 295–312.

P. Wittenburg, H. Brugman, A. Russel, A. Klassmann, and H. Sloetjes. 2006. ELAN: a Professional Framework for Multimodality Research. In *LREC*.

Amir Zeldes, Julia Ritz, Anke Lüdeling, and Christian Chiarcos. 2009. ANNIS: A Search Tool for Multi-Layer Annotated Corpora. In *Proceedings of Corpus Linguistics*.

NEED4Tweet: A Twitterbot for Tweets Named Entity Extraction and Disambiguation

Mena B. Habib
Database Chair
University of Twente
Enschede, The Netherlands
m.b.habib@ewi.utwente.nl

Maurice van Keulen
Database Chair
University of Twente
Enschede, The Netherlands
m.vankeulen@utwente.nl

Abstract

In this demo paper, we present NEED4Tweet, a Twitterbot for named entity extraction (NEE) and disambiguation (NED) for Tweets. The straightforward application of state-of-the-art extraction and disambiguation approaches on informal text widely used in Tweets, typically results in significantly degraded performance due to the lack of formal structure; the lack of sufficient context required; and the seldom entities involved. In this paper, we introduce a novel framework that copes with the introduced challenges. We rely on contextual and semantic features more than syntactic features which are less informative. We believe that disambiguation can help to improve the extraction process. This mimics the way humans understand language.

1 Introduction

Twitter is an important source for continuously and instantly updated information. It contains a large amount of unstructured information about users, locations, events, etc. Shortness and informality of Tweets are challenges for Natural Language Processing (NLP) tasks. Information Extraction (IE) is the NLP field of research that is concerned with obtaining structured information from unstructured text. IE systems attempt to interpret human language text in order to extract information about different types of events, entities, or relationships. Named entity extraction (NEE) is a subtask of IE that aims to locate phrases (mentions) in the text that represent names of persons, organizations, or locations regardless of their type. Named entity disambiguation (NED) is the task of determining which concrete person, place, event, etc. is referred to by a mention. Wikipedia articles are widely used as an entity's reference.

Challenges: NEE and NED in informal text are challenging. Here we summarize the challenges of NEE and NED for Tweets:

- The informal language widely used in Tweets makes the extraction process more difficult. Proper capitalization is a key feature that the state-of-the-art NEE approaches have relied on. However, this feature gets less attention from Twitter users when they write their Tweets.

- The limited length (140 characters) of Tweets forces the senders to provide dense information by using acronyms and informal language. This makes both the extraction and the disambiguation processes more complex.

- The limited coverage of a Knowledge Base (KB) is another challenge facing NED for tweets. According to (Lin et al., 2012), 5 million out of 15 million mentions on the Web cannot be linked to Wikipedia. This means that relying only on a KB for NED leads to around 33% loss in the disambiguated entities. This percentage is higher on Twitter because of its social nature where users also discuss information about seldom entities.

- The processes of NEE and NED involve degrees of uncertainty. For example, in the tweet "*history should show that bush jr should be in jail or at least never should have been president*", for some NEE systems, it may be uncertain whether the word '*jr*' should be part of the mention bush or not. This motivates us to fundamentally consider sets of possible alternatives in an early stage of the extraction and the disambiguation processes and do a later filtration instead of making hard decisions from the beginning.

- Named entity (NE) representation in KBs poses another NED challenge. The YAGO

Proceedings of ACL-IJCNLP 2015 System Demonstrations, pages 31–36,
Beijing, China, July 26-31, 2015. ©2015 ACL and AFNLP

KB (Suchanek et al., 2007) uses the Wikipedia anchor text as a possible mention representation for named entities. However, there may be more representations that do not appear in the Wikipedia anchor text, but are meant to refer to the entity because of a spelling mistake or because of a new abbreviation for the entity.

In this demo, we introduce NEED4Tweet, a Twitterbot for a combined system for NEE and NED in Tweets that uses their interdependency and mimics how humans exploit it in language understanding. The system is based on our work (Habib and van Keulen, 2015). We use a generic open world approach for NED in Tweets for any named entity even though it has no Wikipedia article. Mentions are disambiguated by assigning them to either a Wikipedia article or a home page. We handle the uncertainty involved in the extraction process by considering possible alternatives in an early stage then evaluate these alternatives later based on disambiguation outcomes. The proposed approach is shown to be robust against the coverage of KBs and the informality of the used language.

2 Related work

2.1 Named Entity Disambiguation

NED in Web documents is a topic that is well covered in literature. Recently, researchers have attempted NED for informal short text such as Tweets. Most of this research investigate the problem of entity-oriented disambiguation. Within this theme, (Spina et al., 2011), (Christoforaki et al., 2011), (Yerva et al., 2012) and (Delgado et al., 2012) focus on the task of filtering Tweets containing a given a mention of topic-centric entity, depending whether the Tweet is actually related to the entity or not. They develop a set of features (co-occurrence, Web-based features, collection-based features) to find keywords for positive and negative cases.

Similar to our problem discussed in Section 3.2, is the problem of entity home page finding, which was part of the TREC Web and entity tracks. One of the proposed approaches for this task was (Westerveld et al., 2002). The authors combine content information with other sources as diverse as inlinks, URLs and anchors to find an entry page. Although the TREC problem looks similar to ours, the Tweets' short informal nature makes it more tricky to find an entity reference page.

2.2 Named Entity Extraction

Many tools and services have been developed for the NEE task in web documents written in formal language. In spite of this, few research efforts studied NEE in Tweets. In (Ritter et al.,), the authors built an NLP pipeline to perform NEE. The pipeline involves part-of-speech tagging, shallow parsing, and a novel SVM classifier that predicts the informativeness of capitalization in a Tweet. It trains a Conditional Random Fields (CRF) model with all the aforementioned features for NEE. For classification, LabeledLDA is applied where entity types are used as classes. A bag-of-words-based profile is generated for each entity type, and the same is done with each extracted mention. Classification is done based on the comparison of the two.

The contextual relationship between the microposts is considered by (Jung, 2012). The paper proposes merging the microtexts by discovering contextual relationship between the microtexts. A group of microtexts contextually linked with each other is regarded as a microtext cluster. Once this microtext cluster is obtained, they expect that the performance of NEE can be better. The authors provide some suggestions for Contextual closure, Microtext cluster, Semantic closure, Temporal closure, and Social closure. Those closures are used by Maximum Entropy for the NER task.

Similarly, (Li et al., 2012) exploits the gregarious property in the local context derived from the Twitter stream in an unsupervised manner. The system first leverages the global context obtained from Wikipedia and Web N-Gram corpus to partition Tweets into valid segments (phrases) using a dynamic programming algorithm. Each such Tweet segment is a candidate NE. Afterwards, a ranking approach tries to rank segments according to their probability of being an NE. The highly-ranked segments have a higher chance of being true NEs. Each segment is represented as a node in a graph, and using the Wikipedia and the context of Tweet (adjacent nodes (segments)), a score is assigned to that segment if it is an NE or not.

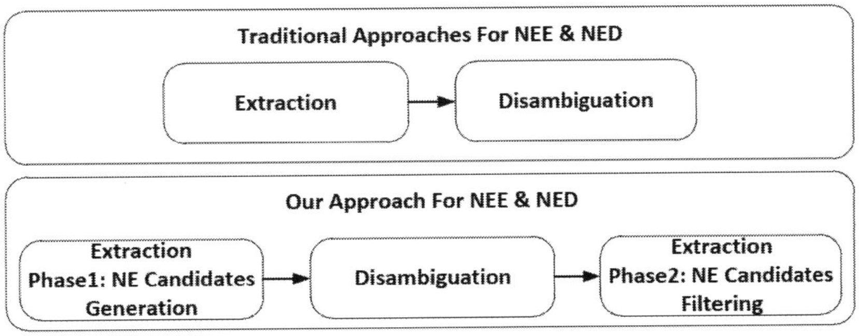

Figure 1: Traditional approaches versus our approach for NEE and NED.

3 NEED4Tweet

Although the logical order for a traditional IE system is to complete the extraction process before commencing with the disambiguation process, we start with an initial extraction-like phase aiming for high recall (i.e. aiming to find as many reasonable mention candidates as possible). We then attempt disambiguation for all the extracted mentions. Finally we classify extracted mention candidates into true and false NE using features (clues) derived from the results of the disambiguation phase such as KB information and entity coherency. Figure 1 illustrates our general approach contrasted with the traditional process.

The potential of this order is that the disambiguation step gives extra clues (such as Entity-Tweet context similarity) about each NE candidate. This information can help in the decision whether the candidate is a true NE or not.

3.1 Mention Candidates Generation

This phase is aiming to find as many reasonable mention candidates as possible. For this task, we unionize the output of the following mention candidates generation methods:

- **Tweet Segmentation**: Tweet text is segmented using the segmentation algorithm described in (Li et al., 2012). Each segment is considered a mention candidate.

- **KB Lookup**: We scan all possible n-grams of the Tweet against the mentions-entities table of YAGO KB. N-grams that matches a YAGO mention are considered mention candidates.

3.2 Disambiguation

For NED, we use a generic open world NED approach where mentions are disambiguated by assigning them to either a Wikipedia article (Wikipedia entity) or a home page (non-Wikipedia entity) (Habib and van Keulen, 2013). The NED approach is composed of three modules; matcher, feature extractor, and SVM ranker.

- **Matcher**: This module is responsible for finding the possible candidate entities of a given mention. For this task, we use the mention-entity table of YAGO KB to get the possible entities for the given mention. Furthermore, we use the mention as an input query for the Google API. The top 18 Web pages retrieved by Google are also considered candidate entities for that mention.

- **Feature Extractor**: For each entity page candidate, we extract a set of context and URL features. Context features (such as language model and overlapping terms between tweet and document) measure the context similarity between mention context (the tweet text) and entity candidates' home pages. URL features (such as path length and mention-URL string similarity) measure the likelihood of the candidate URL being a representative of the entity home page. These features give indicators on how likely the candidate entity page could be a representative to the mention.

- **SVM Ranker**: After extracting the aforementioned set of features, SVM classifier is used to rank candidate entity pages of a mention. We consider the top ranked page to be the entity of the input mention. In this demo, we use an SVM which is trained on the two NED datasets presented in (Habib and van Keulen, 2013).

3.3 Mention Candidates Filtering

After generating the mentions candidate list, we apply our disambiguate approach to disambiguate each mention candidate. After that, we use another SVM classifier to predict which mention candidates are true positives and which ones are not. For each mention candidate, we extract the following set of features :

- **Shape Features**: If the mention candidate is initially or fully capitalized and if it contains digits.
- **Probabilistic Features**:
  - The joint and conditional probability of the mention candidate obtained from the Microsoft Web N-Gram service.
  - The stickiness of the segment as described in (Li et al., 2012).
  - The segment frequency over around 5 million tweets[1].
- **KB Features**:
  - Whether the segment appears in WordNet.
  - Whether the segment appears in the YAGO mention-entity look-up table.
- **Disambiguation Features**: All the features described in Section 3.2 derived from the entity page linked to the given mention candidate.

In this demo, we use an SVM which is trained on four different NEE datasets presented in (Ritter et al.,), (Basave et al., 2013), (Locke and Martin, 2009), and (Habib and van Keulen, 2012).

3.4 Final NE Set Generation

Beside the SVM, we also use a trained CRF model for NEE. We use the CRF model described in (Zhu et al., 2014) trained on the four collections mentioned in Section 3.3. To train the CRF, Tweet text is tokenized using a special tweet tokenizer (Gimpel et al., 2011) and the following features are extracted and used for training:

[1]`http://wis.ewi.tudelft.nl/umap2011/` + TREC 2011 Microblog track collection.

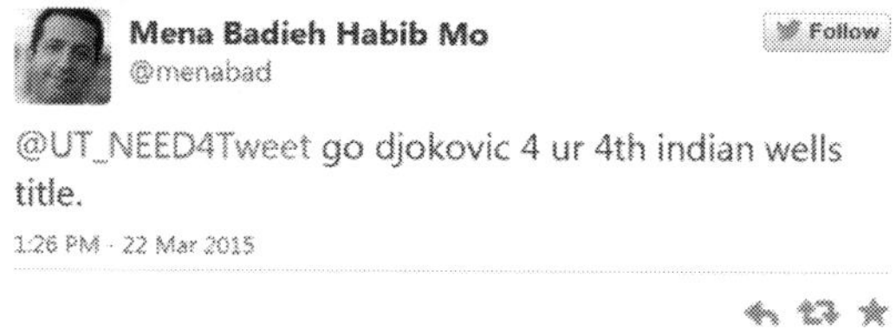

(a) Example 1: Tweet for testing both NEE and NED.

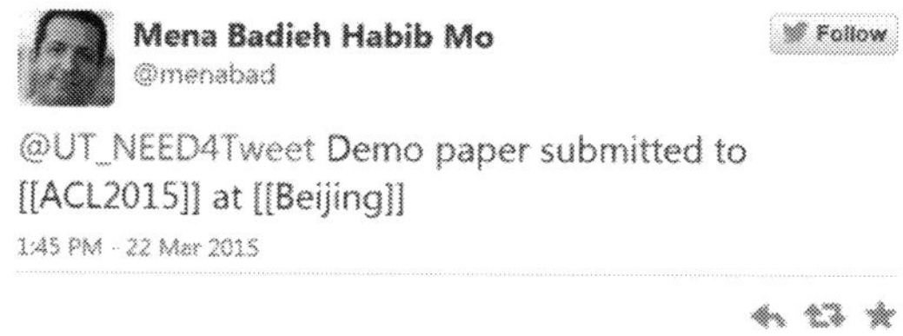

(b) Example 2: Tweet for testing NED only.

(c) Tweet reply.

Processing: @UT_NEED4Tweet go djokovic 4 ur 4th indian wells title.

Mention	Index	Entity
djokovic	18	http://en.wikipedia.org/wiki/Novak_Djokovic
indian wells	36	http://en.wikipedia.org/wiki/BNP_Paribas_Open

(d) Results of example 1

Processing: @UT_NEED4Tweet Demo paper submitted to [[ACL2015]] at [[Beijing]]

Mention	Index	Entity
ACL2015	41	http://acl2015.org/
Beijing	56	http://en.wikipedia.org/wiki/Beijing

(e) Results of example 2

Figure 2: NEED4Tweet Twitterbot

- The Part of Speech (POS) tag of the token provided by a special POS tagger designed for tweets (Gimpel et al., 2011).
- Whether the token's initial is capitalized.
- Whether the token's characters are all capitalized.
- Whether the token has any capital letters.

We consider the best annotation set for the tweet given by the CRF model as true positives. To generate the final NE set, we take the union of the CRF annotation set (after being disambiguated) and the SVM results, after removing duplicate and overlapped extractions. To resolve the overlapped mentions, we select the mention that appears in Yago KB. If both mentions appear in Yago or both don't, we select the one with the longer length.

The idea behind this combination is that the SVM and the CRF work in a different way. The former is a distance based classifier that uses numeric features for classification which CRF can not handle, while the latter is a probabilistic model that can naturally consider state-to-state dependencies and feature-to-state dependencies. On the other hand, SVM does not consider such dependencies. The hybrid approach of both makes use of the strength of each. While the CRF makes better use of the traditional features like POS and Capitalization, the SVM makes better use of the disambiguation (coherency) features.

4 Twitterbot

A Twitterbot is a program used to produce automated posts on the Twitter microblogging service. We developed our system as a Twitterbot which receives the Tweet, processes it and sends a reply message contains a link to a page that shows the generated annotations. We use Twitter API[2] for both receiving the Tweets and sending the replies. To use NEED4Tweet Twitterbot, one should send a Tweet contains either the mention '@UT_NEED4Tweet' or the hashtag '#NEED4Tweet' as shown in Figures 2(a) and 2(b) respectively. Withing few seconds after sending the tweet, the sender will get a reply Tweet (see Figure 2(c)) that includes link to a simple HTML page contains the generated annotations (see Figures 2(d) and 2(e)). The page contains a list of the extracted mentions, their start offset in the Tweet, and their linked entities. It is also possible to test only the disambiguation component by manually coating the mentions required to be disambiguated using double square brackets ([[]])as shown in Figure 2(b).

5 Evaluation

5.1 Data sets

To validate our approach, we use three collections of tweets. The first two data sets are mainly designed for a NER task. We manually construct the NED ground truth by linking each NE to only one appropriate entity page. We give higher priority to Wikipedia pages. When no Wikipedia page exists for a mention, we link it to a non-Wikipedia home page or profile page.

The first data set (Locke collection) is the one used in (Locke and Martin, 2009). The second data set (Habib collection) is the one used in (Habib and van Keulen, 2012) which is relatively small in the number of tweets but rich in the number of NEs. It is composed mainly from tweeted news about sportsmen, celebrities, politics, etc.

The third data set (#Microposts collection) is provided by the #Microposts Named Entity Extraction & Linking (NEEL) Challenge (Cano Basave et al., 2014). The NEEL Challenge task required participants to build systems to extract entity mentions from a tweet and to link the extracted mentions to DBpedia. Note that this data set does not contain any non-Wikipedia entities. We have done the mapping from the YAGO KB to DBpedia by identifying the Wikipedia page as a common property for the identical entities.

(a) Locke collection

	Pre.	Rec.	F1
DBpedia Spotlight	0.1004	0.2669	0.1459
Stanford + AIDA	0.5005	0.2940	0.3704
NEED4Tweet	**0.5455**	**0.5640**	**0.5546**

(b) Habib collection

	Pre.	Rec.	F1
DBpedia Spotlight	0.3711	0.5333	0.4377
Stanford + AIDA	**0.7263**	0.5569	0.6304
NEED4Tweet	0.6861	**0.7157**	**0.7006**

(c) #Microposts collection

	Pre.	Rec.	F1
DBpedia Spotlight	0.1873	0.3349	0.2403
Stanford + AIDA	0.5092	0.2795	0.3609
NEED4Tweet	**0.5337**	**0.5343**	**0.5339**

Table 1: Combined evaluation of NEE and NED.

5.2 Experimental Results

In this experiment, we compare the performance of NEED4Tweet against two competitors: AIDA[3] and DBpedia Spotlight.[4] AIDA is a disambiguation system although it uses Stanford_NER for automatic NE extraction. We consider the combination of Stanford_NER and the AIDA disambiguation system as one competitor to our extraction and disambiguation system. DBpedia Spotlight (Mendes et al., 2011) is a tool for automatically annotating mentions of DBpedia resources in text. We used DBpedia Spotlight through its Annotate Web Service endpoint. We used the

[2] https://dev.twitter.com/

[3] https://d5gate.ag5.mpi-sb.mpg.de/webaida/

[4] https://github.com/dbpedia-spotlight/dbpedia-spotlight/wiki

NESpotter implementation for the extraction configuration. The results in Table 1 show the superiority of NEED4Tweet over DBpedia Spotlight and the combined Stanford and AIDA system. More experimental results and analysis can be found in (Habib and van Keulen, 2015).

6 Conclusion

In this demo paper, we present NEED4Tweet, a Twitterbot for NEE and NED in tweets. The system is composed of three phases. The first phase aims to generate NE candidates with an emphasis on achieving high recall. The second phase aims to disambiguate all the candidates generated in the first phase. For this task, we use a generic non-entity oriented disambiguation approach. Mentions are disambiguated by assigning them to either a Wikipedia article or a home page. Finally, the third phase is to filter the NE candidates using features derived from disambiguation and other shape and KB features. The proposed approach is shown to be robust against the coverage of KBs and the informality of the used language.

References

Amparo Elizabeth Cano Basave, Andrea Varga, Matthew Rowe, Milan Stankovic, and Aba-Sah Dadzie. 2013. Making sense of microposts (#msm2013) concept extraction challenge. In *Making Sense of Microposts (#MSM2013) Concept Extraction Challenge*, pages 1–15.

Amparo Elizabeth Cano Basave, Giuseppe Rizzo, Andrea Varga, Matthew Rowe, Milan Stankovic, and Aba-Sah Dadzie. 2014. Making sense of microposts (#microposts2014) named entity extraction & linking challenge. In *Proc. of (#Microposts2014) Workshop*, pages 54–60.

Maria Christoforaki, Ivie Erunse, and Cong Yu. 2011. Searching social updates for topic-centric entities. In *Proc. of exploreWeb 2011 Workshop*, pages 34–39.

A. D. Delgado, R. Mart'ınez, A. Pérez Garc'ıa-Plaza, and V. Fresno. 2012. Unsupervised Real-Time company name disambiguation in twitter. In *Proc. of RAMSS 2012 Workshop*, pages 25–28.

Kevin Gimpel, Nathan Schneider, Brendan O'Connor, Dipanjan Das, Daniel Mills, Jacob Eisenstein, Michael Heilman, Dani Yogatama, Jeffrey Flanigan, and Noah A. Smith. 2011. Part-of-speech tagging for twitter: annotation, features, and experiments. In *Proc. of ACL 2011*, HLT '11, pages 42–47.

Mena B. Habib and Maurice van Keulen. 2012. Unsupervised improvement of named entity extraction in short informal context using disambiguation clues. In *Proc. of SWAIE 2012 Workshop*, pages 1–10.

Mena B. Habib and M. van Keulen. 2013. A generic open world named entity disambiguation approach for tweets. In *Proc. of KDIR 2013*, pages 267–276.

Mena B. Habib and Maurice van Keulen. 2015. Twitterneed: A hybrid approach for named entity extraction and disambiguation for tweets. *To appear in the journal of Natural Language Engineering*.

Jason J. Jung. 2012. Online named entity recognition method for microtexts in social networking services: A case study of twitter. *Expert Syst. Appl.*, 39(9):8066–8070.

Chenliang Li, Jianshu Weng, Qi He, Yuxia Yao, Anwitaman Datta, Aixin Sun, and Bu-Sung Lee. 2012. Twiner: named entity recognition in targeted twitter stream. In *Proc. of SIGIR 2012*, pages 721–730.

Thomas Lin, Mausam, and Oren Etzioni. 2012. Entity linking at web scale. In *Proc. of AKBC-WEKEX 2012 Workshop*, pages 84–88.

Brian Locke and James Martin. 2009. Named entity recognition: Adapting to microblogging. Senior Thesis, University of Colorado.

Pablo N. Mendes, Max Jakob, Andrés García-Silva, and Christian Bizer. 2011. Dbpedia spotlight: Shedding light on the web of documents. In *Proc. of I-Semantics 2011*, pages 1–8.

A. Ritter, S. Clark, Mausam, and O. Etzioni. Named entity recognition in tweets: An experimental study. In *Proc. of EMNLP 2011*, pages 1524–1534.

Damiano Spina, Enrique Amigó, and Julio Gonzalo. 2011. Filter keywords and majority class strategies for company name disambiguation in twitter. In *Proc. of CLEF 2011*, pages 50–61.

Fabian M. Suchanek, Gjergji Kasneci, and Gerhard Weikum. 2007. Yago: a core of semantic knowledge. In *Proc. of WWW 2007*, pages 697–706.

Thijs Westerveld, Wessel Kraaij, and Djoerd Hiemstra. 2002. Retrieving web pages using content, links, urls and anchors. In *Tenth Text REtrieval Conference, TREC 2001*, volume SP 500, pages 663–672.

Surender Reddy Yerva, Zoltán Miklós, and Karl Aberer. 2012. Entity-based classification of twitter messages. *IJCSA*, 9(1):88–115.

Zhemin Zhu, Djoerd Hiemstra, and Peter Apers. 2014. Linear co-occurrence rate networks (l-crns) for sequence labeling. In *Statistical language and speech processing*, volume 8791 of *Lecture notes in computer science*, pages 185–196.

Visual Error Analysis for Entity Linking

Benjamin Heinzerling
Research Training Group AIPHES
Heidelberg Institute for
Theoretical Studies gGmbH
Schloss-Wolfsbrunnenweg 35
69118 Heidelberg, Germany
benjamin.heinzerling@h-its.org

Michael Strube
Heidelberg Institute for
Theoretical Studies gGmbH
Schloss-Wolfsbrunnenweg 35
69118 Heidelberg, Germany
michael.strube@h-its.org

Abstract

We present the Visual Entity Explorer (VEX), an interactive tool for visually exploring and analyzing the output of entity linking systems. VEX is designed to aid developers in improving their systems by visualizing system results, gold annotations, and various mention detection and entity linking error types in a clear, concise, and customizable manner.

1 Introduction

Entity linking (EL) is the task of automatically linking mentions of entities (e.g. persons, locations, organizations) in a text to their corresponding entry in a given knowledge base (KB), such as Wikipedia or Freebase. Depending on the setting, the task may also require detection of entity mentions[1], as well as identifying and clustering Not-In-Lexicon (NIL) entities.

In recent years, the increasing interest in EL, reflected in the emergence of shared tasks such as the TAC Entity Linking track (Ji et al., 2014), ERD 2014 (Carmel et al., 2014), and NEEL (Cano et al., 2014), has fostered research on evaluation metrics for EL systems, leading to the development of a dedicated scorer that covers different aspects of EL system results using multiple metrics (Hachey et al., 2014).

Based on the observation that representations in entity linking (mentions linked to the same KB entry) are very similar to those encountered in coreference resolution (mentions linked by coreference relations to the same entity), these metrics include ones originally proposed for evaluation of coreference resolutions systems, such as the MUC score (Vilain et al., 1995), B^3 (Bagga and Baldwin, 1998), and *CEAF* (Luo, 2005) and variants thereof (Cai and Strube, 2010).

While such metrics, which express system performance in numeric terms of precision, recall, and *F1* scores, are well-suited for comparing systems, they are of limited use to EL system developers trying to identify problem areas and components whose improvement will likely result in the largest performance increase.

To address this problem, we present the Visual Entity Explorer (VEX), an interactive tool for visually exploring the results produced by an EL system. To our knowledge, there exist no other dedicated tools for visualizing the output of EL systems or similar representations.

VEX is available as free, open-source software for download at `http://github.com/noutenki/vex` and as a web service at `http://cosyne.h-its.org/vex`.

In the remainder of this paper, we first give an overview of VEX (Section 2), proceed to present several usage examples and discuss some of the insights gained from performing a visual error analysis (Section 3), then describe its implementation (Section 4), before concluding and discussing future work (Section 5).

2 The Visual Entity Explorer

After loading system results and gold standard annotations in TAC 2014 or JSON format, as well as the original document text files, VEX displays

[1] This setting is called *Entity Discovery and Linking* (EDL) in the TAC 2014/15 entity linking tracks, and *Entity Recognition and Disambiguation* (ERD) in the Microsoft ERD 2014 challenge.

Proceedings of ACL-IJCNLP 2015 System Demonstrations, pages 37–42,
Beijing, China, July 26-31, 2015.

Figure 1: Screenshot of VEX's main display, consisting of document list (left), entity selectors (bottom right), and the annotated document text (top right).

gold annotations, correct results, and errors as shown in Figure 1. The document to be analyzed can be selected via the clickable list of document IDs on the left. Located bottom right, the entity selectors for gold, true positive, and false positive entities (defined below) can be used to toggle the display of individual entities[2]. The selected entities are visualized in the top-right main area.

Similarly to the usage in coreference resolution, where a cluster of mentions linked by coreference relations is referred to as an *entity*, we define *entity* to mean a cluster of mentions clustered either implicitly by being linked to the same KB entry (in case of non-NIL mentions) or clustered explicitly by performing NIL clustering (in case of NIL mentions).

[2]For space reasons, the entity selectors are shown only partially.

2.1 Visualizing Entity Linking Errors

Errors committed by an EL system can be broadly categorized into mention detection errors and linking/clustering errors. Mention detection errors, in turn, can be divided into partial errors and full errors.

2.1.1 Partial Mention Detection Errors

A partial mention detection error is a system mention span that overlaps but is not identical to any gold mention span. In VEX, partial mention detection errors are displayed using red square brackets, either inside or outside the gold mention spans signified by golden-bordered rectangles (cf. the first and last mention in Figure 2).

2.1.2 Full Mention Detection Errors

A full mention detection error is either (a) a system mention span that has no overlapping gold mention span at all, corresponding to a false positive (FP) detection, i.e. a precision error, or (b) a

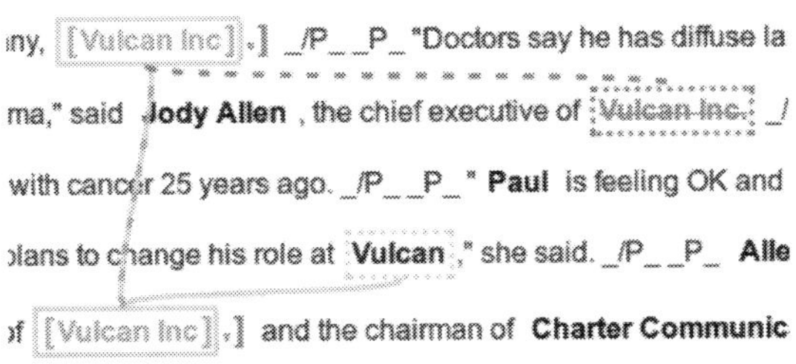

Figure 2: Visualization of various mention detection and entity linking error types (see Section 2 for a detailed description).

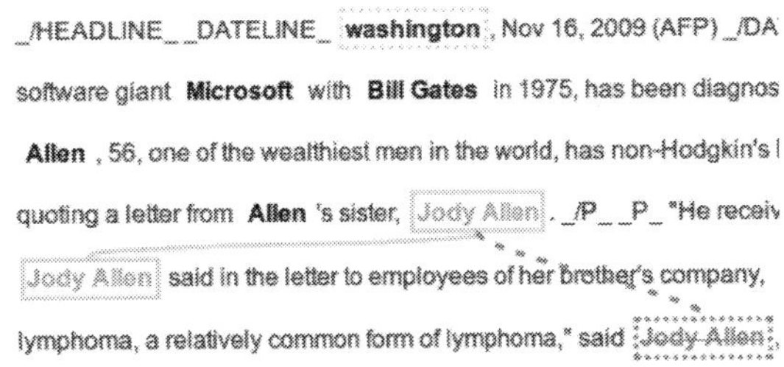

Figure 3: Visualization showing a mention detection error and an annotation error (see Section 3 for a description).

gold mention span that has no overlap with any system mention span, corresponding to a false negative (FN) detection, i.e. a recall error. In VEX, FP mention detections are marked by a dashed red border and struck-out red text (cf. the second mention in Figure 2), and FN mention detections by a dashed gold-colored border and black text (cf. the third mention in Figure 2). For further emphasis, both gold and system mentions are displayed in bold font.

2.1.3 Linking/Clustering Errors

Entities identified by the system are categorized – and possibly split up – into True Positive (TP) and False Positive (FP) entities. The mentions of system entities are connected using dashed green lines for TP entities and dashed red lines for FP entities, while gold entity mentions are connected by solid gold-colored lines. This choice of line styles prevents loss of information through occlusion in case of two lines connecting the same pair of mentions, as is the case with the first and last mention in Figure 2.

Additionally, the text of system mentions linked to the correct KB entry or identified correctly as NIL is colored green and any text associated with erroneous system entity links red.

3 Usage examples

In this section we show how VEX can be used to perform a visual error analysis, gaining insights that arguably cannot be attained by relying only on evaluation metrics.

3.1 Example 1

Figure 2 shows mentions of VULCAN INC.[3] as identified by an EL system (marked red and green) and the corresponding gold annotation[4] (marked in gold color). Of the three gold mentions, two were detected and linked correctly by the system and are thus colored green and connected with a green dashed line. One gold mention is surrounded with a gold-colored dashed box to indicate a FN mention not detected by the system at all. The dashed red box signifies a FP entity, resulting from the system having detected a mention that is not listed in the gold standard. However, rather than a system error, this is arguably an annotation mistake.

Inspection of other entities and other documents reveals that spurious FPs caused by gold annotation errors appear to be a common occurrence (see Figure 3 for another example). Since the supervised machine learning algorithms commonly used for named entity recognition, such as Conditional Random Fields (Sutton and McCallum, 2007), require consistent training data, such inconsistencies hamper performance.

3.2 Example 2

From Figure 2 we can also tell that two mention detection errors are caused by the inclusion of sentence-final punctuation that doubles as abbreviation marker. The occurrence of similar cases in other documents, e.g. inconsistent annotation of "U.S." and "U.S" as mentions of UNITED STATES, shows the need for consistently applied annotation guidelines.

3.3 Example 3

Another type of mention detection error is shown in Figure 3: Here the system fails to detect "washington" as a mention of WASHINGTON, D.C.,

[3]In this paper, SMALL CAPS denote KB entries.

[4]The gold annotations are taken from the TAC 2014 EDL Evaluation Queries and Links (V1.1).

likely due to the non-standard lower-case spelling.

3.4 Example 4

The visualization of the gold mentions of PAUL ALLEN in Figure 1 shows that the EL system simplistically partitioned and linked the mentions according to string match, resulting in three system entities, of which only the first, consisting of the two "Paul Allen" mentions, is a TP. Even though the four "Allen" mentions in Figure 1 align correctly with gold mentions, they are categorized as a FP entity, since the system erroneously linked them to the KB entry for the city of Allen, Texas, resulting in a system entity that does not intersect with any gold entity. The system commits a similar mistake for the mention "Paul".

3.5 Insights

This analysis of only a few examples has already revealed several categories of errors, either committed by the EL system or resulting from gold annotation mistakes:

- mention detection errors due to non-standard letter case, which suggest incorporating truecasing (Lita et al., 2003) and/or a caseless named entity recognition model (Manning et al., 2014) into the mention detection process could improve performance;

- mention detection errors due to off-by-one errors involving punctuation, which suggest the need for clear and consistently applied annotation guidelines, enabling developers to add hard-coded, task-specific post-processing rules for dealing with such cases;

- mention detection errors due to missing gold standard annotations, which suggest performing a simple string match against already annotated mentions to find cases of unannotated mentions could significantly improve the gold standard at little cost;

- linking/clustering errors, likely due to the overly strong influence of features based on string match with Wikipedia article titles, which in some cases appears to outweigh features designed to encourage clustering of mentions if there exists a substring match between them, hence leading to an erroneous partitioning of the gold entity by its various surface forms.

4 Implementation

In this section we describe VEX's implementation and some of the design decisions made to achieve an entity visualization suited for convenient error analysis.

VEX consists of three main components. The `input` component, implemented in Java 8, reads gold and system annotations files, as well as the original documents. Currently, the annotation format read by the official TAC 2014 scorer[5], as well as a simple JSON input format are supported. All system and gold character offset ranges contained in the input files are converted into HTML spans and inserted into the document text. Since HTML elements are required to conform to a tree structure, any overlap or nesting of spans is handled by breaking up such spans into non-overlapping subspans.

At this point, gold NIL clusters and system NIL clusters are aligned by employing the Kuhn-Munkres algorithm[6] (Kuhn, 1955; Munkres, 1957), as is done in calculation of the *CEAF* metric (Luo, 2005). The `input` component then stores all inserted, non-overlapping spans in an in-memory database.

The `processing` component queries gold and system entity data for each document and inventorizes all errors of interest. All data collected by this component is added to the respective HTML spans in the form of CSS classes, enabling simple customization of the visualization via a plain-text stylesheet.

The `output` component employs a template engine[7] to convert the data collected by the `processing` component into HTML and JavaScript for handling display and user interaction in the web browser.

4.1 Design Decisions

One of VEX's main design goals is enabling the user to quickly identify entity linking and clustering errors. Because a naive approach to entity visualization by drawing edges between all possible pairings of mention spans quickly leads to a cluttered graph (Figure 4a), we instead visualize entities using Euclidean minimum spanning trees, inspired by Martschat and Strube's (2014) use of

[5] `http://github.com/wikilinks/neleval`

[6] Also known as Hungarian algorithm.

[7] `https://github.com/jknack/handlebars.java`

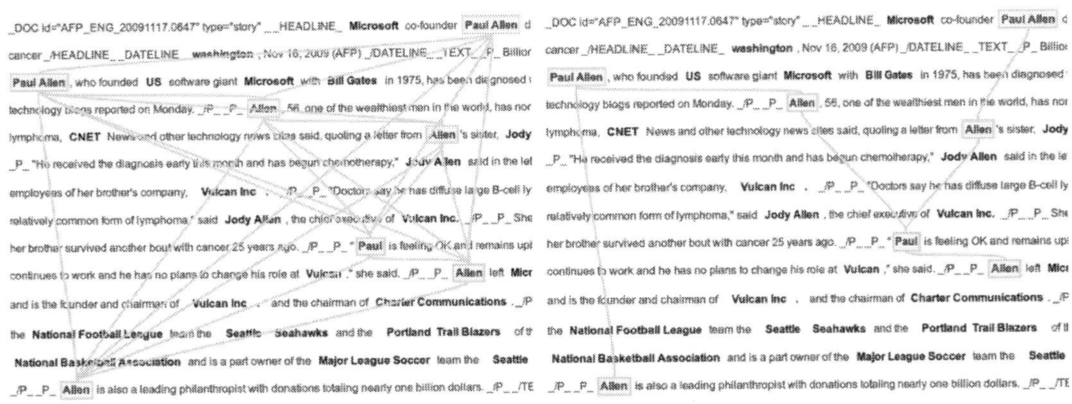

(a) (b)

Figure 4: Cluttered visualization of an entity via its complete graph, drawing all pairwise connections between mentions (a), and a more concise visualization of the same entity using an Euclidean minimum spanning tree, connecting all mentions while minimizing total edge length (b).

spanning trees in error analysis for coreference resolution.

An Euclidean minimum spanning tree is a minimum spanning tree (MST) of a graph whose vertices represent points in a metric space and whose edge weights are the spatial distances between points[8], i.e., it spans all graph vertices while minimizing total edge length. This allows for a much more concise visualization (Figure 4b).

Since the actual positions of mention span elements on the user's screen depend on various user environment factors such as font size and browser window dimensions, the MSTs of displayed entities are computed using a client-side JavaScript library[9] and are automatically redrawn if the browser window is resized. Drawing of edges is performed via jsPlumb[10], a highly customizable library for line drawing in HTML documents.

In order not to overemphasize mention detection errors when displaying entities, VEX assumes a system mention span to be correct if it has a nonzero overlap with a gold mention span. For example, consider the first gold mention "Vulcan Inc" in Figure 2, which has not been detected correctly by the system; it detected "Vulcan Inc." instead. While a strict evaluation requiring perfect mention spans will give no credit at all for this partially correct result, seeing that this mention detection error is already visually signified (by the red square bracket), VEX treats the mention as detected correctly for the purpose of visualizing the entity graph, and counts it as a true positive instance if it has been linked correctly.

While VEX provides sane defaults, the visualization style can be easily customized via CSS, e.g., in order to achieve a finer-grained categorization of error types such as off-by-one mention detection errors, or classification of non-NILs as NILs and vice-versa.

5 Conclusions and Future Work

We presented the Visual Entity Explorer (VEX), a tool for visual error analysis of entity linking (EL) systems. We have shown how VEX can be used for quickly identifying the components of an EL system that appear to have a high potential for improvement, as well as for finding errors in the gold standard annotations. Since visual error analysis of our own EL system revealed several issues and possible improvements, we believe performing such an analysis will prove useful for other developers of EL systems, as well.

In future work, we plan to extend VEX with functionality for visualizing additional error types, and for exploring entities not only in a single document, but across documents. Given the structural similarities entities in coreference resolution and

[8]In our case, the metric space is the DOM document being rendered by the web browser, a point is the top-left corner of a text span element, and the distance metric is the pixel distance between the top-left corners of text span elements.

[9]`https://github.com/abetusk/euclideanmst.js`. This library employs Kruskal's algorithm (Kruskal, 1956) for finding MSTs.

[10]`http://www.jsplumb.org`

entities in entity linking share, we also will add methods for visualizing entities found by coreference resolution systems.

Acknowledgements

This work has been supported by the German Research Foundation as part of the Research Training Group "Adaptive Preparation of Information from Heterogeneous Sources" (AIPHES) under grant No. GRK 1994/1, and partially funded by the Klaus Tschira Foundation, Heidelberg, Germany. We would like to thank our colleague Sebastian Martschat who commented on earlier drafts of this paper.

References

Amit Bagga and Breck Baldwin. 1998. Algorithms for scoring coreference chains. In *Proceedings of the 1st International Conference on Language Resources and Evaluation,* Granada, Spain, 28–30 May 1998, pages 563–566.

Jie Cai and Michael Strube. 2010. Evaluation metrics for end-to-end coreference resolution systems. In *Proceedings of the SIGdial 2010 Conference: The 11th Annual Meeting of the Special Interest Group on Discourse and Dialogue,* Tokyo, Japan, 24–25 September 2010, pages 28–36.

Amparo E. Cano, Giuseppe Rizzo, Andrea Varga, Matthew Rowe, Milan Stankovic, and Aba-Sah Dadzie. 2014. Making sense of microposts named entity extraction & linking challenge. In *Proceedings of the 4th Workshop on Making Sense of Microposts,* Seoul, Korea, 7 April 2014, pages 54–60.

David Carmel, Ming-Wei Chang, Evgeniy Gabrilovich, Bo-June Paul Hsu, and Kuansan Wang. 2014. ERD'14: Entity recognition and disambiguation challenge. In *ACM SIGIR Forum,* volume 48, pages 63–77. ACM.

Ben Hachey, Joel Nothman, and Will Radford. 2014. Cheap and easy entity evaluation. In *Proceedings of the 52nd Annual Meeting of the Association for Computational Linguistics (Volume 2: Short Papers),* Baltimore, Md., 22–27 June 2014, pages 464–469.

Heng Ji, Joel Nothman, and Ben Hachey. 2014. Overview of TAC-KBP2014 entity discovery and linking tasks. In *Proceedings of the Text Analysis Conference,* National Institute of Standards and Technology, Gaithersburg, Maryland, USA, 17–18 November 2014.

Joseph B. Kruskal. 1956. On the shortest spanning subtree of a graph and the traveling salesman problem. *Proceedings of the American Mathematical society,* 7(1):48–50.

Harold W. Kuhn. 1955. The Hungarian method for the assignment problem. *Naval Research Logistics Quarterly,* 2(1-2):83–97.

Lucian Vlad Lita, Abe Ittycheriah, Salim Roukos, and Nanda Kambhatla. 2003. Truecasing. In *Proceedings of the 41st Annual Meeting of the Association for Computational Linguistics,* Sapporo, Japan, 7–12 July 2003, pages 152–159. Association for Computational Linguistics.

Xiaoqiang Luo. 2005. On coreference resolution performance metrics. In *Proceedings of the Human Language Technology Conference and the 2005 Conference on Empirical Methods in Natural Language Processing,* Vancouver, B.C., Canada, 6–8 October 2005, pages 25–32.

Christopher D. Manning, Mihai Surdeanu, John Bauer, Jenny Finkel, Steven J. Bethard, and David McClosky. 2014. The Stanford CoreNLP natural language processing toolkit. In *Proceedings of the 52nd Annual Meeting of the Association for Computational Linguistics: System Demonstrations,* Baltimore, Md., 22–27 June 2014, pages 55–60. Association for Computational Linguistics.

Sebastian Martschat and Michael Strube. 2014. Recall error analysis for coreference resolution. In *Proceedings of the 2014 Conference on Empirical Methods in Natural Language Processing,* Doha, Qatar, 25–29 October 2014, pages 2070–2081.

James Munkres. 1957. Algorithms for the assignment and transportation problems. *Journal of the Society for Industrial & Applied Mathematics,* 5(1):32–38.

Charles Sutton and Andrew McCallum. 2007. An introduction to conditional random fields for relational learning. In L. Getoor and B. Taskar, editors, *Introduction to Statistical Relational Learning,* pages 93–128. MIT Press, Cambridge, Mass.

Marc Vilain, John Burger, John Aberdeen, Dennis Connolly, and Lynette Hirschman. 1995. A model-theoretic coreference scoring scheme. In *Proceedings of the 6th Message Understanding Conference (MUC-6),* pages 45–52, San Mateo, Cal. Morgan Kaufmann.

A Web-based Collaborative Evaluation Tool for Automatically Learned Relation Extraction Patterns

Leonhard Hennig, Hong Li, Sebastian Krause, Feiyu Xu, and Hans Uszkoreit
Language Technology Lab, DFKI
Berlin, Germany
{leonhard.hennig,lihong,skrause,feiyu,uszkoreit}@dfki.de

Abstract

Patterns extracted from dependency parses of sentences are a major source of knowledge for most state-of-the-art relation extraction systems, but can be of low quality in distantly supervised settings. We present a linguistic annotation tool that allows human experts to analyze and categorize automatically learned patterns, and to identify common error classes. The annotations can be used to create datasets that enable machine learning approaches to pattern quality estimation. We also present an experimental pattern error analysis for three semantic relations, where we find that between 24% and 61% of the learned dependency patterns are defective due to preprocessing or parsing errors, or due to violations of the distant supervision assumption.

1 Introduction

Dependency parse trees of sentences have been shown to be very useful structures for relation extraction (RE), since they often capture syntactic and semantic properties of a relation and its arguments more compactly than more surface-oriented representations (Grishman, 2012). Typically, shortest-path or similar algorithms are used to extract a pattern from a sentence's dependency parse that connects the relation's arguments. Such patterns can be directly applied to parsed texts to identify novel instances of a relation (Krause et al., 2012), or they can be used as features in a supervised learning approach (Mintz et al., 2009). They are also useful by themselves, as linguistic resources that capture the different ways in which a given human language expresses semantic relations (Uszkoreit and Xu, 2013).

In recent years, distant supervision has become a very important approach to relation extraction (Mintz et al., 2009; Surdeanu et al., 2012; Ritter et al., 2013), due to the availability of large-scale structured knowledge bases such as Freebase (Bollacker et al., 2008). While typically yielding a high recall of relation mentions, distant supervision makes several strong assumptions that may significantly affect the quality of extracted dependency patterns. First, it assumes that for each relation tuple $r_i(e_{i_1},\ldots,e_{i_k})$ in a knowledge base, every sentence containing mentions of $e_{i_1},\ldots,e_{i_k}$ (or a subset thereof) expresses the relation r_i (Surdeanu et al., 2012). This assumption typically does not hold for most sentences, i.e., entity mentions may co-occur without the sentence expressing the target relation. Dependency patterns extracted from such sentences should be discarded to improve the precision of an RE system. Furthermore, distant supervision assumes that the knowledge base is complete: entity mention co-occurrences with no known relations are ignored or treated as negative training examples, lowering the discriminative capabilities of a learned model (Ritter et al., 2013).

Automatically estimating the quality of extracted patterns, e.g., by using data-driven statistical metrics, or by learning weights in a supervised setting, leads to indirect measures of pattern quality, but tells us only very little about the (grammatical) correctness and the semantic appropriateness of the patterns themselves. We are hence interested in a more direct, expert-driven analysis of dependency patterns and their properties, which will hopefully guide us towards better automatic quality metrics. To this end, we have developed a linguistic annotation tool, *PatternJudge*, that allows human experts to evaluate relation-specific dependency patterns and their associated source sentences. Our contributions in this paper are:

- We present a linguistic annotation tool for human expert-driven quality control of dependency patterns (Section 3)

Proceedings of ACL-IJCNLP 2015 System Demonstrations, pages 43–48,
Beijing, China, July 26-31, 2015.

- We describe an annotation process for pattern evaluation and the guidelines we developed for it (Section 4)

- We present and discuss common error classes observed in an initial study of three semantic relations (Section 5)

2 Pattern Extraction

In this section, we briefly describe our approach for extracting relation-specific dependency patterns in a distantly supervised setting, called Web-DARE (Krause et al., 2012). In contrast to most other approaches, we consider not only binary, but arbitrary n-ary relations, with $n >= 2$. For example, we can define a 4-ary *marriage* relation with the spouses as essential (required) arguments, and optional arguments such as the wedding date and location. Given a knowledge base (KB) containing such relations and their arguments, we select a set of seed relation instances from the KB. We then collect sentences from a large text corpus that mention at least the essential arguments of a given seed relation instance.

Sentences are preprocessed with a standard NLP pipeline, including tokenization, named entity recognition (NER) and linking, lemmatization, part-of-speech tagging and word sense disambiguation (WSD).[1] We also apply a dependency parser producing Stanford dependency relations. Given a preprocessed sentence and the seed relation instance which matches this sentence, the pattern extraction algorithm first identifies the argument mentions of the seed relation instance occurring in the sentence, and then determines and composes the set of shortest paths connecting the arguments in the dependency parse in a bottom-up manner. Figure 1 visualizes the pattern extraction process for an example sentence expressing the *marriage* relation. The extracted pattern is shown in attribute-value-matrix (AVM) notation in Figure 1c. For more details on the algorithm we refer the interested reader to the DARE pattern extraction method described in Xu et al. (2007).

3 Evaluation tool – PatternJudge

To facilitate the manual evaluation of dependency patterns, we have developed a web-based annotation tool, dubbed *PatternJudge*. With *PatternJudge*, annotators can inspect patterns and source sentences for a given relation, and evaluate their grammatical and semantic correctness. The tool is realized as a browser-based client with a back end web server for data management. It is available online at *http://sargraph.dfki.de/pattern_judge*.

Figure 2 shows a screen shot of the user interface. The interface is split into three main components. The left part displays a list of available relations and patterns, and allows searching for specific patterns or sentences. The center part visualizes the currently selected dependency pattern in AVM notation. In this notation, the INPUT element contains the dependency pattern, and the OUTPUT element lists the relation arguments extracted by this pattern. In the example pattern shown in Figure 2, these correspond to the spouses and the wedding date. Thus, the patterns also contain the semantic role label information of the target relation for the corresponding linguistic arguments, which is not included in most traditional pattern extraction approaches (e.g., Stevenson and Greenwood (2005)).

The area below the representation of the pattern lists the source sentences that it was observed in, as well as some statistics about the frequency of the pattern. Sentences are formatted to highlight the important elements of the pattern. Relation arguments are marked in red, content words occurring in the pattern are marked in blue. Listing the source sentences is important because it enables the human expert to verify both the extracted dependency pattern (e.g., to detect a parse error), and the semantic correctness of the pattern, i.e., whether the sentences express the target relation.

The annotation tab on the right-hand side collects the human expert's feedback on the quality of the selected pattern. Currently available options include labeling the pattern as "CORRECT", "CORRECT, BUT TOO SPECIFIC", "INCORRECT" or "UNCERTAIN/DON'T KNOW". We describe the intended scope and meaning of these feedback categories in Section 4. Note that this set of categories is not fixed, but simply reflects what we have found to be useful distinctions thus far for annotating patterns. Annotators can also provide a comment, and, if desired, view the annotations and comments of previous annotators of this pattern. Since multiple experts can collaboratively annotate the same pattern, these comments are

[1] We use the Stanford CoreNLP pipeline (`nlp.stanford.edu/software/corenlp.shtml`), and our own implementation of Babelfy (`babelfy.org`) for WSD and entity linking.

Brad Pitt married Jennifer Aniston in a private wedding ceremony in Malibu on July 29, 2000.

(a) Sentence with a mention of the *marriage* relation.

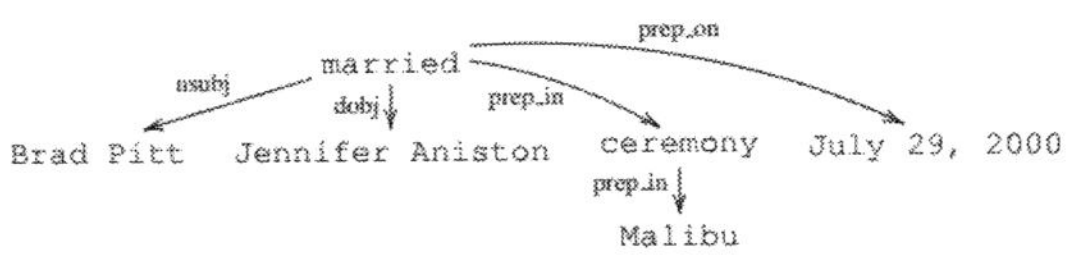

(b) Dependency pattern extracted from the sentence in (a).

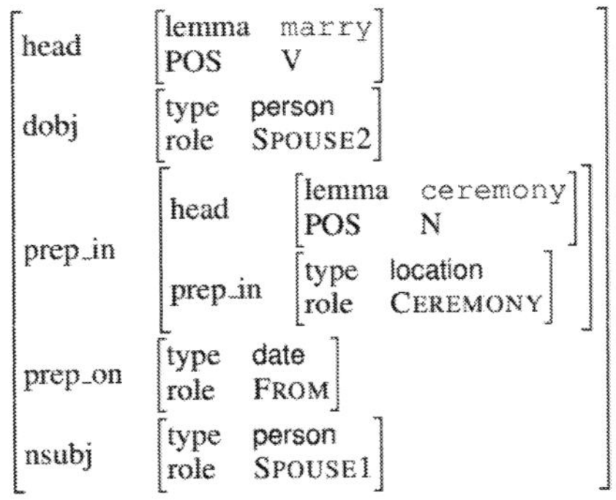

(c) Generalized dependency pattern derived from (b).

Figure 1: Data flow for gathering dependency patterns from distantly labeled text.

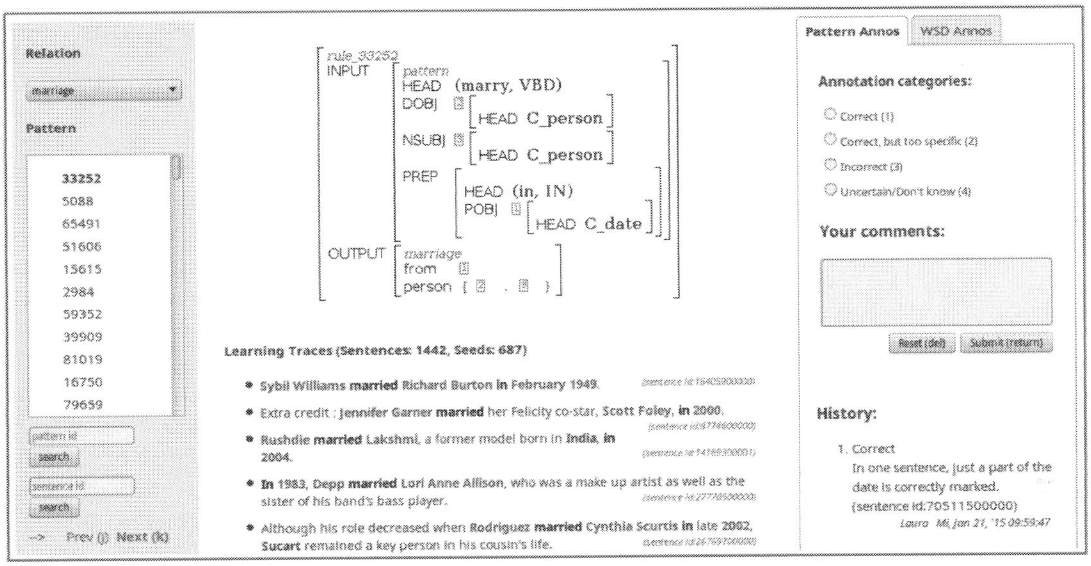

Figure 2: User interface of the *PatternJudge* tool. The tool allows annotators to judge the quality of automatically learned dependency patterns.

mainly used for discussion and clarification, but also for adding error class information in cases where an annotator decided to label a pattern as "INCORRECT".

In a separate tab (not shown in the Figure), annotators can inspect the word senses of the pattern's lemmas. Per lemma, we display a distribution over word senses, since the sentence-level WSD decisions may differ from each other. Annotators can use this view to label the correct word senses for a pattern. Word senses are directly linked to BabelNet[2] for reference. The *PatternJudge* tool also includes a basic user management component to keep track of different annotators, and for undoing or updating previous judgments. All pattern judgments are persisted in a NoSQL data base, and can be exported to CSV or other standard formats for statistical analysis.

4 Expert-driven quality control

We use the *PatternJudge* tool for an experimental analysis of dependency patterns. The analysis has two major goals: to validate interesting, productive dependency patterns, and to identify common error classes of defective patterns. In this section,

[2] http://babelnet.org/

we describe the guidelines that we developed for the manual evaluation process, and the experimental dataset. We report the results of our analysis in Section 5.

4.1 Quality control guidelines

We define three qualitative categories, "CORRECT", "CORRECT, BUT TOO SPECIFIC" and "INCORRECT", as well as a set of annotation guidelines for the evaluation of dependency patterns. We label a relation-specific pattern as "CORRECT" if it is grammatically and semantically correct. A pattern is grammatically correct if there are no parsing or other preprocessing errors, and it is semantically correct if its source sentences express the target relation. Correspondingly, we label a dependency pattern as "INCORRECT" if it is grammatically incorrect, or if its sentences do not express the target relation. Typically, the annotators aim to identify one or more of the error classes discussed in Section 5 to decide whether a pattern is incorrect.

For deciding whether a sentence expresses a given relation, we use the ACE annotation guidelines' conceptual definition of relations and their mentions (Doddington et al., 2004), and define the semantics of relations based on Freebase descriptions. In contrast to the ACE tasks, we also consider n-ary relations in addition to binary relations. Sentences must express the target relation explicitly, e.g., *"Obama was awarded the Nobel Peace Prize."* explicitly expresses the relation *award honor*. We treat implicit mentions as semantically incorrect, e.g., the previous example only implies an *award nomination*.

A third feedback category, "CORRECT, BUT TOO SPECIFIC", was added based on our initial analysis of the dataset, and applies to dependency patterns mostly found in the long tail of the frequency distribution. Too specific patterns, while both grammatically and semantically correct, are patterns that are overly complex and / or include irrelevant parts of the sentence specific to a particular relation instance. Such patterns do not generalize well, and are unlikely to be very productive when applied to novel text.

4.2 Dataset

We apply the pattern extraction approach described in Section 2 to create a dataset for 25 relations from the domains *awards, business* and *personal relationships*. We use Freebase as our knowledge base, and retrieve 200K relation instances as seed knowledge. We then create a text corpus by querying Bing with the seeds as input, and retrieving the top 100 results per query. From these documents, we extract more than 3M sentences mentioning a seed relation instance. The resulting pattern dataset contains 1.5M unique patterns. Since a manual evaluation of all these patterns would be too resource-intensive, we select a subset based on the pattern filtering algorithm proposed by Moro et al. (2013).

We then sample a small set of sentences ($3-5$) for each pattern, and conduct an initial pass over the data with human annotators that judge whether these sentences express the target relation or not. We discard all patterns whose sentences do not express the relation. The final dataset for manual evaluation consists of more than 8K patterns with all their source sentences.

5 Pattern observations

Three annotators evaluated 1185 patterns for the relations *award honor* (510 patterns), *acquisition* (224) and *marriage* (451), using the guidelines described in the previous section. Each annotator evaluated the patterns of a single relation.[3]

5.1 Error classes

The annotators identified six main error classes, which are listed in Table 1. Three of the classes relate to preprocessing errors (*PIPE-S, PIPE-NER, PIPE-PT*), the other three encompass semantic mistakes in patterns or source sentences (*NEX-P, NEX-S, IMP-S*).

The error class *PIPE-S* is used for ungrammatical sentences and patterns resulting from sentence boundary detection errors. In example (1) in Table 1, the category label tokens "Personal life" are interpreted as relevant elements of the extracted pattern. *PIPE-NER* errors refer to patterns with arguments that are semantically or grammatically incongruent with the ones tagged in the sentence, as well as entity type errors. In example (2), the title of the book has not been recognized as an entity, and the lemmas "leave" and "us" are included as lexical elements in the pattern. The category *PIPE-PT* is applied to patterns derived from defective dependency parse trees. In example (3),

[3]We used a separate relation, *siblings*, to establish a shared set of evaluation principles among the annotators. In future work, we plan to have multiple annotations per pattern, e.g., to analyze inter-annotator agreement.

#	Error class	Description	Example
1	PIPE-S	Sentence segmentation error	Personal life On July 5, 2003, Banks married sportswriter and producer Max Handelman, who had been her boyfriend since she met him on her first day at college, September 6, 1992. *(marriage)*
2	PIPE-NER	NER tagging error	Rahna Reiko Rizzuto is the author of the novel, Why She Left Us, which won an American Book Award in 2000. *(award honor)*
3	PIPE-PT	Dependency parsing error	*Say won a Caldecott Medal for his illustrations in Grandfather's Journey. *(award honor)*
4	NEX-P	Relation is not expressed in pattern	Julian joined Old Mutual in August 2000 as Group Finance Director, moving on to become CEO of Skandia following its purchase by Old Mutual in February 2006. *(acquisition)*
5	NEX-S	Relation is not expressed in text	The 69th Annual Peabody Awards ceremony will be held on May 17 at the Waldorf-Astoria in New York City and will be hosted by Diane Sawyer, the award-winning anchor of ABCs World News. *(award honor)*
6	IMP-S	Relation is too implicit	The looming expiration of Lipitors patent in 2012 is a big reason Pfizer felt compelled to buy a company like Wyeth. *(acquisition)*

Table 1: Common error classes of dependency patterns for the relations *marriage*, *acquisition* and *award honor*. Underlined token sequences denote relation arguments, concepts with a dashed underline are additional pattern elements.

the parser interpreted the proper name *Say* as a finite verb.

The category *NEX-P* is used for dependency patterns that do not include any relation-relevant content words. In example (4), the most explicit word expressing an acquisition is the lemma "purchase". The pattern, however, extracts other parts of the source sentence. *NEX-S* applies to patterns that are based on sentences which do not express the relation of interest. In example (5), the target relation *award honor* is not expressed, instead, the host of the ceremony is erroneously identified as the winner of the prize. Finally, the category *IMP-S* marks patterns that are derived from sentences in which a relation is expressed merely implicitly. Judging from the source sentence in example (6), we cannot be entirely sure whether or not an acquisition took place because "felt compelled to" might only express a momentary mindset of the company's leaders that was not followed by action.

5.2 Pattern statistics

Table 2 summarizes the distribution of correct and incorrect dependency patterns for the three relations *marriage*, *award honor* and *acquisition*. We find that between 24% and 61% of the learned dependency patterns are defective, between 21% and 55% are labeled as correct. For the relation *acquisition*, more than 60% of the patterns are labeled as "INCORRECT", which is much higher than for the other two relations. "CORRECT, BUT TOO SPECIFIC" patterns make up between 12% and 30% of the total number of patterns.

	award honor	*acquisition*	*marriage*
Correct	54.7%	21.0%	40.0%
Correct, but too specific	12.4%	14.7%	29.9%
Incorrect	24.3%	60.7%	24.6%
Uncertain	8.6%	3.6%	5.5%

Table 2: Distribution of pattern categories

Table 3 gives details on the distribution of the error classes for the same relations. The two predominant error classes are PIPE-NER and NEX-S. The distribution of error classes varies significantly between the different relations. *PIPE-NER* is the category most frequently found in *award honor*. Sentences in this category often mention the titles of works the prize was awarded for. If those titles are not recognized as entities by the NER tagger, the dependency parsing fails and parts of the title can erroneously end up in the pattern. For the *acquisition* relation, the vast majority of errors can be assigned to the category *NEX-S*. In these cases, a relation between two or more or-

	award honor	*acquisition*	*marriage*
PIPE-S	1	2	11
PIPE-NER	78	2	10
PIPE-PT	33	4	14
NEX-P	3	19	26
NEX-S	2	107	2
IMP-S	5	1	34
Other	2	1	13

Table 3: Distribution of error classes

ganizations is often expressed in the source sentences, e.g., that "company X is a subsidiary of company Y", but no statement is made about the act of purchase. For the *marriage* relation, the most frequent error type was *IMP-S*, mainly resulting from sentences stating a divorce, which we do not consider as explicit mentions of the *marriage* relation. A final observation that can be made from Table 3 is that 42% of the errors are preprocessing pipeline errors.

6 Conclusions and future work

We presented *PatternJudge*, a linguistic annotation tool for manual evaluation of dependency patterns. The tool allows human experts to inspect dependency patterns and their associated source sentences, to categorize patterns, and to identify error classes. The annotated patterns can be used to create datasets that enable machine learning approaches to pattern quality estimation and relation extraction. We showed how the tool can be used to perform a pattern error analysis on three semantic relations. Our study indicates that textual entailment may play an important role for relation extraction, since many relations are not expressed explicitly in texts. We also observe that close interactions among semantically similar relations should be reflected in the pattern discovery approach. In future work, we will extend the *PatternJudge* tool to provide a better interface for defining and assigning error classes. In addition, our annotators are currently evaluating the pattern dataset for a larger set of semantic relations, which will allow us to extend the initial study presented in this work.

Acknowledgments

This research was partially supported by the German Federal Ministry of Education and Research (BMBF) through the projects ALL SIDES (01IW14002) and BBDC (01IS14013E), by the German Federal Ministry of Economics and Energy (BMWi) through the project SDW (01MD15010A), and by Google through a Focused Research Award granted in July 2013.

References

Kurt Bollacker, Colin Evans, Praveen Paritosh, Tim Sturge, and Jamie Taylor. 2008. Freebase: A Collaboratively Created Graph Database for Structuring Human Knowledge. In *Proc. of SIGMOD*, pages 1247–1250.

George R Doddington, Alexis Mitchell, Mark A Przybocki, Lance A Ramshaw, Stephanie Strassel, and Ralph M Weischedel. 2004. The Automatic Content Extraction (ACE) Program - Tasks, Data, and Evaluation. In *Proc. of LREC*.

Ralph Grishman. 2012. Information Extraction: Capabilities and Challenges. Technical report, NYU Dept. CS.

Sebastian Krause, Hong Li, Hans Uszkoreit, and Feiyu Xu. 2012. Large-Scale Learning of Relation-Extraction Rules with Distant Supervision from the Web. In *Proc. of ISWC*, pages 263–278.

Mike Mintz, Steven Bills, Rion Snow, and Dan Jurafsky. 2009. Distant Supervision for Relation Extraction Without Labeled Data. In *Proc. of ACL-IJCNLP*, pages 1003–1011.

Andrea Moro, Hong Li, Sebastian Krause, Feiyu Xu, Roberto Navigli, and Hans Uszkoreit. 2013. Semantic Rule Filtering for Web-Scale Relation Extraction. In *Proc. of ISWC*, pages 347–362.

Alan Ritter, Luke Zettlemoyer, Mausam, and Oren Etzioni. 2013. Modeling Missing Data in Distant Supervision for Information Extraction. *TACL*, 1:367–378.

Mark Stevenson and Mark Greenwood. 2005. A semantic approach to IE pattern induction. In *Proc. of ACL*, pages 379–386.

Mihai Surdeanu, Julie Tibshirani, Ramesh Nallapati, and Christopher D. Manning. 2012. Multi-instance Multi-label Learning for Relation Extraction. In *Proc. of EMNLP*, pages 455–465.

Hans Uszkoreit and Feiyu Xu. 2013. From Strings to Things – Sar-Graphs: A New Type of Resource for Connecting Knowledge and Language. In *Proc. of WS on NLP and DBpedia*.

Feiyu Xu, Hans Uszkoreit, and Hong Li. 2007. A Seed-driven Bottom-up Machine Learning Framework for Extracting Relations of Various Complexity. In *Proc. of ACL*, pages 584–591.

A Dual-Layer Semantic Role Labeling System

Lun-Wei Ku
Institute of Information Science
Academia Sinica, Taiwan
lwku@iis.sinica.edu.tw

Shafqat Mumtaz Virk
Institute of Information Science
Academia Sinica, Taiwan
virk.shafqat@gmail.com

Yann-Huei Lee
Institute of Information Science
Academia Sinica, Taiwan
andycyrus.gmail.com

Abstract

We describe a well-performed semantic role labeling system that further extracts concepts (smaller semantic expressions) from unstructured natural language sentences language independently. A dual-layer semantic role labeling (SRL) system is built using Chinese Treebank and Propbank data. Contextual information is incorporated while labeling the predicate arguments to achieve better performance. Experimental results show that the proposed approach is superior to CoNLL 2009 best systems and comparable to the state of the art with the advantage that it requires no feature engineering process. Concepts are further extracted according to templates formulated by the labeled semantic roles to serve as features in other NLP tasks to provide semantically related cues and potentially help in related research problems. We also show that it is easy to generate a different language version of this system by actually building an English system which performs satisfactory.

1 Introduction

Semantic roles are utilized to find concepts automatically and assure their meaningfulness. Semantic role labeling is a research problem which finds in a given sentence the predicates and their arguments (identification), and further labels the semantic relationship between predicates and arguments, that is, their semantic roles (classification). There are several labeling sets. Researchers have widely adopted the semantic role labels defined in Propbank (Bonial *et al.*, 2010) like predicate (PRED), numbered arguments 0 to 5 (ARG0, ARG1, ARG2, ARG3, ARG4, ARG5), or modifier arguments (ARGM-X); finer labels are those defined in Sinica Treebank (Huang *et al.*, 2000) like agent, theme, target, which are labeled on each node of the parse tree; those defined in FrameNet (Ruppenhofer *et al.*, 2006) are the finest but most expressive. Each set provides semantic information. As long as the semantic relationship between terms derives from their semantic role labels, we are able to determine whether they should be extracted from the current sentence to construct a concept.

The word *concept* usually refers to an abstract or general idea inferred or derived from specific instances. Therefore, the extraction of concepts from text is often defined as extracting terms that are in some way related to one another. These terms could be predefined by people in resources such as ontologies, or they could be typical words in texts. In this paper, we view concepts as the continuous or discontinuous meaningful units in a sentence and hence they are tightly related to semantic roles. We propose a dual-layer semantic role labeling system which provides extracted concepts according to the reported labels, and then demonstrate the functions of this system. Experimental results will show the merit of the proposed framework.

2 Related Work

Previous studies related to this work can be divided into two groups: semantic role labeling and concept extraction. Semantic role labeling (SRL) has sparked much interest in NLP (Shen and Lapata, 2007; Liu and Gildea, 2010). The first automatic SRL systems were reported by Gildea and Jurafsky in 2002 (Gildea and Jurafsky 2002); since then, their ideas have dominated the field. In their approach, they emphasize the selection of appropriate lexical and syntactical features for SRL, the use of statistical classifiers and their combinations, and ways to handle data sparseness. Many researchers have tried to build on their work by augmenting and/or altering the feature set (Xue 2004), by experimenting with various classification approaches (Pradhan et al. 2004; Park and Rim 2005), and by attempting different ways to handle data sparseness

Proceedings of ACL-IJCNLP 2015 System Demonstrations, pages 49–54,
Beijing, China, July 26-31, 2015. ©2015 ACL and AFNLP

(Zapirain, Agirre, and Màrquez 2007). Moreover, some researchers have tried to extend it in novel ways. For example, Ding and Chang (2008) used a hierarchical feature selection strategy, while Jiang, Li, and Ng (2005) proposed exploiting argument interdependence, that is, the fact that the semantic role of one argument can depend on the semantic roles of other arguments.

Many researchers have tried to extract concepts from texts (Gelfand *et al.*, 1998; Hovy *et al.*, 2009; Villalon and Calvo, 2009; Dinh and Tamine, 2011; Torii *et al.*, 2011). Hovy narrowed the domain of interest into concepts "below" a given seed term. Villalon and Calvo extract concepts from student essays for concept map mining, which generates a directed relational graph of the extracted concepts in an essay. For specific domains, biological or medical concepts are of greatest interest to researchers (Jonnalagadda et al., 2011). Two relatively new and related approaches are the Concept parser (Rajagopal et al. 2013), a part of the SenticNet project (Cambria, Olsher, and Rajagopal 2014) and ConceptNet (Liu and Singh 2004). The former is a tool to decompose unrestricted natural language text to a bag of concepts, which is similar to our work. However, in the final phase a semantic knowledge base is used to express a concept in all its different forms and their concept-parser does not use any semantic knowledge during decomposition. The latter is a semantic network based on the Open Mind Common Sense (OMCS) knowledge base. As it is a knowledge base, its construction process is quite different from the work described here of automatically extracting concepts from sentences.

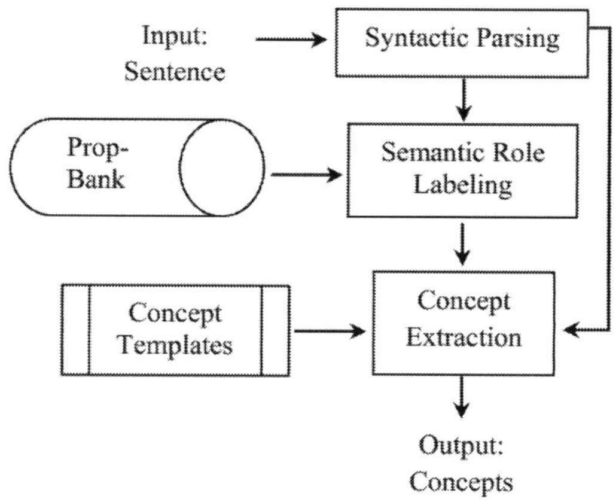

Figure 1: System Framework.

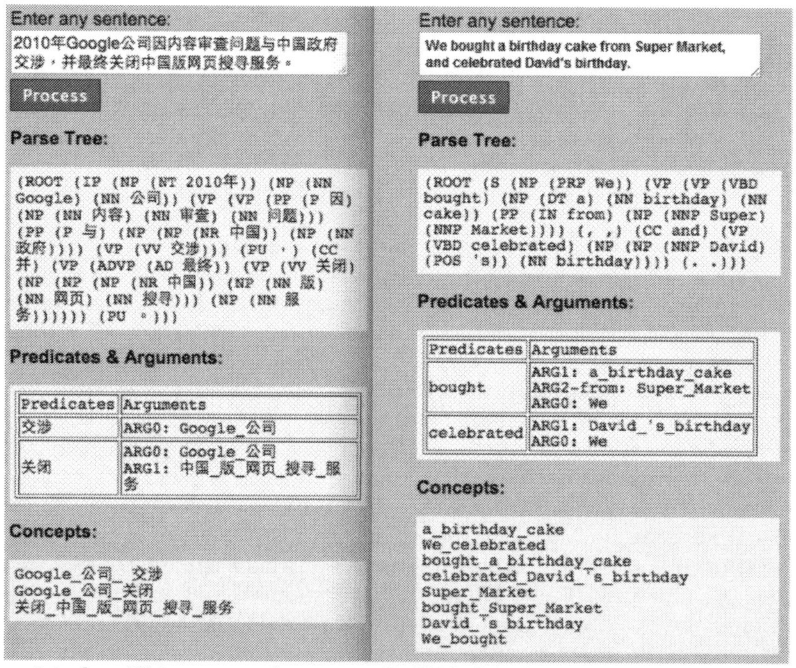

Figure 2: System Interface (Chinese example sentence: In 2010, Google company negotiated with the China government on the issue of results censoring, and eventually shut down the web search service.)

3 System

The proposed system includes three major components: a syntactic parser, a semantic role labeler, and a concept formulation component. The framework is shown in Figure 1. The input sentence is first transformed into a syntactic parse tree through a syntactical analysis step that almost all automatic semantic role labeling systems require (Johansson and Nugues 2008). Here the Stanford parser (Klein and Manning 2003) is utilized. Figure 2 shows the system interface. The left part is the English system and the right part is the Chinese system. After users input a sentence, the system will automatically parse, label semantic roles and report the related concepts for it.

3.1 Semantic Role Labeling

To develop a SRL system, a total of 33 features including features related to the head word related features, target word related features, grammar related features, and semantic type related features, are collected from related work (Xue, 2008; Ding and Chang, 2008; Sun and Jurafsky 2004; Gildea and Jurafsky 2002). Then the baseline maximum entropy system is developed using these features (Manning and Schutze, 1999). Two sets of data – Chinese Treebank 5.0 together with Propbank 1.0 and Chinese Treebank 6.0 with Propbank 2.0 – are separated into the training and testing sets, and are then used to build models to identify and classify semantic labels, and also to evaluate the performance, respectively. As Chinese data was selected for experiments, the hypernyms of words from E-Hownet[1], a Chinese word ontology, are utilized as the semantic type of words. When applying the whole system on data in other languages, for major languages it is not difficult to find resources to obtain hypernyms. For minor languages, it is fine to just ignore these features. According to our experience, this will yield F-Score reductions of only 1% to 2%.

We further exploit argument interdependence to enhance performance by the dual-layer framework shown in Figure 2. Suppose for any given predicate *P* in a sentence, the system has identified the three potential arguments A1, A2, and A3 of the predicate. Next, to predict the semantic role labels of those three arguments, a critical observation made by (Jiang, Li, and Ng 2005) is that the semantic roles of arguments may depend on each other; this phenomenon is known as argument interdependence. A common way to escape argument interdependence is to adopt sequence labeling, and use the features extracted from the arguments around the current argument together with the features of the current one to predict the label for the current argument. For example, while predicting the label of argument A2, features extracted from arguments A1 and A3 are also used. Although window sizes can be used to set the scope of this interdependence, the window-size strategy has some practical limits: the typically large feature set necessitates the use of smaller window sizes (a window size of [-1,1] is common). However, small window sizes can make it impossible to capture long dependency phenomena.

To overcome the limitations of the window-size strategy, we use all the surrounding arguments' predicted labels – window size [$-\infty,\infty$], as opposed to their features – to predict the label of the current node. This also conforms to the rule that when a role is taken by the other argument, it is less likely that the current argument is of the same role. We implement this idea using the dual-layer classification framework shown in Figure 3.

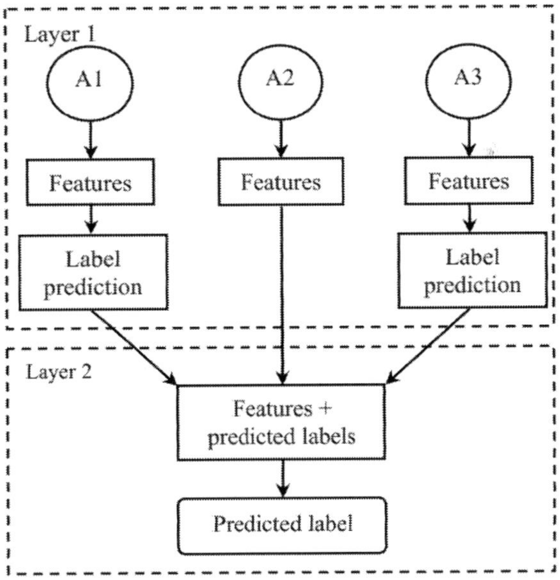

Figure 3: SRL classification framework.

In layer 1 the baseline system is used to predict the labels for identified nodes. Then in layer 2, these predicted labels of all surrounding arguments (in this example, A1 and A3) together with other features of the current node (A2) are used

[1] http://ckip.iis.sinica.edu.tw/CKIP/conceptnet.htm

to predict the label of the current node. Note as this approach is under no window size limitation, the labels of all arguments under the same predicate are taken into account. Experimental resu lts show that this strategy works better than the window-size strategy. Table 1 shows the system accuracies for the single- and dual-layer frameworks. The predicted dual-layer framework utilized the SRL labels predicted in layer 1, while the gold dual-layer framework used as features the gold SRL labels of the surrounding arguments.

System	Accuracy
Ding and Chang, 2008 (state of the art)	94.68
Single-layer framework	94.60
Dual-layer framework (predicted)	**94.86**
Dual-layer framework (gold)	95.40

Table 1. Accuracy of SRL classification phase.

To further evaluate the performance of the proposed system and offer comparisons, we applied it on Chinese Treebank 6.0 with Propbank 2.0 in the same way as in the CoNLL 2009 SRL-only task data according to the information provided by the CoNLL organizers. Table 2 shows the results of the proposed system. Table 3 further shows the performance of the best systems in CoNLL 2009.

	Identification	Classification	SRL
Precision	94.38	90.22	86.89
Recall	96.24		80.11
F-Score	95.30		**83.36**
Accuracy	97.92		96.25

Table 2. SRL results on Propbank 2.0.

System name	Type	Score
Nugus (Björkelund *et al.*, 2009)	Closed challenge, SRL-only	78.50 (F-Score)
Meza-Ruiz (Meza-Ruiz and Riedel, 2009)	Closed challenge, SRL-only	82.66 (Precision)
Täckström (Täckström, 2009)	Closed challenge, SRL-only	79.31 (Recall)
Che (Che *et al.*, 2009)	Open challenge, Joint Task	76.42 (F-Score)

Table 3. CoNLL 2009 SRL performance[2].

The CoNLL 2009 task builds dependency-based SRL systems, while the proposed system works on the constituent-based parsing trees. Also the settings of the proposed system are not all the same as the CoNLL 2009 SRL systems. In CoNLL 2009, as noted in Table 5, participants can participate in open or closed challenges, and can choose whether they want to attempt both syntactic and semantic labeling tasks (joint task) or only to attempt the SRL task. The setting of the proposed system is open challenge, SRL-only, while researchers working on the Chinese data selected only two other different settings: closed challenge, SRL only and open challenge, joint task. However, Table 5 shows that the proposed system outperforms the CoNLL 2009 best systems in terms of precision (86.89 vs. 82.66), recall (80.11 vs. 79.31), and f-score (83.36 vs. 78.50). Moreover, lately, dependency-based SRL has shown advantages over constituent-based SRL (Johansson and Nugues, 2008); thus we expect to show better results if working on dependency-based parsed data. Therefore, we believe the proposed system is comparable or even superior to other systems.

3.2 Concept-Formulations

Once the sentence has been annotated semantically, the concepts are formulated by concept templates designed according to Propbank SRL labels. Propbank provides semantic role labels of two types. One type is numbered arguments Arg0, Arg1, and so on until Arg5; the other type is modifiers with function tags, which give additional information about when, where, or how the event occurred. Tables 4 and 5 list the descriptions of the Propbank arguments utilized for the concept template generation. Table 6 then lists the generated concept templates.

As shown in Table 6, the predicate and its arguments are placed in various orders to build a list of concepts according to their semantic roles. These role combinations serve as templates which can capture a complete and important piece of information described in one sentence to form a concept. Additionally, the arguments (i.e., the subjects and objects of the predicate) in themselves can represent useful concepts, and for this reason, the arguments alone are also included in extracted concepts. For comparison, in Table 7 the extracted concepts are listed with those from the SenticNet concept parser.

[2] http://ufal.mff.cuni.cz/conll2009-st/results/results.php

Numbered Argument	Description
Arg0	agent, causer, experiencer
Arg1	theme, patient
Arg2	instrument, benefactive, attribute
Arg3	starting point, benefactive, attribute
Arg4	ending point
Arg5	Direction

Table 4. Propbank numbered arguments.

Modifier	Desc	Modifier	Desc
ArgM-LOC	Location	ArgM-COM	Comitative
ArgM-TMP	Time	ArgM-DIR	Direction
ArgM-GOL	Goal	ArgM-EXT	Extent
ArgM-MNR	Manner	ArgM-NEG	Negation
ArgM-CAU	Cause	ArgM-PRP	Purpose

Table 5. Propbank modifier auguments.

#	**Concept Template**
1	ARG0_Pred
2	Pred_ARG1
3	Pred_ARG1_ARG2
4	Pred_ARG1_ARG2_ARG3
5	Pred_ARG1_ARG2_ARG3_ARG4
6	Pred_ARG1_ARG2_ARG3_ARG4_ARG5
7	Pred_with_ARGM-COM
8	Pred_in_ARGM-LOC
9	Pred_in_order_to_ARGM-PRP
10	Pred_in_the_direction_ARGM-DIR
11	Pred_because_ARGM-CAU
12	Pred_when_ARGM-TMP
13	Pred_ARGM-GOL
14	Pred_by_ARGM-EXT
15	Pred_ARGM-MNR
16	Pred_ARGM-NEG
17	ARGX's
18	ARGM's

Table 6. Concept templates.

Proposed System
a_birthday_cake, bought_Super_Market, bought_a_birthday_cake, Super_Market, celebrated_David's_birthday, We_bought, David's_birthday, We_celebrated
SenticNet Concept Parser
birthday_cake, birthday_from_market, buy_birthday_cake, birthday_cake, birthday_david, buy_from_market, super_market, celebrate_david

Table 7. Concepts generated by the proposed system and the SenticNet Concept Parser.

4 Conclusion

We have presented a system to decompose a sentence into a set of concepts through the proposed well-performed semantic role labeling system (http://doraemon.iis.sinica.edu.tw/srl-concept/), which differs from previous related attempts. We demonstrated that this dual-layer semantic role labeling framework that exploits argument interdependence performs slightly better than the state of the art, and that it is relatively simple as no feature selection or engineering processes are required. We easily generated another English system under the same framework, which showcased the language independency of the system. In addition, it reached an F-Score 0.84, which was considered satisfactory. In the future, we plan to investigate how to further represent and utilize these extracted concepts efficiently in more NLP tasks which call for deep language understanding.

Acknowledgement

Research of this paper was partially supported by National Science Council, Taiwan, under the contract NSC101-2628-E-224-001-MY3.

References

Björkelund, A., Hafdell, L., & Nugues, P. 2009. Multilingual semantic role labeling. In Proceedings of the Thirteenth Conference on Computational Natural Language Learning: Shared Task, 43-48.

Bonial, C.; Babko-Malaya, O.; Choi, J. D.; Hwang, J.; and Palmer, M. 2010. Propbank annotation guidelines. Center for Computational Language and Edu-cation Research Institute of Cognitive Science Uni-versity of Colorad at Boulder.

Cambria, E.; Olsher, D.; and Rajagopal, D. 2014. Senticnet 3: A common and common-sense knowledge base for cognition-driven sentiment anal-ysis. In Proceedings of AAAI, 1515–1521.

Che, W., Li, Z., Li, Y., Guo, Y., Qin, B., & Liu, T. 2009. Multilingual dependency-based syntactic and semantic parsing. In Proceedings of the Thirteenth Conference on Computational Natural Language Learning: Shared Task, 49-54.

Dinh, D., & Tamine, L. 2011. Biomedical concept extraction based on combining the content-based and word order similarities. In Proceedings of the 2011 ACM Symposium on Applied Computing, 1159-1163. ACM.

Gelfand, B., Wulfekuler, M., & Punch, W. F. 1998. Automated concept extraction from plain text.

In AAAI 1998 Workshop on Text Categorization, 13-17.

Gildea, D., and Jurafsky, D. 2002. Automatic labeling of semantic roles. Comput. Linguist. 28(3):245–288.

Hovy, E., Kozareva, Z., & Riloff, E. 2009. Toward completeness in concept extraction and classification. In Proceedings of the 2009 Conference on Empirical Methods in Natural Language Processing: Volume 2-Volume 2, 948-957.

Huang, C. R., Chen, F. Y., Chen, K. J., Gao, Z. M., & Chen, K. Y. (2000, October). Sinica Treebank: design criteria, annotation guidelines, and on-line interface. In Proceedings of the second workshop on Chinese language processing: held in conjunction with the 38th Annual Meeting of the Association for Computational Linguistics-Volume 12, 29-37.

Jiang, Z. P.; Li, J.; and Ng, H. T. 2005. Semantic argu-ment classification exploiting argument inter-depend-ence. In Proceedings of the 19th International Joint Conference on Artificial Intelligence, IJCAI'05, 1067–1072.

Johansson, R., & Nugues, P. 2008. The effect of syntactic representation on semantic role labeling. In Proceedings of the 22nd International Conference on Computational Linguistics-Volume 1, 393-400.

R. Johansson and P. Nugues. 2008. Dependency-based semantic role labeling of PropBank. In Proceedings of the 2008 Conference on Empirical Methods in Natural Language Processing.

Jonnalagadda, S., Cohen, T., Wu, S., & Gonzalez, G. 2012. Enhancing clinical concept extraction with distributional semantics. Journal of biomedical informatics, 45(1), 129-140.

Klein, D., and Manning, C. D. 2003. Accurate unlexical-ized parsing. In Proceedings of the 41st Annual Meeting on Association for Computational Linguis-tics - Volume 1, ACL '03, 423–430.

D. Liu and D. Gildea. 2010. Semantic role features for machine translation. In Proceedings of the 23rd International Conference on Computational Linguistics.

Liu, H., and Singh, P. 2004. Conceptnet: A practical commonsense reasoning toolkit. BT TECHNOLOGY JOURNAL 22:211–226.

Manning, Christopher D. and Schutze, Hinrich. 1999. Foundations of statistical natural language processing, Cambridge, Mass.: MIT Press.

Meza-Ruiz, I., & Riedel, S. 2009. Multilingual semantic role labelling with markov logic. In Proceedings of the Thirteenth Conference on Computational Natural Language Learning: Shared Task, 85-90.

Park, K.-M., and Rim, H.-C. 2005. Maximum entropy based semantic role labeling. In Proceedings of the Ninth Conference on Computational Natural Language Learning, CONLL '05, 209–212.

Pradhan, S.; Ward, W.; Hacioglu, K.; and Martin, J. H. 2004. Shallow semantic parsing using support vector machines. In Proceedings of the Conference on the Human Language Technologies and North American Association for Computational Linguistics (HLT-NAACL 2004), 233–240.

Rajagopal, D.; Cambria, E.; Olsher, D.; and Kwok, K. 2013. A graph-based approach to commonsense concept extrac- tion and semantic similarity detection. In Proceedings of the 22Nd International Conference on World Wide Web Companion, WWW '13 Companion, 565–570.

Ruppenhofer, J., Ellsworth, M., Petruck, M. R., Johnson, C. R., & Scheffczyk, J. (2006). FrameNet II: Extended theory and practice.

D. Shen and M. Lapata. 2007. Using semantic roles to improve question answering. In Proceedings of the Conference on Empirical Methods in Natural Language Processing and on Computational Natural Language Learning.

Täckström, O. 2009. Multilingual semantic parsing with a pipeline of linear classifiers. In Proceedings of the Thirteenth Conference on Computational Natural Language Learning: Shared Task, 103-108.

Torii, M., Wagholikar, K., & Liu, H. 2011. Using machine learning for concept extraction on clinical documents from multiple data sources. Journal of the American Medical Informatics Association, amiajnl-2011.

Villalon, J., & Calvo, R. A. 2009. Concept extraction from student essays, towards concept map mining. In Proceedings of Ninth IEEE International Conference on Advanced Learning Technologies, 221-225.

Xue, N. 2004. Calibrating features for semantic role labeling. In Proceedings of EMNLP 2004, 88–94.

Xue, N. 2008. Labeling chinese predicates with seman-tic roles. Comput. Linguist. 34(2):225–255.

Zapirain, B.; Agirre, E.; and Màrquez, L. 2007. Ub-cupc: Sequential srl using selectional preferences: An approach with maximum entropy markov models. In Proceedings of the 4th International Workshop on Semantic Evaluations, SemEval '07, 354–357.

A system for fine-grained aspect-based sentiment analysis of Chinese

Janna Lipenkova
Anacode
janna.lipenkova@anacode.de

Abstract

This paper presents a pipeline for aspect-based sentiment analysis of Chinese texts in the automotive domain. The input to the pipeline is a string of Chinese characters; the output is a set of relationships between evaluations and their targets. The main goal is to demonstrate how knowledge about sentence structure can increase the precision, insight value and granularity of the output. We formulate the task of sentiment analysis in two steps, namely unit identification and relation extraction. In unit identification, we identify fairly well-delimited linguistic units which describe features, emotions and evaluations. In relation extraction, we discover the relations between evaluations and their "target" features.

1 Introduction

Whereas most work on sentiment analysis, and especially on less covered languages such as Chinese, is based on probabilistic models and the use of general sentiment lexica, we believe that a holistic approach should also take into account general linguistic knowledge. On the one hand, this allows to leverage the results of several decades of research in theoretical linguistics. On the other hand, the hard-coding of general principles of language structure allows us to create a linguistically adequate training space for further application of probabilistic models.

In the following, we present the "bottom-up" component of our sentiment system which builds opinion representations by a progression along three levels - the lexical, the phrasal and the sentence level. The system has been conceptualized manually and bootstrapped on a corpus of about 1 mio. automotive reviews with an average length of 135 Chinese characters.[1] We use a prebuilt lexicon with ca. 2000 entries which contains opinion words, their modifiers, car features as well as a large number of functional categories relevant for the syntactic analysis of phrases and sentences. The performance of the system is evaluated on a testset of 800 annotated sentences. In practice, the presented model is complemented by a probabilistic model which performs topic and polarity classification on the sentence and the document levels; this component will not be described below due to space limitations.

The basic assumption on which the model builds is that language follows rules. Many of these rules have been extensively studied in the linguistic literature and have been taken to a level of abstraction which allows for a straightforward encoding. Incorporating these rules spares us the construction of probabilistic models for the discovery of already established general knowledge about linguistic structure. For example, it has long been observed that Chinese phrase structure is largely head-final (Huang 1982, Li 1990, *i. a.*): nominal modifiers precede their head nouns, whereas degree and negation adverbs normally precede the adjectives or verbs they modify. Due to the relative rigidity of word order in Chinese on the phrasal level, a small set of corresponding phrase-level rules achieves a high coverage on our dataset. Rules do not perform as well on sentence level; nevertheless, some general observations are possible: for example, AP targets precede their APs. These high-level observations form the basis of a sequence classifier which determines whether a sequence of words between two syntactic phrases establishes or disrupts one of the target relations between these phrases.

The paper is structured as follows: after a very brief review of research on aspect-based sentiment analysis (henceforth ABSA), we formulate

[1] The reviews were crawled from popular automotive sites: http://www.autohome.com.cn, http://auto.16888.com, http://auto.qq.com.

Proceedings of ACL-IJCNLP 2015 System Demonstrations, pages 55–60,
Beijing, China, July 26-31, 2015.

our task and, specifically, present the output format of the system (Section 3). In the second step, we briefly describe the categories used in our lexical resources (Section 4). In the third step, we describe the three levels of processing (Section 5). Finally, we present the evaluation of our system (Section 6).

2 Previous work

ABSA has been exploited as a refined alternative to sentiment analysis on the sentence and the document level: whereas the latter targets the general sentiment or polarity of a piece of text, ABSA outputs a mapping from specific aspects of the discussed topic to their evaluations. Different ABSA approaches have been exploited; thus, Popescu and Etzioni (2005) and Kim and Hovy (2006) present unsupervised algorithms for extracting aspects and determining sentiment in review text. Ding et al. (2008) and Liu (2012) describe approaches based on rules of semantic composition and distance metrics for the identification of relations between aspects and their opinions. Due to the relatively fine granularity of the task, parsing-based approaches have been proposed to capture the aspect/sentiment relations based on sentence structure (Jiang et al. 2011, Boiy and Moens 2009, *i. a.*). Further, the SemEval-2014 task on ABSA (Pontiki et al., 2014) has been addressed with a number of promising approaches and also significantly contributed to a unified understanding of ABSA.

Still, most research is focussed on the English language; for Chinese, most approaches to sentiment analysis are targeted on lexicon construction (e. g. Liu et al. 2013) or sentence/document-level sentiment classification.[2] Only few contributions aim at a finer-grained analysis at the aspect level (Ku et al. (2009), Su et al. (2008)).

3 Task

The goal of aspect-based sentiment analysis is to derive the opinions of a speaker about an entity and its features (Liu, 2012, p. 58). In our framework, opinions can be subclassified into evaluations and emotions. Evaluations express how the author evaluates a specific feature (e. g. *good*, *expensive*), whereas emotions express how the author feels about a specific feature (e. g. *to please*, *angry*).

We formulate the task in two stages - the identification of syntactic units and the extraction of relations between the syntactic units. Thus, given an opinion statement on a specific product, we "translate" the statement into a set of $(feature, < evaluation|emotion >)$ pairs in two processing steps:

1. Build three sets of syntactic units F (features), EV (evaluations) and EM (emotions). For convenience, we will use $E = EM \cup EV$ in cases where the evaluation/emotion distinction is not relevant.

2. For each $e \in E$, find whether it has an opinion target $f \in F$.

A word is in place about the semantic organization of evaluations and emotions in our system. It has long been observed that many evaluation words come with implicit features; for example, the evaluation *beautiful* implicitly contains the feature VisualAppearance. In order to preserve this meaning, we adopt a scalar representation of evaluations (cf. Kennedy and McNally (2005) for a linguistic analysis of scalar expressions): evaluations are represented as pairs of a feature and a numerical value which "maps" the evaluation to some point on the feature scale [-3, 3]. Thus, *beautiful* gets the representation (VisualAppearance, 2), whereas *ugly* gets the representation (VisualAppearance, -2). Similarly, emotions are also represented as pairs of the emotion concept and a numerical value representing the intensity of the emotion (e. g. *angry*: (Anger, 2)).

The final mapping goes from sequences of features to numerical evaluations. In a feature sequence $[f_1, f_2 \dots f_n]$, features are ordered by the subfeature relation, such that f_i (with $i > 0$) is a subfeature of f_{i-1}. Consider the following feature expression:

(1) 方向盘 的 指针
steering.wheel DE indicator
the indicator of the steering wheel

Our representation is [SteeringWheel, Indicator], whereby Indicator is interpreted as a subfeature of SteeringWheel.

Further, implicit features that are contained in associated evaluations are also "moved" into the feature sequence:

[2] Cf. Proceedings of the evaluation task on polarity analysis organized by the Professional Committee of Information Retrieval (中文倾向性分析评测委员会) 2008 - 2014.

(2) 方向盘 的 指针 很 精准。
steering.wheel DE indicator very precise
The indicator of the steering wheel is very precise.

This sentence contains the evaluation 'precise'. According to the above description, it is decomposed into a feature (Precision) and a positive evaluation. The feature is moved into the feature sequence. The resulting mapping is as follows:

(3) [SteeringWheel, Indicator, Precision] → +2

Thus, instead of limiting ourselves to entities and restricted sets of their immediate features, we adapt a "higher-order" view and allow a hierarchical feature sequence of arbitrary depth. This structure seamlessly integrates implicit features and flexibly captures any granularity that is intended by the author of the text. At the same time, the value of the evaluation is reduced to a single numerical value, which allows for a straightforward aggregation of the final results.

4 Lexical basis

Out lexical resources contain functional and semantic categories. Members of "functional" categories (e. g. conjunctions, phrase-final markers) are only relevant for the syntactic analysis. Semantic categories are relevant for the interpretation of opinions. The top-level semantic categories are:

- Features, e. g. 外观 ('look'), 座椅 ('seat'), 颜色 ('color')
- Evaluations:
  - with implicit features, e. g. 好看 ('beautiful' → VisualAppearance), 便宜 ('cheap' → Price)
  - without implicit features, e. g. 不错 ('not bad'), 一般 ('ordinary'), 还可以 ('OK')
- Emotions, e. g. 赞美 ('admire'), 烦人 ('annoying')
- Degree adverbs and negation words, e. g. 非常 ('very'), 稍微 ('a little bit'), 不 ('not')

Each of these categories is in turn subclassified into more fine-grained classes which capture information about the linguistic use of the subclass members.

5 Processing steps

Figure illustrates the in- and output, the three processing steps as well as the resources involved in these steps.

5.1 Preprocessing

We use the third-party tool jieba[3] for word segmentation and POS tagging; both steps are customized in order to achieve a better performance on domain- and task-specific data. Specifically, the dictionary provided by the tool is intersected with a user-specified dictionary. This user-specified dictionary contains all words from our lexical resources. The user-added words are annotated with customized POS tags, such as 'F' for feature, 'EV' for evaluation etc. The following two examples depict the same sentence as output by jieba without and with customization:

(4) a. original jieba output without customization:
后排/vn 空间/n 已经/d 做/v 得/ud
rear.row space already make DE
很/d 不错/a 了/ul 。/x
very not.bad PFV
The rear space is already quite not bad.

b. after customization:
后排空间/F 已经/d 做/v 得/ud
rear.space already make DE
很/D 不错/EV 了/ul 。/x
very not.bad PFV
The rear space is already quite not bad.

Thus, we see that the two words 后排 ('rear row') and 空间 ('space') are merged into one word in the customized output since this combination occurs frequently in automotive texts and has a quasi-lexicalized meaning; the resulting word gets our custom POS tag 'F' (feature). Further, the POS tag of 不错 is changed from the original jieba tag 'a' to the custom tag 'EV' (evaluation).

5.2 Unit identification

In the next step, we identify phrasal units corresponding to features, evaluations, emotions. We use a phrase rule grammar which is based on regular expressions involving the POS tags of the

[3] https://github.com/fxsjy/jieba

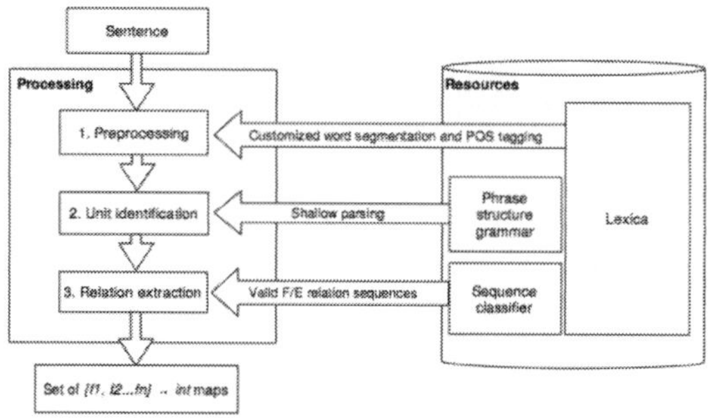

Figure 1: Overall architecture of the system

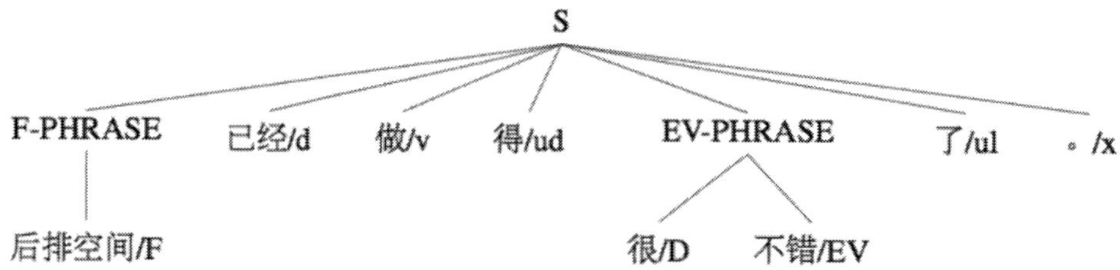

Figure 2: Phrasal analysis of the sentence 后排空间 已经 做 得 很 不错 了。

words. Figure 2 shows the parsed version of example (4b).

In the following, we present some of the most common phrase structures for features and evaluations/emotions that are used in our system.

Feature phrases Besides simple NPs consisting only of one feature word, the most frequent types of feature phrases are phrases with nominal modifiers, coordinated NPs and NPs with pronominal modifiers:

(5) NP modifier:

座椅 的 材料
seat DE material

the material of the seats

(6) 它 的 设计
it DE design
its design

(7) 前排 （跟/和） 后排
front.row (and) rear.row
the front and the rear row

Evaluation and emotion chunks The class of evaluations consists of adjectives, whereas the class of emotions consists both of adjectives and verbs. However, evaluations and emotions get a unified treatment at the unit level, since Chinese stative verbs behave similarly to adjectives: they can also be modified by degree adverbs, used in comparative constructions etc.

Besides simple lexical units, the following are the most frequent phrase types for the E class:

(8) a. Verb or adjective preceded by negation or degree adverb:
很 难受
very difficult.to.bear
very difficult to bear

b. Adjective followed by degree adverb:
小 了 点
small PFV a.bit
a bit small

Evaluations can be coordinated in various ways; for example, coordination can be expressed by simple juxtaposition, with a comma or in the 又 E1 又 E2 construction:

(9) a. juxtaposition / punctuation:
精准 （，）灵活
precise (,) flexible
precise and flexible

b. 又 E1 又 E2:
又 精准 又 灵活
CONJ precise CONJ flexible
both precise and flexible

Besides, evaluations are often expressed by so-called "possessed features": the evaluation value is derived from the "amount" to which a feature is possessed by the discussed entity:

(10) 没 有 活力
NEG have vigor
not vigorous

5.3 Relation extraction

After identifying the syntactic units of interest, we proceed with identifying sentence-level relations between these units. In the literature, there are two major approaches to the identification of relations between evaluations and their targets. On the one hand, some authors recur to parsing and identify evaluation targets based on dependency relations (Wu et al. 2009, Jiang et al. 2011, *i. a.*). On the other hand, distance metrics can be used (Ding et al., 2008; Liu, 2012). Since we want to avoid the overhead of full-fledged syntactic parsing, but also want to improve the accuracy of simple distance metrics, we develop a sequence classifier which determines whether a given sequence of words between a feature and an evaluation/emotion phrase indicates a target relation.

The two semantic relations of interest are the *causer* and the *theme* relation. Additionally, the system analyzes a third non-semantic relation – the *topic* – which provides relevant discourse-structural information on the overall aspect discussed in a sentence.

The *causer* relation The causer relation is a fairly well-delimited relation which describes the causer of some state of event. In our model, it is applied to emotions caused by specific features. In the most basic cases, the causer is expressed as subject of one of the causative verbs (让, 令 etc.):

(11) 动力 让 我 非常 失望。
power CAUS me very desperate
The power really makes me desperate.

The *theme* relation The *theme* relation is expressed differently for evaluations and emotions. In the case of evaluations, it can be realized as the single argument of an AP or the nominal head of an adjectival modifier:

(12) a. Single argument of an AP:
设计 特别 时尚。
design particularly fashionable
The design is particularly fashionable.

b. Nominal head of an adjectival modifier:
特别 时尚 的 设计
particularly fashionable DE design
a particularly fashionable design

With respect to emotions, the *theme* relation is only relevant for verbs; the feature targets of adjectives are covered by the causer relation. Thus, themes can be expressed as (possibly topicalized) objects of emotion verbs:

(13) a. Object in canonical postverbal position:
我 很 喜欢 它 的 设计。
me very like it DE design
I like its design a lot.

b. Topicalized object:
设计 很 喜欢， ...
design very like , ...
The design, I like it a lot, ...

5.4 Relation extraction

In the above examples, relations hold between adjoined constituents and can thus be easily recognized. However, in many cases, several words occur between the evaluation/emotion and its target:

(14) 后排空间 已经 做 得 很 不错 了。
rear.row space already make DE very not.bad PFV
The rear space is already quite not bad.

From our corpus, we bootstrap the most frequent sequences that occur between themes and emotions/evaluations, emotions and themes as well as causers and emotions. We then apply a simple classifier for the classification of unseen sequences.

6 Evaluation

The system is evaluated on a testset of 800 sentences annotated for feature, evaluation and emotion phrases and for relations between them. The annotation was carried out according to previously developed annotation guidelines; we worked with

	Precision	Recall
F-phrases	87.43%	85.37%
EV-phrases	89.21 %	84.29%
EM-phrases	88.56%	85.32%

Table 1: Results of unit identification

	Precision	Recall
F-EV relations - theme	89.2%	87.33%
F-EM relations - theme	84.01%	83.10%
F-EM relations - causer	86.49%	87.90%

Table 2: Results of relation extraction

two independent annotators - a native Chinese student without specialized linguistic knowledge and a non-native linguist with very good mastery of the Chinese language. They proceeded in three steps: at the phrase level, the total F-score of inter-annotator agreement was 91.3%. The diverging items were discussed with a third team member to create a unified phrase-level annotation. The reviewed corpus was then annotated for relations between opinion and their targets; in this step, inter-annotator agreement reached 93.4%.

Table 1 shows the results achieved in unit identification; table 2 shows the results achieved for relation extraction on the test set with finalized annotation of F/EV/EM phrases.

7 Outlook

We have shown that the use of a prebuilt lexicon together with the application of general language rules allows to achieve a considerable accuracy in ABSA for Chinese. Currently, the presented system is being extended with a number of more complex sentence-level relations, specifically comparative structures and modal operators. Further,

References

Boiy, Erik and Moens, Marie-Francine. 2009. A machine learning approach to sentiment analysis in multilingual Web texts. *Inf. Retr.* 12(5), 526–558.

Ding, Xiaowen, Liu, Bing and Yu, Philip S. 2008. A Holistic Lexicon-based Approach to Opinion Mining. In *Proceedings of WSDM'08*, WSDM '08, pages 231–240.

Huang, James C.-T. 1982. *Logical relations in Chinese and the theory of grammar*. Ph. D.thesis, MIT, Massachusetts.

Jiang, Long, Yu, Mo, Zhou, Ming, Liu, Xiaohua and Zhao, Tiejun. 2011. Target-dependent Twitter Sentiment Classification. In *Proceedings of ACL'11 - Volume 1*, pages 151–160.

Kennedy, Christopher and McNally, Louise. 2005. Scale structure, degree modification, and the semantics of gradable predicates. *Language* 81, 345 – 381.

Kim, Soo-Min and Hovy, Eduard. 2006. Extracting Opinions, Opinion Holders, and Topics Expressed in Online News Media Text. In *Proceedings of the Workshop on Sentiment and Subjectivity in Text*, SST '06, pages 1–8.

Ku, Lunwei, Huang, Tinghao and Chen, Hsinhsi. 2009. Using Morphological and Syntactic Structures for Chinese Opinion Analysis. In *Proceedings of EMNLP'09*, pages 1260–1269.

Li, Audrey Yen-Hui. 1990. *Order and Constituency in Mandarin Chinese*. Studies in Natural Language and Linguistic Theory, Dordrecht: Kluwer Academic Publishers.

Liu, Bing. 2012. Sentiment Analysis and Opinion Mining.

Liu, Lizhen, Lei, Mengyun and Wang, Hanshi. 2013. Combining Domain-Specific Sentiment Lexicon with Hownet for Chinese Sentiment Analysis. *Journal of Computers* 8(4).

Pontiki, Maria, Galanis, Dimitris, Pavlopoulos, John, Papageorgiou, Harris, Androutsopoulos, Ion and Manandhar, Suresh. 2014. SemEval-2014 Task 4: Aspect Based Sentiment Analysis. In *Proceedings of the SemEval'14*, pages 27–35, Dublin, Ireland: ACL and Dublin City University.

Popescu, Ana Maria and Etzioni, Oren. 2005. Extracting Product Features and Opinions from Reviews. In *Proceedings of HLT & EMNLP'05*, pages 339–346, Stroudsburg, USA.

Su, Qi, Xu, Xinying, Guo, Honglei, Guo, Zhili, Wu, Xian, Zhang, Xiaoxun, Swen, Bin and Su, Zhong. 2008. Hidden Sentiment Association in Chinese Web Opinion Mining. In *Proceedings of WWW'08*.

Wu, Yuanbin, Zhang, Qi, Huang, Xuanjing and Wu, Lide. 2009. Phrase Dependency Parsing for Opinion Mining. In *Proceedings of EMNLP'09*, pages 1533–1541, Stroudsburg, USA.

Plug Latent Structures and Play Coreference Resolution

Sebastian Martschat, Patrick Claus and **Michael Strube**
Heidelberg Institute for Theoretical Studies gGmbH
Schloss-Wolfsbrunnenweg 35
69118 Heidelberg, Germany
(sebastian.martschat|patrick.claus|michael.strube)@h-its.org

Abstract

We present *cort*, a modular toolkit for devising, implementing, comparing and analyzing approaches to coreference resolution. The toolkit allows for a unified representation of popular coreference resolution approaches by making explicit the structures they operate on. Several of the implemented approaches achieve state-of-the-art performance.

1 Introduction

Coreference resolution is the task of determining which mentions in a text refer to the same entity. Machine learning approaches to coreference resolution range from simple binary classification models on mention pairs (Soon et al., 2001) to complex structured prediction approaches (Durrett and Klein, 2013; Fernandes et al., 2014).

In this paper, we present a toolkit that implements a framework that unifies these approaches: in the framework, we obtain a unified representation of many coreference approaches by making explicit the *latent structures* they operate on.

Our toolkit provides an interface for defining structures for coreference resolution, which we use to implement several popular approaches. An evaluation of the approaches on CoNLL shared task data (Pradhan et al., 2012) shows that they obtain state-of-the-art results. The toolkit also can perform end-to-end coreference resolution.

We implemented this functionality on top of the coreference resolution error analysis toolkit *cort* (Martschat et al., 2015). Hence, this toolkit now provides functionality for devising, implementing, comparing and analyzing approaches to coreference resolution. *cort* is released as open source[1] and is available from the Python Package Index[2].

[1] http://smartschat.de/software

[2] http://pypi.python.org/pypi. Install it via pip install cort.

2 A Framework for Coreference Resolution

In this section we briefly describe a structured prediction framework for coreference resolution.

2.1 Motivation

The popular mention pair approach (Soon et al., 2001; Ng and Cardie, 2002) operates on a *list* of mention pairs. Each mention pair is considered individually for learning and prediction. In contrast, antecedent tree models (Yu and Joachims, 2009; Fernandes et al., 2014; Björkelund and Kuhn, 2014) operate on a *tree* which encodes all anaphor-antecedent decisions in a document.

Conceptually, both approaches have in common that the structures they employ are not annotated in the data (in coreference resolution, the annotation consists of a mapping of mentions to entity identifiers). Hence, we can view both approaches as instantiations of a generic structured prediction approach with latent variables.

2.2 Setting

Our aim is to learn a prediction function f that, given an input document $x \in \mathcal{X}$, predicts a pair $(h, z) \in \mathcal{H} \times \mathcal{Z}$. h is the (unobserved) latent structure encoding the coreference relations between mentions in x. z is the mapping of mentions to entity identifiers (which is observed in the training data). Usually, z is obtained from h by taking the transitive closure over coreference decisions encoded in h. $\mathcal{H}$ and $\mathcal{Z}$ are the spaces containing all such structures and mappings.

2.3 Representation

For a document $x \in \mathcal{X}$, we write $M_x = \{m_1, \ldots, m_n\}$ for the mentions in x. Following previous work (Chang et al., 2012; Fernandes et al., 2014), we make use of a *dummy mention* which we denote as m_0. If m_0 is predicted as the

Proceedings of ACL-IJCNLP 2015 System Demonstrations, pages 61–66,
Beijing, China, July 26-31, 2015.

antecedent of a mention m_i, we consider m_i non-anaphoric. We define $M_x^0 = \{m_0\} \cup M_x$.

Inspired by previous work (Bengtson and Roth, 2008; Fernandes et al., 2014; Martschat and Strube, 2014), we adopt a graph-based representation of the latent structures $h \in \mathcal{H}$. In particular, we express structures by *labeled directed graphs* with vertex set M_x^0.

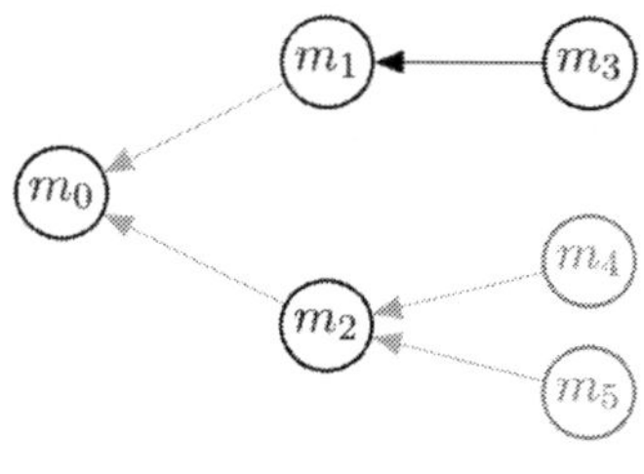

Figure 1: Latent structure underlying the mention ranking and the antecedent tree approach. The black nodes and arcs represent one substructure for the mention ranking approach.

Figure 1 shows a structure underlying the mention ranking and the antecedent tree approach. An arc between two mentions signals coreference. For antecedent trees (Fernandes et al., 2014), the whole structure is considered, while for mention ranking (Denis and Baldridge, 2008; Chang et al., 2012) only the antecedent decision for one anaphor is examined. This can be expressed via an appropriate segmentation into subgraphs which we refer to as *substructures*. One such substructure encoding the antecedent decision for m_3 is colored black in the figure.

Via arc labels we can express additional information. For example, mention pair models (Soon et al., 2001) distinguish between *positive* and *negative* instances. This can be modeled by labeling arcs with appropriate labels, such as $+$ and $-$.

2.4 Inference and Learning

As is common in natural language processing, we model the prediction of (h, z) via a linear model. That is,

$$f(x) = f_\theta(x) = \underset{(h,z) \in \mathcal{H} \times \mathcal{Z}}{\arg\max} \langle \theta, \phi(x, h, z) \rangle,$$

where $\theta \in \mathbb{R}^d$ is a parameter vector and $\phi\colon \mathcal{X} \times \mathcal{H} \times \mathcal{Z} \to \mathbb{R}^d$ is a joint feature representation for inputs and outputs. When employing substructures, one maximization problem has to be solved for each substructure (instead of one maximization problem for the whole structure).

To learn the parameter vector $\theta \in \mathbb{R}^d$ from training data, we employ a latent structured perceptron (Sun et al., 2009) with cost-augmented inference (Crammer et al., 2006) and averaging (Collins, 2002).

3 Implementation

We now describe our implementation of the framework presented in the previous section.

3.1 Aims

By expressing approaches in the framework, researchers can quickly devise, implement, compare and analyze approaches for coreference resolution. To facilitate development, it should be as easy as possible to define a coreference resolution approach. We first describe the general architecture of our toolkit before giving a detailed description of how to implement specific coreference resolution approaches.

3.2 Architecture

The toolkit is implemented in Python. It can process raw text and data conforming to the format of the CoNLL-2012 shared task on coreference resolution (Pradhan et al., 2012). The toolkit is organized in four modules: the `preprocessing` module contains functionality for processing raw text, the `core` module provides mention extraction and computation of mention properties, the `analysis` module contains error analysis methods, and the `coreference` module implements the framework described in the previous section.

3.2.1 `preprocessing`

By making use of NLTK[3], this module provides classes and functions for performing the preprocessing tasks necessary for mention extraction and coreference resolution: tokenization, sentence splitting, parsing and named entity recognition.

3.2.2 `core`

We employ a rule-based mention extractor, which also computes a rich set of mention attributes, including tokens, head, part-of-speech tags, named entity tags, gender, number, semantic class, grammatical function and mention type. These attributes, from which features are computed, can be extended easily.

[3] `http://www.nltk.org/`

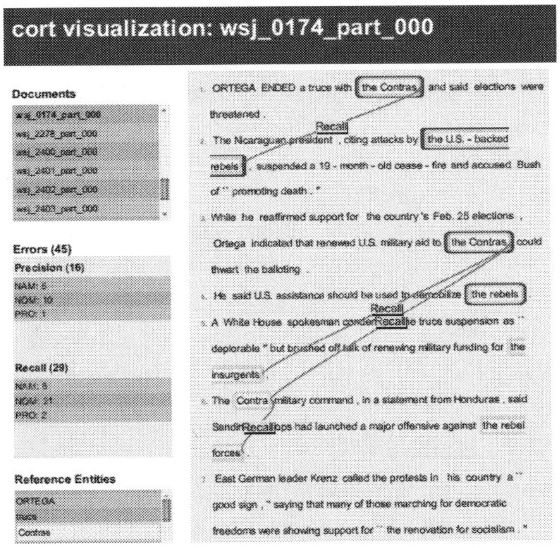

Figure 2: Visualization of errors.

3.2.3 `analysis`

To support system development, this module implements the error analysis framework of Martschat and Strube (2014). Users can extract, analyze and visualize recall and precision errors of the systems they are working on. Figure 2 shows a screenshot of the visualization. A more detailed description can be found in Martschat et al. (2015).

3.2.4 `coreference`

This module provides features for coreference resolution and implements the machine learning framework described in the previous section.

We implemented a rich set of features employed in previous work (Ng and Cardie, 2002; Bengtson and Roth, 2008; Björkelund and Kuhn, 2014), including lexical, rule-based and semantic features. The feature set can be extended by the user.

The module provides a structured latent perceptron implementation and contains classes that implement the workflows for training and prediction. As its main feature, it provides an interface for defining coreference resolution approaches. We already implemented various approaches (see Section 4).

3.3 Defining Approaches

The toolkit provides a simple interface for devising coreference resolution approaches via structures. The user just needs to specify two functions: an *instance extractor*, which defines the search space for the optimal (sub)structures, and a *decoder*, which, given a parameter vector, finds optimal (sub)structures. The toolkit then performs training and prediction using these user-specified functions. The user can further customize the approach by defining *cost functions* to be used during cost-augmented inference, and *clustering algorithms* to extract coreference chains from latent structures, such as closest-first (Soon et al., 2001) or best-first (Ng and Cardie, 2002).

In the remainder of this section, we present an example implementation of the mention ranking model with latent antecedents (Chang et al., 2012) in our toolkit.

Listing 1 Instance extraction for the mention ranking model with latent antecedents.

```
def extract_substructures(doc):
  substructures = []

  # iterate over mentions
  for i, ana in enumerate(
      doc.system_mentions):
    ana_arcs = []

    # iterate in reversed order over
    # candidate antecedents
    for ante in sorted(
        doc.system_mentions[:i],
        reverse=True):
      ana_arcs.append((ana, ante))

    substructures.append(ana_arcs)

  return substructures
```

Listing 2 Decoder for the mention ranking model with latent antecedents.

```
class RankingPerceptron(
    perceptrons.Perceptron):
  def argmax(self, substructure,
             arc_information):
    best_arc, best_arc_score, \
    best_cons_arc, best_cons_arc_score, \
    consistent = self.find_best_arcs(
      substructure, arc_information)

    return ([best_arc], [],
            [best_arc_score],
            [best_cons_arc], [],
            [best_cons_arc_score],
            consistent)
```

3.3.1 Instance Extractors

The instance extractor receives a document as input and defines the search space for the maximization problem to be solved by the decoder. To do so, it needs to output the segmentation of the la-

Listing 3 Cost function for the mention ranking model with latent antecedents.

```
def cost_based_on_consistency(arc):
    ana, ante = arc

    consistent = \
      ana.decision_is_consistent(ante)

    # false new
    if not consistent and \
        ante.is_dummy():
      return 2
    # wrong link
    elif not consistent:
      return 1
    # correct
    else:
      return 0
```

tent structure for one document into substructures, and the candidate arcs for each substructure.

Listing 1 shows source code of the instance extractor for the mention ranking model with latent antecedents. In this model, each antecedent decision for a mention corresponds to one substructure. Therefore, the extractor iterates over all mentions. For each mention, arcs to all preceding mentions are extracted and stored as candidate arcs for one substructure.

3.3.2 Decoders

The decoder solves the maximization problems for obtaining the highest-scoring latent substructures consistent with the gold annotation, and the highest-scoring cost-augmented latent substructures.

Listing 2 shows source code of a decoder for the mention ranking model with latent antecedents. The input to the decoder is a *substructure*, which is a set of arcs, and a mapping from arcs to information about arcs, such as features or costs. The output is a tuple containing

- a list of arcs that constitute the highest-scoring substructure, together with their labels (if any) and scores,
- the same for the highest-scoring substructure consistent with the gold annotation,
- the information whether the highest-scoring substructure is consistent with the gold annotation.

To obtain this prediction, we invoke the auxiliary function `self.find_best_arcs`. This function searches through a set of arcs to find the overall highest-scoring arc and the overall highest-scoring arc consistent with the gold annotation. Furthermore, it also outputs the scores of these arcs according to the model, and whether the prediction of the best arc is consistent with the gold annotation.

For the mention ranking model, we let the function search through all candidate arcs for a substructure, since these represent the antecedent decision for one anaphor. Note that the mention ranking model does not use any labels.

The update of the parameter vector is handled by our implementation of the structured perceptron.

3.3.3 Cost Functions

Cost functions allow to bias the learner towards specific substructures, which leads to a large margin approach. For the mention ranking model, we employ a cost function that assigns a higher cost to erroneously determining anaphoricity than to selecting a wrong link, similar to the cost functions employed by Durrett and Klein (2013) and Fernandes et al. (2014). The source code is displayed in Listing 3.

3.3.4 Clustering Algorithms

The mention ranking model selects one antecedent for each anaphor, therefore there is no need to cluster antecedent decisions. Our toolkit provides clustering algorithms commonly used for mention pair models, such as *closest-first* (Soon et al., 2001) or *best-first* (Ng and Cardie, 2002).

3.4 Running *cort*

cort can be used as a Python library, but also provides two command line tools `cort-train` and `cort-predict`.

4 Evaluation

We implemented a mention pair model with best-first clustering (Ng and Cardie, 2002), the mention ranking model with closest (Denis and Baldridge, 2008) and latent (Chang et al., 2012) antecedents, and antecedent trees (Fernandes et al., 2014). Only slight modifications of the source code displayed in Listings 1 and 2 were necessary to implement these approaches. For the ranking models and antecedent trees we use the cost function described in Listing 3.

We evaluate the models on the English test data of the CoNLL-2012 shared task on multilingual coreference resolution (Pradhan et al., 2012). We use the reference implementation of the CoNLL

Model	MUC R	MUC P	MUC F_1	B^3 R	B^3 P	B^3 F_1	$CEAF_e$ R	$CEAF_e$ P	$CEAF_e$ F_1	Average F_1
CoNLL-2012 English test data										
Fernandes et al. (2014)	65.83	75.91	70.51	51.55	65.19	57.58	50.82	57.28	53.86	60.65
Björkelund and Kuhn (2014)	67.46	74.30	70.72	54.96	62.71	58.58	52.27	59.40	55.61	61.63
Mention Pair	67.16	71.48	69.25	51.97	60.55	55.93	51.02	51.89	51.45	58.88
Ranking: Closest	67.96	76.61	72.03	54.07	64.98	59.03	51.45	59.02	54.97	62.01
Ranking: Latent	68.13	76.72	72.17	54.22	66.12	59.58	52.33	59.47	55.67	62.47
Antecedent Trees	65.34	78.12	71.16	50.23	67.36	57.54	49.76	58.43	53.75	60.82

Table 1: Results of different systems and models on CoNLL-2012 English test data. Models below the dashed lines are implemented in our toolkit.

scorer (Pradhan et al., 2014), which computes the average of the evaluation metrics MUC (Vilain et al., 1995), B^3, (Bagga and Baldwin, 1998) and $CEAF_e$ (Luo, 2005). The models are trained on the concatenation of training and development data.

The evaluation of the models is shown in Table 1. To put the numbers into context, we compare with Fernandes et al. (2014), the winning system of the CoNLL-2012 shared task, and the state-of-the-art system of Björkelund and Kuhn (2014).

The mention pair model performs decently, while the antecedent tree model exhibits performance comparable to Fernandes et al. (2014), who use a very similar model. The ranking models outperform Björkelund and Kuhn (2014), obtaining state-of-the-art performance.

5 Related Work

Many researchers on coreference resolution release an implementation of the coreference model described in their paper (Lee et al., 2013; Durrett and Klein, 2013; Björkelund and Kuhn, 2014, inter alia). However, these implementations implement only one approach following one paradigm (such as mention ranking or antecedent trees).

Similarly to *cort*, research toolkits such as BART (Versley et al., 2008) or Reconcile (Stoyanov et al., 2009) provide a framework to implement and compare coreference resolution approaches. In contrast to these toolkits, we make the latent structure underlying coreference approaches explicit, which facilitates development of new approaches and renders the development more transparent. Furthermore, we provide a generic and customizable learning algorithm.

6 Conclusions

We presented an implementation of a framework for coreference resolution that represents approaches to coreference resolution by the structures they operate on. In the implementation we placed emphasis on facilitating the definition of new models in the framework.

The presented toolkit *cort* can process raw text and CoNLL shared task data. It achieves state-of-the-art performance on the shared task data.

The framework and toolkit presented in this paper help researchers to devise, analyze and compare representations for coreference resolution.

Acknowledgements

We thank Benjamin Heinzerling for helpful comments on drafts of this paper. This work has been funded by the Klaus Tschira Foundation, Germany. The first author has been supported by a HITS Ph.D. scholarship.

References

Amit Bagga and Breck Baldwin. 1998. Algorithms for scoring coreference chains. In *Proceedings of the 1st International Conference on Language Resources and Evaluation*, Granada, Spain, 28–30 May 1998, pages 563–566.

Eric Bengtson and Dan Roth. 2008. Understanding the value of features for coreference resolution. In *Proceedings of the 2008 Conference on Empirical Methods in Natural Language Processing*, Waikiki, Honolulu, Hawaii, 25–27 October 2008, pages 294–303.

Anders Björkelund and Jonas Kuhn. 2014. Learning structured perceptrons for coreference resolution with latent antecedents and non-local features.

In *Proceedings of the 52nd Annual Meeting of the Association for Computational Linguistics (Volume 1: Long Papers),* Baltimore, Md., 22–27 June 2014, pages 47–57.

Kai-Wei Chang, Rajhans Samdani, Alla Rozovskaya, Mark Sammons, and Dan Roth. 2012. Illinois-Coref: The UI system in the CoNLL-2012 shared task. In *Proceedings of the Shared Task of the 16th Conference on Computational Natural Language Learning,* Jeju Island, Korea, 12–14 July 2012, pages 113–117.

Michael Collins. 2002. Discriminative training methods for Hidden Markov Models: Theory and experiments with perceptron algorithms. In *Proceedings of the 2002 Conference on Empirical Methods in Natural Language Processing,* Philadelphia, Penn., 6–7 July 2002, pages 1–8.

Koby Crammer, Ofer Dekel, Joseph Keshet, Shai Shalev-Shwartz, and Yoram Singer. 2006. Online passive-aggressive algorithms. *Journal of Machine Learning Research,* 7:551–585.

Pascal Denis and Jason Baldridge. 2008. Specialized models and ranking for coreference resolution. In *Proceedings of the 2008 Conference on Empirical Methods in Natural Language Processing,* Waikiki, Honolulu, Hawaii, 25–27 October 2008, pages 660–669.

Greg Durrett and Dan Klein. 2013. Easy victories and uphill battles in coreference resolution. In *Proceedings of the 2013 Conference on Empirical Methods in Natural Language Processing,* Seattle, Wash., 18–21 October 2013, pages 1971–1982.

Eraldo Fernandes, Cícero dos Santos, and Ruy Milidiú. 2014. Latent trees for coreference resolution. *Computational Linguistics,* 40(4):801–835.

Heeyoung Lee, Angel Chang, Yves Peirsman, Nathanael Chambers, Mihai Surdeanu, and Dan Jurafsky. 2013. Deterministic coreference resolution based on entity-centric, precision-ranked rules. *Computational Linguistics,* 39(4):885–916.

Xiaoqiang Luo. 2005. On coreference resolution performance metrics. In *Proceedings of the Human Language Technology Conference and the 2005 Conference on Empirical Methods in Natural Language Processing,* Vancouver, B.C., Canada, 6–8 October 2005, pages 25–32.

Sebastian Martschat and Michael Strube. 2014. Recall error analysis for coreference resolution. In *Proceedings of the 2014 Conference on Empirical Methods in Natural Language Processing,* Doha, Qatar, 25–29 October 2014, pages 2070–2081.

Sebastian Martschat, Thierry Göckel, and Michael Strube. 2015. Analyzing and visualizing coreference resolution errors. In *Proceedings of the 2015 Conference of the North American Chapter of the Association for Computational Linguistics: Demonstrations,* Denver, Col., 31 May – 5 June 2015, pages 6–10.

Vincent Ng and Claire Cardie. 2002. Improving machine learning approaches to coreference resolution. In *Proceedings of the 40th Annual Meeting of the Association for Computational Linguistics,* Philadelphia, Penn., 7–12 July 2002, pages 104–111.

Sameer Pradhan, Alessandro Moschitti, Nianwen Xue, Olga Uryupina, and Yuchen Zhang. 2012. CoNLL-2012 Shared Task: Modeling multilingual unrestricted coreference in OntoNotes. In *Proceedings of the Shared Task of the 16th Conference on Computational Natural Language Learning,* Jeju Island, Korea, 12–14 July 2012, pages 1–40.

Sameer Pradhan, Xiaoqiang Luo, Marta Recasens, Eduard Hovy, Vincent Ng, and Michael Strube. 2014. Scoring coreference partitions of predicted mentions: A reference implementation. In *Proceedings of the 52nd Annual Meeting of the Association for Computational Linguistics (Volume 2: Short Papers),* Baltimore, Md., 22–27 June 2014, pages 30–35.

Wee Meng Soon, Hwee Tou Ng, and Daniel Chung Yong Lim. 2001. A machine learning approach to coreference resolution of noun phrases. *Computational Linguistics,* 27(4):521–544.

Veselin Stoyanov, Claire Cardie, Nathan Gilbert, Ellen Riloff, David Buttler, and David Hysom. 2009. Reconcile: A coreference resolution research platform. Technical report, Cornell University.

Xu Sun, Takuya Matsuzaki, Daisuke Okanohara, and Jun'ichi Tsujii. 2009. Latent variable perceptron algorithm for structured classification. In *Proceedings of the 21th International Joint Conference on Artificial Intelligence,* Pasadena, Cal., 14–17 July 2009, pages 1236–1242.

Yannick Versley, Simone Paolo Ponzetto, Massimo Poesio, Vladimir Eidelman, Alan Jern, Jason Smith, Xiaofeng Yang, and Alessandro Moschitti. 2008. BART: A modular toolkit for coreference resolution. In *Companion Volume to the Proceedings of the 46th Annual Meeting of the Association for Computational Linguistics,* Columbus, Ohio, 15–20 June 2008, pages 9–12.

Marc Vilain, John Burger, John Aberdeen, Dennis Connolly, and Lynette Hirschman. 1995. A model-theoretic coreference scoring scheme. In *Proceedings of the 6th Message Understanding Conference (MUC-6),* pages 45–52, San Mateo, Cal. Morgan Kaufmann.

Chun-Nam John Yu and Thorsten Joachims. 2009. Learning structural SVMs with latent variables. In *Proceedings of the 26th International Conference on Machine Learning,* Montréal, Québec, Canada, 14–18 June 2009, pages 1169–1176.

SCHNÄPPER: A Web Toolkit for Exploratory Relation Extraction

Thilo Michael and **Alan Akbik**
Technische Universität Berlin
Einsteinufer 17, 10587 Berlin
{thilo.michael,alan.akbik}@tu-berlin.de

Abstract

We present SCHNÄPPER, a web toolkit for *Exploratory Relation Extraction* (ERE). The tool allows users to identify relations of interest in a very large text corpus in an exploratory and highly interactive fashion. With this tool, we demonstrate the ease-of-use and intuitive nature of ERE, as well as its applicability to large corpora. We show how users can formulate exploratory, natural language-like pattern queries that return relation instances. We also show how automatically computed suggestions are used to guide the exploration process. Finally, we demonstrate how users create extractors with SCHNÄPPER once a relation of interest is identified.

1 Introduction

Relation Extraction (RE) is the task of extracting instances of semantic relations between entities in unstructured data such as natural language text. Common examples are the BORNIN relationship between a person and its birthplace, or the CHILDOF relation between a parent and its child. A principal challenge in RE is how to build high quality extractors for a given set of relations at minimal effort.

One line of approaches to RE are *rule-based*, where users manually define rule-sets consisting of extraction patterns that if observed point to instances of a relation. Advantages associated with rule-based RE are a high level of direct control over the extraction process: Ideally, rule-writers build interpretable and maintainable rule-sets, enabling both the extension and error analysis of rule-based extractors (Chiticariu et al., 2013). Indeed, in a number of recent works, rule-based RE approaches have been found to outperform previous machine-learning based state-of-the-art systems, for tasks such as temporal expression detection (Strötgen and Gertz, 2010) and OpenIE (Del Corro and Gemulla, 2013).

Exploratory search for relations. Recently, in (Akbik et al., 2014), we introduced the paradigm of *Exploratory Relation Extraction* (ERE). We argued that workflows and tooling can be developed in such a way as to enable an interactive and *open ended* search for relations. With ERE, relations therefore do not need to be precisely defined in advance. Rather, users can start a process of *exploration* for interesting relations even if their information needs are only vaguely defined.

We outlined key ideas in order to enable the exploratory workflow: First, extraction patterns should be very easy to define and quick to test, much in the same way as exploratory keyword queries in a web search engine (Marchionini, 2006). Second, the exploration process should be guided through suggestions computed from the available data and previous user interactions. Third, there should be a high level of interactivity. Appropriate tooling is therefore required.

Contributions. With this demo, we present SCHNÄPPER, a web-based tool for ERE that demonstrates the incremental, data-guided workflow introduced in (Akbik et al., 2014). The demo is intended to underline a central claim of ERE, which is that non-experts can use it to easily explore a corpus for relational information and build extractors. Additionally, by using a large portion of the CLUEWEB09[1] corpus as dataset, we aim to highlight the applicability of such an approach to very large datasets.

Paper outline. We first give a quick overview over the ERE workflow in Section 2. We then present SCHNÄPPER, our web interface (Section 3) and walk through an example workflow with the tool. We then briefly give an overview over related work and give an outlook of possible future additions to

[1] http://www.lemurproject.org/clueweb09/index.php

Proceedings of ACL-IJCNLP 2015 System Demonstrations, pages 67–72,
Beijing, China, July 26-31, 2015.

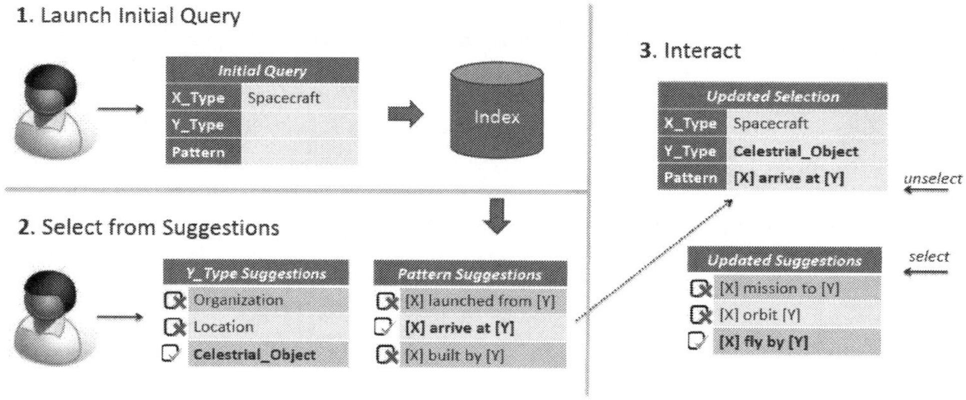

Figure 1: Illustration of the Exploratory Relation Extraction example workflow discussed in Section 2.2.

the toolkit and the method itself.

2 Exploratory Relation Extraction

We demonstrate an approach to finding *binary relations* in text that has been proposed in (Akbik et al., 2014). Each relation holds between two entities: a *subject* and an *object* entity. Users explore a corpus for information by selecting and composing extraction patterns.

2.1 Pattern Language

Extraction patterns consist of two components:

1. Dependency subtrees. The first component is the lexico-syntactic pattern that connects two entities in a sentence. Here, we allow *arbitrary* subtrees in a sentence's dependency tree, as long as they span two entities of interest. To generalize the patterns, they are stemmed and the two entities are replaced by the placeholders "`[X]` and `[Y]`". Examples of subtree patterns are "`[X] and [Y] married`" and "`[X] 's father [Y]`"[2]. However, since any subtree is a possible pattern, many subtrees with less obvious meanings are also possible; in the end, it is up to the user to make the decision which patterns are relevant and which are not.

2. Entity type restrictions Optionally, patterns may be further restricted to match only entities of certain fine-grained types, such as PERSON, LOCATION, LANGUAGE or MOVIE. The type restrictions may be set individually for each subject and object entities. Since the subject is replaced with the placeholder `[X]` in a pattern, its restriction is referred to as *X_Type*, while the object restriction is referred to as *Y_Type*.

Preemptive pattern extraction. Following the idea of preemptive Information Extraction (Shinyama and Sekine, 2006), we pre-extract and store all subtrees and entity types from a given corpus for each sentence with at least two named entities. This allows not only fast retrieval of matching entity pairs for a given set of subtrees and type restrictions, but also allows us to compute pattern correlations over the entire dataset for the presently selected setup. In the next section, we show how fast retrieval and pattern correlations are used to aid the exploration process.

2.2 Example Workflow

We illustrate the exploration process with an example workflow, the first steps of which are depicted in Figure 1. Assume that our user is interested in relations that involve "spacecraft", but is unsure of what types of relations may be found for such entities in the given corpus.

Initial query (1). The user starts by issuing an initial query that is strongly underspecified: By setting *X_Type* to SPACECRAFT and leaving the *Pattern* and *Y_Type* fields in the query unspecified, the user searches for all sentences that contain at least one entity of the desired type. At this point, there are no other restrictions to the query with regards to patterns or object entity types.

Explore by reacting to suggestions (2). After issuing the query, the system responds with both a list of sentences that match the query (not illustrated in Figure 1) and well as, more importantly, suggestions for patterns and object entity type re-

[2] For the purpose of readability, we do not display the deep syntactic information from the subtrees. Instead, we only show the lexical portion of the patterns. Here, some verbs, such as participles and gerunds, are not stemmed for readability purposes.

strictions that correlate with the user query.

The user can now choose from the suggestions: For instance, by selecting the object type LOCATION and the pattern "`[X] launched from [Y]`", the user may direct the exploration process towards relations that indicate locations (cities, countries, sites) from which a spacecraft was launched. Similarly, by choosing ORGANIZATION as object type and "`[X] built by [Y]`" as pattern, the user may select organizations (contractors, space agencies) that constructed or designed spacecraft as the focus of interest.

In the example shown in Figure 1, the user instead selects the object type CELESTIALOBJECT and the pattern "`[X] arrive at [Y]`". This directs the search towards relations that indicate spacecraft missions to celestial objects.

User interactions (3). This user interaction updates both the query as well as the suggestions for patterns and restrictions. Now pattern suggestions are more specific to the previous selection; For instance, by selecting either the pattern "`[X] orbit [Y]`" or "`[X] fly by [Y]`", the user can specify relations for spacecraft that have achieved orbit around celestial objects, or have made flybys. By following a process of querying, inspecting results, selecting and unselecting subtrees and restrictions, the user can interactively explore the given corpus for relations of interest. Once an interesting relation is identified, the user utilizes the same approach to build an extractor by compiling a list of relevant patterns from the suggestions. Typically, the more patterns a user selects, the higher the recall of the created extractor will be.

Store extractor. When the user has identified an interesting relation and selected a list of relevant patterns, she can export the extraction results (i.e. all relation instances found by the extractor). The user can also save the extractor and provide a descriptive name for the relation for possible later reuse.

3 Web Demonstration

We now present SCHNÄPPER[3], our web toolkit for Exploratory Relation Extraction.

[3]The tool was named after the *Petroicidae* famliy of birds, which in German are called *Schnäpper*. This name stems from the verb *schnappen* (Schmitthenner, 1837), which translates as "*to grab*" or "*to catch*". We found this fitting since the tool is used to "grab" or "catch" information.

3.1 Web Interface

In order to make the use of SCHNÄPPER as straightforward as possible, the user interface is clearly structured into four panels that fit onto one screen. The top half of the screen consists of three panels in which the user can select patterns and entity type restrictions. The bottom half of the screen is the result panel which displays a sample of extraction results for the currently selected patterns and entity type restrictions. See Figure 2 for the screen and a breakdown of the panels, which we explain in more detail in the following:

Pattern panel (1) Of the three panels in the upper half of the screen, the pattern panel assumes the center stage. Here, the user can enter keywords in the search field to find appropriate patterns. If at least one user interaction has already been made (e.g. one pattern or type restriction selected), a list of pattern suggestions is presented in gray. Single clicking on a pattern suggestion gives a small number of example sentences and entity pairs for which this pattern holds (this is illustrated in field **(6)** in Figure 2). Double-clicking on a pattern adds it to the extractor; it is then highlighted blue and suggestions as well as the result panel are updated to reflect the selection. By double-clicking on a selected pattern, users may remove it again from the selection.

Entity type restriction panels (2) Extractors may also have entity type restrictions which restrict lexico-syntactic patterns to only apply to entities of certain types. The top right and top left panels are used to define restrictions for the subject and object of a binary relation respectively. Here, users have a choice between three different ways of selecting entity type restrictions. The first and default option is to use FREEBASE entity types (Bollacker et al., 2008). I.e. the user can select the subject of a relation to be only of the FREEBASE type SPACECRAFT, ORGANIZATION or CELESTIALOBJECT.

The user can also restrict a relation to one specific entity. For instance, by restricting the object of a BORNIN relation to be the country "Finland", the extractor will only find persons born in Finland.

Finally, the user can restrict entities to those found with a previously created extractor. Users can embed extractors in this way to find more complex relations. For instance, an extractor that

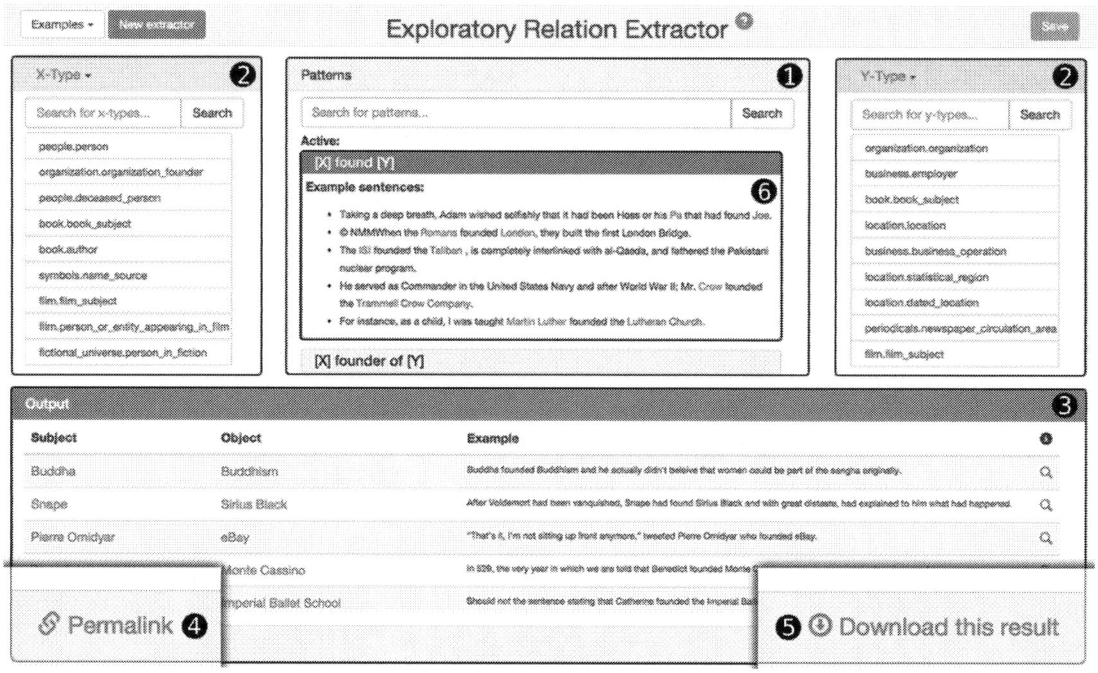

Figure 2: Screen capture of the SCHNÄPPER tool showing the *pattern panel (1)* with an activated pattern showing a list of example sentences (6), the *entity type restriction panels (2)* and the *result panel (3)*. The *permalink button (4)* and the *download button (5)* are located at the bottom.

finds "Persons born in Finland" may be used to restrict the subject entity of another extractor. The other extractor can then find a relation between "Persons born in Finland" and, for example, entities of type BUILDING ("Buildings designed by persons from Finland").

Similar to the pattern panel, double-clicking is used to select or unselect type restrictions. Upon each interaction, the suggestions as well as the result panel are updated to reflect the current selection.

Result panel (3) The lower half of the screen is the result panel which lists a set of entity pairs that are found with the presently selected patterns and restrictions. Each entity pair is displayed along with the sentence that matches the pattern. By clicking the magnifying glass symbol next to an entity pair, more details are shown, including the entity pair's FREEBASE ids and a list of sentences that match the selected patterns.

Storing and exporting extractors After finishing building an extractor, users can export the setup as a JSON by clicking the download button in the lower right corner of the screen (see field **(5)** in Figure 2). This exports the selected patterns and restrictions, together with a result list of entity pairs found with the extractor. In addition, users can generate a "permalink" by clicking the button in the lower left corner of the screen (see field **(4)** in Figure 2). This allows users to generate links to created extractors and share them electronically.

3.2 Example Usage

We now briefly give an example of using the tool. Assume a user is interested in a relation between persons and the companies they founded.

There are several entry points the user may choose from. For instance, the user might search for appropriate entity types in the *X_Type* and *Y_Type* panels. Another option is to start by looking for appropriate patterns. For this, the user can use the search box in the pattern panel **(1)** to search for the general term "found". This results in a list of patterns being displayed, which includes the pattern "`[X] found [Y]`". By single-clicking on it, the user can see a list of sentences that include this pattern. This is illustrated in field **(6)** in Figure 2.

The user activates the pattern by double-clicking it. He sees the output of the extractor in the result panel **(3)** as well as patterns and entity types that are suggested based on the current selection. Scanning through the result panel, the user finds that while many matching sentences do indeed express the desired relation (like *"Pierre Omidyar founded eBay"*), some others do not (*"Snape found Sirius Black"*).

The tool however also presents three sets of suggestions that the user can use to refine the patterns. For instance, for both *X_Type* and *Y_Type* a ranked list of suggestions highlighted gray appears **(2)**. As illustrated in Figure 2, it suggests PERSON as *X_Type* and ORGANIZATION as *Y_Type*. The user can affirm suggestions by double clicking on them. When selecting ORGANIZATION as *Y_Type*, the result panel is updated to reflect the most recent changes. Scanning through the results the user sees that the extraction quality has greatly improved as there are far fewer false positives in the list.

The user may now try to further improve the extractor by selecting more specific patterns. The tool suggests the pattern "`[X] be founder of [Y]`", which more accurately describes the relation the user wants to extract. Again by single-clicking on the suggestion, the user can see example sentences that match this pattern, as well as the selected entity type restrictions. Double-clicking on the pattern adds it to the extractor, which now consists of two patterns. With multiple patterns selected, the tool is now able to suggest patterns more accurately, offering patterns such as "`[Y] founded by [X]`", "`[X] start [Y]`" and "`[X] co-found [Y]`". By selecting them and implicitly rejecting those suggestions that do not reflect the desired relation (like the correlated patterns "`[X] president of [Y]`" or "`[X] CEO of [Y]`"), the user incrementally creates an extractor.

After multiple iterations of selecting suggested patterns and entity type restrictions the user is able to download the results of the extractor by using the download button (5) at the bottom of the page.

3.3 Implementation Details

We use CLUEWEB09 as corpus and make use of FACC1 annotations (Gabrilovich et al., 2013) to determine entity mentions and their FREEBASE types. We extract all English sentences that contain at least 2 FREEBASE entities, yielding over 160 million sentences. We then parse these sentences using the CLEARNLP pipeline (Choi and McCallum, 2013) and preemptively generate all subtrees for all entity pairs in all sentences. Together with information on the entity types, we store all information in a Lucene index for fast retrieval.

3.4 Hands-on Demonstration

We plan a hands-on demonstration in which users work with SCHNÄPPER to explore the CLUEWEB09 corpus for relations of interest. Our purpose is twofold: One the one hand we would like to make the case for the simplicity and intuitive nature of the proposed approach. One the other hand, we would like to gather feedback from the NLP community for possible future improvements to the approach. In particular some of the more advanced features such as embedding extractors within other extractors may be interesting to discuss in a hands-on demo[4].

4 Previous Work

Recent work in the field of rule-based RE has investigated workflows and tooling to facilitate the creation of extractors. (Li et al., 2012) presented a wizard-like approach to guide users in the process of building extractors. In (Akbik et al., 2013), we presented an example-driven workflow that allows even users who are unfamiliar with NLP to write extractors using lexico-syntactic patterns over dependency trees. Similarly, (Grishman and He, 2014) create a toolkit for persons who are experts in a *domain* of interest, but not in NLP. Users create extractors for pre-defined entities and relations by seeding example instances in a semi-supervised fashion. (Gupta and Manning, 2014) use a similar bootstrapping approach and create a tool for visualizing learned patterns for diagnostic purposes. Finally, (Freedman et al., 2011) focus on reducing effort in a user-driven process by including elements from active learning and bootstrapping, but target their tool at NLP experts.

Unlike the approach presented with this demo, these approaches are mostly intended for traditional RE in which relations of interest are specified in advance. With this demo, we instead support an *exploratory* workflow in which relations of interest may be discovered through user interactions with available data at little effort.

[4]The tool is also publicly available online. It can be reached through Alan Akbik's web page.

5 Outlook

While SCHNÄPPER is currently focused on binary relations only, we are investigating the application of comparable workflows at the entity level. Ideally, we would like to be able to create extractors that find named entities of custom types and embed them into custom relation extractors. While, as the demo shows, it is already possible to embed extractors into other extractors, more research is required fully develop the process of creating entity extractors, which possibly includes developing a different pattern language for the entity level. With more extensive capabilities of creating custom entity extractors, such tooling could conceivably be used to use the approach for knowledge base population tasks (Surdeanu and Ji, 2014). The approach could be also used to quickly create custom knowledge bases for specialized topics such as the biomedical domain (Hunter and Cohen, 2006). Another point of interest is that, since the tooling is Web-based, collaborative aspects of creating custom knowledge bases can be investigated in this context.

References

Alan Akbik, Oresti Konomi, and Michail Melnikov. 2013. Propminer: A workflow for interactive information extraction and exploration using dependency trees. In *ACL System Demonstrations*. Association for Computational Linguistics.

Alan Akbik, Thilo Michael, and Christoph Boden. 2014. Exploratory relation extraction in large text corpora. In *COLING 2014, 25th International Conference on Computational Linguistics, Proceedings of the Conference: Technical Papers, August 23-29, 2014, Dublin, Ireland*, pages 2087–2096.

Kurt Bollacker, Colin Evans, Praveen Paritosh, Tim Sturge, and Jamie Taylor. 2008. Freebase: a collaboratively created graph database for structuring human knowledge. In *Proceedings of the 2008 ACM SIGMOD international conference on Management of data*, pages 1247–1250. ACM.

Laura Chiticariu, Yunyao Li, and Frederick R Reiss. 2013. Rule-based information extraction is dead! long live rule-based information extraction systems! In *Proceedings of the 2013 Conference on Empirical Methods in Natural Language Processing*, pages 827–832.

Jinho D. Choi and Andrew McCallum. 2013. Transition-based dependency parsing with selectional branching. In *Proceedings of the 51st Annual Meeting of the Association for Computational Linguistics*.

Luciano Del Corro and Rainer Gemulla. 2013. Clausie: clause-based open information extraction. In *Proceedings of the 22nd international conference on World Wide Web*, pages 355–366. International World Wide Web Conferences Steering Committee.

Marjorie Freedman, Lance Ramshaw, Elizabeth Boschee, Ryan Gabbard, Gary Kratkiewicz, Nicolas Ward, and Ralph Weischedel. 2011. Extreme extraction: machine reading in a week. In *Proceedings of the Conference on Empirical Methods in Natural Language Processing*, pages 1437–1446. Association for Computational Linguistics.

Evgeniy Gabrilovich, Michael Ringgaard, and Amarnag Subramanya. 2013. FACC1: freebase annotation of ClueWeb corpora, version 1 (release date 2013-06-26, format version 1, correction level 0).

Ralph Grishman and Yifan He. 2014. An information extraction customizer. In *Text, Speech and Dialogue*, pages 3–10. Springer.

Sonal Gupta and Christopher D Manning. 2014. Spied: Stanford pattern-based information extraction and diagnostics. *Sponsor: Idibon*, page 38.

Lawrence Hunter and K Bretonnel Cohen. 2006. Biomedical language processing: what's beyond pubmed? *Molecular cell*, 21(5):589–594.

Yunyao Li, Laura Chiticariu, Huahai Yang, Frederick R Reiss, and Arnaldo Carreno-fuentes. 2012. Wizie: a best practices guided development environment for information extraction. In *Proceedings of the ACL 2012 System Demonstrations*, pages 109–114. Association for Computational Linguistics.

Gary Marchionini. 2006. Exploratory search: from finding to understanding. *Communications of the ACM*, 49(4):41–46.

Friedrich Schmitthenner. 1837. *Kurzes deutsches Wörterbuch für Etymologie, Synonymik und Orthographie*. Jonghaus.

Yusuke Shinyama and Satoshi Sekine. 2006. Preemptive information extraction using unrestricted relation discovery. In *Proceedings of the main conference on Human Language Technology Conference of the North American Chapter of the Association of Computational Linguistics*, pages 304–311. Association for Computational Linguistics.

Jannik Strötgen and Michael Gertz. 2010. Heideltime: High quality rule-based extraction and normalization of temporal expressions. In *Proceedings of the 5th International Workshop on Semantic Evaluation*, pages 321–324. Association for Computational Linguistics.

Mihai Surdeanu and Heng Ji. 2014. Overview of the english slot filling track at the tac2014 knowledge base population evaluation. In *Proc. Text Analysis Conference (TAC2014)*.

OMWEdit - The Integrated Open Multilingual Wordnet Editing System

Luís Morgado da Costa and Francis Bond
Linguistics and Mulitingual Studies
Nanyang Technological University
Singapore
{luis.passos.morgado@gmail.com, bond@ieee.org}

Abstract

Wordnets play a central role in many natural language processing tasks. This paper introduces a multilingual editing system for the Open Multilingual Wordnet (OMW: Bond and Foster, 2013). Wordnet development, like most lexicographic tasks, is slow and expensive. Moving away from the original Princeton Wordnet (Fellbaum, 1998) development workflow, wordnet creation and expansion has increasingly been shifting towards an automated and/or interactive system facilitated task. In the particular case of human edition/expansion of wordnets, a few systems have been developed to aid the lexicographers' work. Unfortunately, most of these tools have either restricted licenses, or have been designed with a particular language in mind. We present a web-based system that is capable of multilingual browsing and editing for any of the hundreds of languages made available by the OMW. All tools and guidelines are freely available under an open license.

1 Introduction

Lexical semantic resources, such as wordnets (WNs), play a central role in many Natural Language Processing (NLP) tasks. Word Sense Disambiguation (WSD), for example, relies heavily on existing lexical semantic resources. Likewise, many other unsolved problems of NLP (e.g. Machine Translation, Q&A Systems) rely on WSD and, consequently, indirectly, rely also on the existence of resources like WNs.

This explains why substantial resources have been employed in the development of high quality lexical semantic resources. The Princeton Wordnet (PWN: Fellbaum, 1998) pioneered the development of such a resource for English. Following its steps, many other projects followed PWN into building similar resources for different languages.

The lexicographic work-flow for these early projects included hand-typing linked complex data structures in electronic text files. The result was a huge net of concepts, senses and definitions linked through a variety of relations. This kind of work is ultimately very time consuming and prone to mistakes. The direct manipulation of text files makes it extremely easy to unintentionally violate the data syntax. In recent times, the creation and expansion of these resources has been increasingly shifting into an automated and/or interactive system facilitated task. Simple and intuitive user interfaces can help to both speed-up and to immediately check for inconsistencies in the data (e.g. relatedness to nonexistent keys, reduplicated information, typos or omission of minimal required information). Using modern relational databases and web-serviced interactive platforms has also allowed for remote and parallel collaboration, as well as effective journaling systems.

As the coverage of dictionaries is never complete, WNs are in constant development. Even should the main lexicon of a language be described, as languages evolve, new words and senses appear, while old senses fade away. For this reason, maintaining a WN is a demanding task that should be facilitated in every possible way.

In this paper we present a web-based system designed to exploit the OMW multilingual structure, allowing a multilingual editing environment (e.g. allow multilingual lexicographers to edit multiple languages at the same time), to allow remote parallel access to the editing environment, requiring minimal to no technical knowledge from the lexicographers side to install/run the editing interface, and to facilitate the management overhead of mantaining a WN.[1]

The system has been tested by the developers

[1] `http://compling.hss.ntu.edu.sg/omw/`

Proceedings of ACL-IJCNLP 2015 System Demonstrations, pages 73–78,
Beijing, China, July 26-31, 2015.

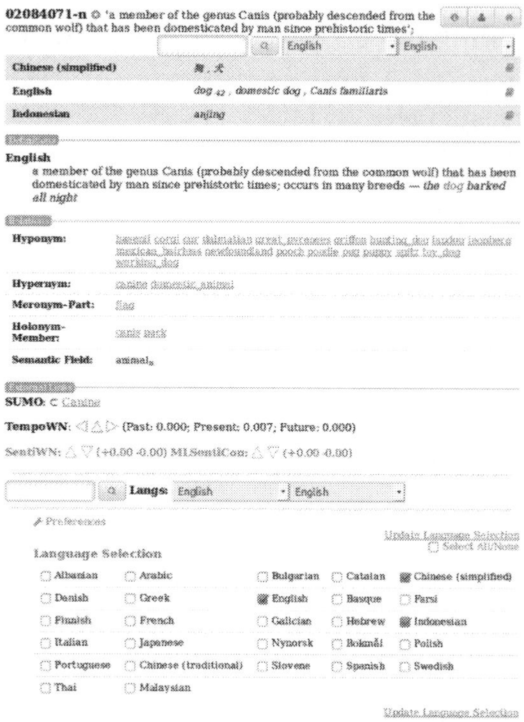

Figure 1: OMW Browsing / Language Selection

and ten annotators (linguistics students) for over 10 months, who made feature requests and gave feedback during the development. The lexicographic work was done in parallel with the semantic annotation of a portion of the NTU Multilingual Corpus (NTU-MC: Tan and Bond, 2012) in (Mandarin) Chinese, English, Indonesian and Japanese (Bond et al., 2015).

The remainder of this paper is arranged as follows. In Section 2 we discuss related work, including the OMW and other similar tools available. The main functionality of our system are described in Section 3. Section 4 will summarize and point to our current and future work.

2 Related Work

2.1 The Open Multilingual Wordnet (OMW)

The OMW is a combination of open-licenced wordnets, along with data extracted from Wiktionary and the Unicode Common Locale Data Repository. In total, OMW has over 2 million senses for over 100 thousand concepts, linking over 1.4 million words in hundreds of languages (Bond and Foster, 2013). It is used as a source of data for projects such as BabelNet (Navigli and Ponzetto, 2012) and Google translate. OMW uses the basic structure of the Princeton Wordnet (PWN: Fellbaum, 1998) to pivot other languages around PWN3.0 synset IDs. Even though it is a single resource, data from each language and project is available separately, respecting their individual licenses. Figure 1 shows the language selection menu that allows browsing this resource as a monolingual or a multilingual resource. The OMW is also fully integrated with the tools currently in use for the development of the NTU Multilingual Corpus (Tan and Bond, 2012). Even though the specifics of this integration go beyond the scope of this paper, it is important to note that most of the development that tested this tool was according to the needs of the semantic annotation of the NTU-MC.

2.2 Other Available Systems

Building and expanding large lexical semantic resources is not an easy task. More importantly, many realized early on that building a WN is not a simple translation task (e.g., Vossen, 1998a). Being able to modify its hierarchy and creating new concepts is important when expressing individual languages semantic hierarchies. Still, due to the lack of resources, many WN projects bootstrap themselves by translating the PWN. However, as individual projects grow, they tend to move away from the inherited English concept hierarchy. This is the moment when systems to support easy manipulation and expansion of their WNs are needed.

Among the available systems we can find VisDic (Horák et al., 2004) (later developed into DEBVisDic, Horák et al., 2006), used for the development of BalkaNet (Tufis et al., 2004), plWordNetApp (succeeded by WordNetLoom (Piasecki et al., 2013)) used for the construction of the Polish Wordnet (Derwojedowa et al., 2008), GernEdiT, the GermaNet editing tool (Henrich and Hinrichs, 2010), KUI (Sornlertlamvanich et al., 2008, used in the Asian Wordnet) and Polaris (Louw, 1998) used in the development of EuroWordnet (Vossen, 1998b).

Out of the above mentioned, we excluded Polaris as not being released. Even though GernEdiT seemed well designed, it was mainly developed for a monolingual environment and a restrictive license (i.e. it does not allow redistribution or commercial use). WordNetLoom, the successor of plWordNetApp, develops an interesting editing mode based directly on the WN hierarchy graph, but the fact that it was not offered as a web-service limited our interest. VisDic was originally developed in response to Polaris commercial licence, but the direct manipulation of XML limited its usefulness when compared to the original work-flow of direct manipulation of text files. DEBVisDic was later developed on top of VisDic, enhacing it many ways. It can be served as a web application and it supports the development of multiple link wordnets. Unfortunately, while experimenting with it, we found that its installation and user experience was not intuitive. Its development and usability is strongly dependent on Mozilla's Firefox, making any further development less appealing. And, most importantly, its license also restricts use of the tool to noncommercial, nonprofit internal research purposes only. KUI was open source, but only contained functionality for adding lemmas, not making changes to the wordnet structure. We decided we had enough motivation to start the development of a new tool.

3 System Overview and Architecture

OMWEdit follows a simple yet powerful web-based architecture. It is built on an SQLite database, allowing fast querying and reliable storage. It is fully tested for Firefox, Chrome and Safari browsers. Its main focus is on semi-automation and consistency checking of the WN development work, supporting the lexicographer's work. In this section we discuss the OMWEdit's main functionality.

3.1 Browsing and Authentication

The OMW can be browsed either monolingually or multilingually. Figure 1 shows how languages can be filtered through the navigation interface. Filtering languages is an important feature for both browsing and editing since many concepts have data for over 100 languages. This amount of information can be overwhelming, especially within the edition interface. The OMW interface also integrates an authentication menu. As guests, users are free to browse through the resource. Once logged in (provided they are given access), a user can access the editing mode. All changes committed are immediately available for further browsing, editing and usage by linked tools (i.e. the OMW is currently linked to a set of corpus annotation tools).

3.2 Creating and Editing Concepts

The lexicographic work centers around editing existing concepts and adding new concepts, senses or relations to the WN. For this reason, our system has been optimized for these two tasks.

Our system integrates the lexical, concept and relation levels in a single semi-automated process. Most of the above mentioned systems sustain a separate development between lexical entries and concepts (e.g. in order to be linked to a concept, a lexical unit has to be previously created as a separate entity). Contrary to this practice, the OMWEdit has a fully automated lexical management — e.g. the creation, linking, unlinking, correction and deletion of lexical entries is fully automated behind the concept creation/edition screen. In order to add a lemma to a concept, for example, a lexicographer has simply to type the word form in the appropriate field of creation/editing concept view. The system then verifies if a new lexical entry needs to be created. In the event that the lexical entry already exists, its ID is automatically fetched and bound to the concept. Otherwise, a new lexical entry is created and linked to the concept ID. Likewise, correcting an existing lexical entry within a concept will trigger a similar process. The system checks if a lexical entry that matches the corrected version already exists, or if needs to be created. The link between the previously corrected lexical unit is dropped and a new link is created for the newly corrected form. Lexical entries that are not linked to any concept are periodically removed from the database.

Similar processes are put in practice for the main components of a concept. We currently allow to edit/add lemmas, definitions, examples and synset relations. The web interface was designed to be intuitive and as automated as possible, in order to shield the lexicographer's work to include checking. The editing interfaces include quick guidelines that summarize the workflow of that particular task. Typos are avoided by either checking inputs with regular expressions or through the use of closed selection lists (see Figure 2). The inputs are processed for further consistency before being written in the database (e.g. white-space and punctuation stripping).

Fields such as definitions, examples and lemmas are associated with languages. Most of our lexicographers are, at least, bilingual. Having the possibility of creating multilingual concepts is a single submission is, therefore, most efficient. The languages displayed and available when creating/editing a concept are constrained by the se-

Figure 2: Adding a new concept

lected browsing languages, as seen in Figure 1. It is especially important to be able to constrain the languages in the editing mode, since too much information quickly becomes hard to manage.

The creation of a new synset has been optimized to fall under one of three categories. Named Entities have a quick creation setting where only minimal information is required (not shown) – as this system knows where to place them in the hierarchy. The creation of new concepts can also be done from scratch (Figure 2), or through the selection of a linked concept. In this case, the information available for the linked concept is displayed and some information is copied across into the creation form for further edition.

The tool has a link to a multiple lexicon search, where the lexicographers can simultaneously query multiple lexicons for different languages (e.g. wiktionary, JMDict for Japanese, CC-edict for Chinese and so on). This makes it easy to check the meanings of words without relying too much on a single source.

Other consistency checks are enforced by the system. For example, when creating new entries, the minimal information required to constitute a concept (name, pos, definition in English, link to existing synset, at least one lemma) is enforced by the interface, making it impossible to unwittingly create an ill-formed entry.

3.3 Journaling and Reporting System

Although the wordnets are stored in a relational database, they can easily be exported as other standard formats such as Wordnet LMF (Vossen et al., 2013) or plain text triples.

The WN development is done directly into this database. All editable tables are associated with triggers that record every change committed to the database, along with the authorship and the timestamp of the event. By keeping the metadata in a separate table, we ensure that the wordnet itself does not get unwieldy. Both manual and scripted manipulation of a data is dated and signed. Individual lexicographers have to go through an online login system to be able to see the editing interface. The authorship of scripted manipulation of data is often the name of the script — this allows us to keep track of what was changed when. The ease of manipulation of the data by scripts is important to the development — it is easy to develop new data as a separate project and import it when it is ready.

This careful database journaling keeps a tractable history of all the changes in the OWN. This information allows a better management of the lexicographers' workflow, and also a better control of the quality of data that is inserted. Management of the lexicographic work is facilitated by a reporting interface that displays the rate/progress of each contributor's work (Figure 3). This interface allows the coordinators to adjudicate and revert any changes they deem fit, to assert the work pace of individual contributors and also to judge the quality of the lexicographer's work. This interface also provides some consistency checks to the quality of the information contained in the synset, for example lack of senses or definitions, and how often it appears in the corpus.

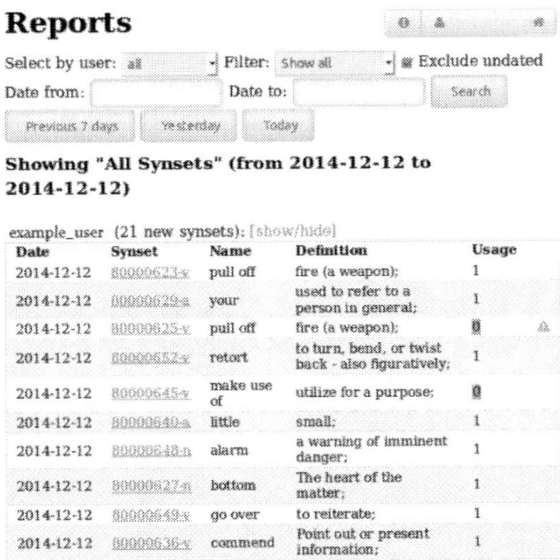

Figure 3: Reporting Interface (extract of list)

4 Summary and Future Work

We have described the architecture and main functionality of the OMWEdit. Considering its short development history, our system has proved itself an increasingly stable and useful tool for the expansion of a few major Wordnet projects. Our web-based system architecture has proved itself ideal for a medium to large scale lexicographic team, regardless of the location of each member. During the development of this system, we were able to confirm an increase in the speed of the lexicographer's workflow. The managing overhead, such as maintaining consistency and quality of the introduced changes has also become a much easier task to accomplish.

Nevertheless, we are aware that the nature of this kind of system is always open ended, and we hope to keep supporting and developing it further. We are aware of some shortcomings and have a list of ongoing planned development of future implementation. This list includes (but is not restricted to):

- the ability to change and/or add lexical relations and verb frames
- the ability to easily comment on entries and watch entries for changes
- the ability to express all relations (both lexical and between concepts) by language — allowing to move away from only using the hierarchy given by the PWN
- the ability to seed a new concept by copying a similar concept (with all its internal structure and relations)
- the ability to do a live check for similarity scores in definitions, accounting for probable matching/mergeable concepts
- further development of the reporting interface
- the development of a graphic component to help visualizing the best placement of a new concept in the hierarchy
- Also, considering our multilingual context, to further develop our support for multilingual users by translating the user interface.

Even though our system was developed with the goal of expanding and correcting wordnets, we believe that our system can also be used to help create new wordnets that use the PWN hierarchy as their backbone. Though the hierarchical relations are still currently imposed by the PWN, we have abolished the limitation to a fixed concept inventory by allowing the creation of new concepts.

Although the tool is far from perfect, we encourage existing and new projects to use the OMW and OMWEdit as a platform to for their WN development. Furthermore, we intend to feedback the changes committed to the individual wordnet projects: the Princeton Wordnet (Fellbaum, 1998), the Japanese Wordnet (Isahara et al., 2008), the Wordnet Bahasa (Nurril Hirfana *et al.* 2011) and the Chinese Open Wordnet (Wang and Bond, 2013), respectively, so that changes committed to the OMW can be incorporated to the original WN projects.

Acknowledgments

This research was supported in part by the MOE Tier 2 grant *That's what you meant: a Rich Representation for Manipulation of Meaning* (MOE ARC41/13) and Fuji-Xerox Co. Ltd (Joint Research on *Multilingual Semantic Analysis*). We would also like to thank our lexicographers for their feedback during the system's development.

References

Francis Bond, Luís Morgado da Costa, and Tuấn Anh Lê. 2015. IMI — a multilingual semantic annotation environment. In *ACL-2015 System Demonstrations*. (this volume).

Francis Bond and Ryan Foster. 2013. Linking and extending an open multilingual wordnet. In *51st Annual Meeting of the Association for Computational Linguistics: ACL-2013*, pages 1352–1362. Sofia. URL `http://aclweb.org/anthology/P13-1133`.

Magdalena Derwojedowa, Maciej Piasecki, Stanisław Szpakowicz, Magdalena Zawisławska, and Bartosz Broda. 2008. Words, concepts and relations in the construction of polish wordnet. In *Proceedings of the Global WordNet Conference, Seged, Hungary*, pages 162–177.

Christine Fellbaum, editor. 1998. *WordNet: An Electronic Lexical Database*. MIT Press.

Verena Henrich and Erhard W Hinrichs. 2010. Gernedit-the germanet editing tool. In *ACL (System Demonstrations)*, pages 19–24.

Aleš Horák, Karel Pala, Adam Rambousek, Martin Povolný, et al. 2006. Debvisdic–first version of new client-server wordnet browsing and editing tool. In *Proceedings of the Third International Wordnet Conference (GWC-06), Jeju Island, Korea*.

Aleš Horák, Pavel Smrž, et al. 2004. Visdic–wordnet browsing and editing tool. In *Proceedings of the Second International WordNet Conference–GWC*, pages 136–141.

Hitoshi Isahara, Francis Bond, Kiyotaka Uchimoto, Masao Utiyama, and Kyoko Kanzaki. 2008. Development of the Japanese WordNet. In *Sixth International conference on Language Resources and Evaluation (LREC 2008)*. Marrakech.

Michael Louw. 1998. Polaris user's guide. *EuroWordNet (LE-4003), Deliverable D023D024*.

Nurril Hirfana Mohamed Noor, Suerya Sapuan, and Francis Bond. 2011. Creating the open Wordnet Bahasa. In *Proceedings of the 25th Pacific Asia Conference on Language, Information and Computation (PACLIC 25)*, pages 258–267. Singapore.

Roberto Navigli and Simone Paolo Ponzetto. 2012. BabelNet: The automatic construction, evaluation and application of a wide-coverage multilingual semantic network. *Artificial Intelligence*, 193:217–250.

Maciej Piasecki, Michał Marcińczuk, Radosław Ramocki, and Marek Maziarz. 2013. Wordnetloom: a wordnet development system integrating form-based and graph-based perspectives. *International Journal of Data Mining, Modelling and Management*, 5(3):210–232.

Virach Sornlertlamvanich, Thatsanee Charoenporn, Kergrit Robkop, and Hitoshi Isahara. 2008. KUI: Self-organizing multi-lingual wordnet construction tool. In Attila Tanács, Dóra Csendes, Veronika Vincze, Christiane Fellbaum, and Piek Vossen, editors, *4th Global Wordnet Conference: GWC-2008*, pages 417–427. Szeged, Hungary.

Liling Tan and Francis Bond. 2012. Building and annotating the linguistically diverse NTU-MC (NTU-multilingual corpus). *International Journal of Asian Language Processing*, 22(4):161–174.

Dan Tufis, Dan Cristea, and Sofia Stamou. 2004. Balkanet: Aims, methods, results and perspectives. a general overview. *Romanian Journal of Information science and technology*, 7(1-2):9–43.

Piek Vossen, editor. 1998a. *Euro WordNet*. Kluwer.

Piek Vossen. 1998b. *A multilingual database with lexical semantic networks*. Springer.

Piek Vossen, Claudia Soria, and Monica Monachini. 2013. LMF - lexical markup framework. In Gil Francopoulo, editor, *LMF - Lexical Markup Framework*, chapter 4. ISTE Ltd + John Wiley & sons, Inc.

Shan Wang and Francis Bond. 2013. Building the Chinese Open Wordnet (COW): Starting from core synsets. In *Proceedings of the 11th Workshop on Asian Language Resources, a Workshop at IJCNLP-2013*, pages 10–18. Nagoya.

SACRY: Syntax-based Automatic Crossword puzzle Resolution sYstem

Gianni Barlacchi[†], **Massimo Nicosia**[†] and **Alessandro Moschitti**
[†]Dept. of Computer Science and Information Engineering, University of Trento
38123 Povo (TN), Italy
ALT, Qatar Computing Research Institute, Hamad Bin Khalifa University
5825 Doha, Qatar
{gianni.barlacchi, m.nicosia, amoschitti}@gmail.com

Abstract

In this paper, we present our Crossword Puzzle Resolution System (SACRY), which exploits syntactic structures for clue reranking and answer extraction. SACRY uses a database (DB) containing previously solved CPs in order to generate the list of candidate answers. Additionally, it uses innovative features, such as the answer position in the rank and aggregated information such as the min, max and average clue reranking scores. Our system is based on WebCrow, one of the most advanced systems for automatic crossword puzzle resolution. Our extensive experiments over our two million clue dataset show that our approach highly improves the quality of the answer list, enabling the achievement of unprecedented results on the complete CP resolution tasks, i.e., accuracy of 99.17%.

1 Introduction

Crossword Puzzles (CPs) are the most famous language games played around the world. The automatic resolution of CPs is an open challenge for the artificial intelligence (AI) community, which mainly employs AI techniques for filling the puzzle grid with candidate answers. Basic approaches try to optimize the overall probability of correctly filling the grid by exploiting the likelihood of each candidate answer, while satisfying the grid constraints.

Previous work (Ernandes et al., 2005) clearly suggests that providing the solver with an accurate list of answer candidates is an important step for the CP resolution task. These can be retrieved using (i) the Web, (ii) Wikipedia, (iii) dictionaries or lexical databases like WordNet or, (iv) most importantly, recuperated from the DBs of previously solved CP. Indeed, CPs are often created reusing the same clues of past CPs, and thus querying the DB with the target clue allows for recuperating the same (or similar) clues of the target one. It is interesting to note that, for this purpose, all previous automatic CP solvers use standard DB techniques, e.g., SQL Full-Text query. Existing systems for automatic CP resolution, such as Proverb (Littman et al., 2002) and Dr. Fill (Ginsberg, 2011), use several different modules for generating candidate answer lists. These are merged and used for defining a Constraint Satisfaction Problem, resolved by the CP solver.

Our CP system, SACRY, is based on innovative QA methods for answering CP clues. We employ (i) state-of-the-art IR techniques to retrieve the correct answer by querying the DB of previously solved CPs, (ii) learning to rank methods based on syntactic structure of clues and structural kernels to improve the ranking of clues that can potentially contain the answers and (iii) an aggregation algorithm for generating the final list containing unique candidate answers. We implemented a specific module based on these approaches and we plugged it into an automatic CP solver, namely WebCrow (Ernandes et al., 2005). The latter is one of the best systems for CP resolution and it has been kindly made available by the authors.

We tested our models on a dataset containing more than two million clues and their associated answers. This dataset is an interesting resource that we will make available to the research community. It can be used for tasks such as: (i) similar clue retrieval/reranking, which focuses on improving the rank of clues c_i retrieved by a search engine, and (ii) answer reranking, which targets the list of a_{c_i}, i.e., their aggregated clues. We tested SACRY on an end-to-end task by solving ten crossword puzzles provided by two of the most famous CP editors from The New York Times and the Washington Post. SACRY obtained an impressive CP resolution accuracy of 99.17%.

Proceedings of ACL-IJCNLP 2015 System Demonstrations, pages 79–84,
Beijing, China, July 26-31, 2015.

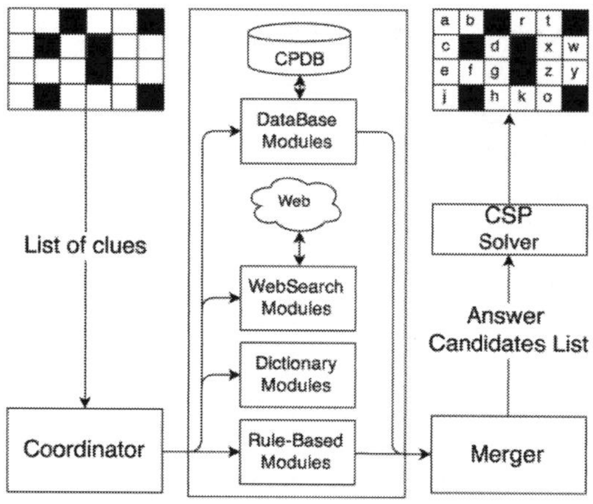

Figure 1: The architecture of WebCrow

In the reminder of this paper, Sec. 2 introduces WebCrow and its architecture. Our models for similar clues retrieval and answers reranking are described in Sec. 3 while Sec. 4 illustrates our experiments. Finally, the conclusions and directions for future work are presented in Sec. 5.

2 The WebCrow Architecture

Our approaches can be used to generate accurate candidate lists that CP solvers can exploit to improve their overall accuracy. Therefore, the quality of our methods can be also implicitly evaluated on the final resolution task. For this purpose, we use an existing CP solver, namely WebCrow, which is rather modular and accurate and it has been kindly made available by the authors. Its architecture is illustrated in Figure 1. In the following, we briefly introduce the database module of WebCrow, which is the one that we substituted with ours.

WebCrow's solving process can be divided in two phases. In the first phase, the input list of clues activate a set of answer search modules, which produce several lists of possible solutions for each clue. These lists are then merged by a specific *Merger* component, which uses the confidence values of the lists and the probability that a candidate in a list is correct. Eventually, a single list of answers with their associated probabilities is built for each input clue. In the second phase WebCrow fills the crossword grid by solving a constraint-satisfaction problem. WebCrow selects a single answer from each merged list of candidates, trying to satisfy the imposed constraints. The goal of this phase is to find an admissible solution that maximizes the number of correctly inserted words. It is done using an adapted version of the WA* algorithm (Pohl, 1970) for CP resolution.

2.1 CrossWord Database module (CWDB)

Gathering clues contained in previously published CPs is essential for solving new puzzles. A large portion of clues in new CPs has usually already appeared in the past. Clues may share similar wording or may be restated in a very different way. Therefore, it is important to identify the clues that have the same answer. WebCrow uses three different modules to retrieve clues identical or similar to a given clue from the database: the CWDB-EXACT module, which retrieves DB clues that match exactly with a target clue, and weights them by the frequency they have in the clue collection. The CWDB-PARTIAL module, which uses the MySQL's partial matching function, query expansion and positional term distances to compute clue-similarity scores, along with the Full-Text search functions. The CWDB-DICTIO module, which simply returns the full list of words of correct length, ranked by their number of occurrences in the initial list.

We outperform the previous approach by applying learning-to-rank algorithms based on SVMs and tree kernels on clue lists generated by state-of-the-art passage retrieval systems.

3 Crossword Puzzle Database (CPDB) Module

WebCrow creates answer lists by retrieving clues from the DB of previously solved crosswords. It simply uses the classical SQL operators and full-text search. We instead index the DB clues and their answers with the open source search engine Lucene (McCandless et al., 2010), using the state-of-the-art BM25 retrieval model. This alone significantly improves the quality of the retrieved clue list, which is further refined by applying reranking. The latter consists in promoting the clues that potentially have the same answer of the query clue.

We designed a relatively complex pipeline shown in Fig. 2. We build a training set using some training clues for querying our search engine, which retrieves correct and incorrect candidates from the indexed clues. At classification time, the new clues are used as a search query and the retrieved similar candidate are reranked by our models. The next sections show our approach for building rerankers that can exploit structures for solving the ineffectiveness of the simple word representation.

3.1 Reranking framework based on Kernels

The basic architecture of our reranking framework is relatively simple: it uses a standard preference kernel reranking approach and is similar to the one proposed in (Severyn and Moschitti, 2012) for QA tasks. However, we modeled different kernels suitable for clue retrieval.

The framework takes a query clue and retrieves a list of related candidate clues using a search engine (applied to the CPDB), according to some similarity criteria. Then, the query and the candidates are processed by an NLP pipeline. Our pipeline is built on top of the UIMA framework (Ferrucci and Lally, 2004) and contains many text analysis components. The components used for our specific tasks are: the tokenizer[1], sentence detector[1], lemmatizer[1], part-of-speech (POS) tagger[1] and chunker[2].

The annotations produced by these standard processors are input to our components that extract structures as well as traditional features for representing clues. This representation is employed to train kernel-based rerankers for reordering the candidate lists provided by a search engine. Since the syntactic parsing accuracy can impact the quality of our structures and consequently the accuracy of our learning to rank algorithms, we preferred to use shallow syntactic trees over full syntactic representations.

In the reranker we used the Partial Tree Kernel (PTK) (Moschitti, 2006). Given an input tree, it generates all possible connected tree fragments, e.g., sibling nodes can also be separated and be part of different tree fragments. In other words, a fragment (which is a feature) is any possible tree path, from whose nodes other tree paths can depart. Thus, it can generate a very rich feature space resulting in higher generalization ability.

We combined the structural features with other traditional ones. We used the following groups:

iKernels features (iK), which include similarity features and kernels applied intra-pairs, i.e., between the query and the retrieved clues:
– *Syntactic similarities*, i.e., cosine similarity measures computed on n-grams (with $n = 1, 2, 3, 4$) of word lemmas and part-of-speech tags.
– *Kernel similarities*, i.e., string kernels and tree kernels applied to structural representations.

DKPro Similarity (DKP), which defines features used in the Semantic Textual Similarity (STS) challenge. These are encoded by the UKP Lab (Bär et al., 2013):
– *Longest common substring measure* and *Longest common subsequence measure*. They determine the length of the longest substring shared by two text segments.
– *Running-Karp-Rabin Greedy String Tiling*. It provides a similarity between two sentences by counting the number of shuffles in their subparts.
– *Resnik similarity*. The WordNet hierarchy is used to compute a measure of semantic relatedness between concepts expressed in the text.
The aggregation algorithm in (Mihalcea et al., 2006) is applied to extend the measure from words to sentences.
– *Explicit Semantic Analysis* (ESA) similarity (Gabrilovich and Markovitch, 2007), which represents documents as weighted vectors of concepts learned from Wikipedia, WordNet and Wiktionary.
– *Lexical Substitution* (Biemann, 2013). A supervised word sense disambiguation system is used to substitute a wide selection of high-frequency English nouns with generalizations. Resnik and ESA features are computed on the transformed text.

WebCrow features (WC), which are the similarity measures computed on the clue pairs by WebCrow (using the Levenshtein distance) and the Search Engine score.

Kernels for reranking, given a query clue q_c and two retrieved clues c_1, c_2, we can rank them by using a reranking model, namely **(RR)**. It uses two pairs $P = \langle p_q^1, p_q^2 \rangle$ and $P' = \langle p_{q'}^1, p_{q'}^2 \rangle$, the member of each pair are clues from the same list generated by q and q', respectively. In this case, we use the kernel, $K_{RR}(P, P') = PTK(\langle q, c_1 \rangle, \langle q', c'_1 \rangle) + PTK(\langle q, c_2 \rangle, \langle q', c'_2 \rangle) - PTK(\langle q, c_1 \rangle, \langle q', c'_2 \rangle) - PTK(\langle q, c_2 \rangle, \langle q', c'_1 \rangle)$, which corresponds to the scalar product between the vectors, $(\phi(p_q^1) - \phi(p_q^2)) \cdot (\phi(p_{q'}^1) - \phi(p_{q'}^2))$, in the fragment vector space generated by PTK.

3.2 Learning to rank aggregated answers

Groups of similar clues retrieved from the search engine can be associated with the same answers. Since each clue receives a score from the reranker, a strategy to combine the scores is needed. We

[1] `http://nlp.stanford.edu/software/corenlp.shtml`

[2] `http://cogcomp.cs.illinois.edu/page/software_view/13`

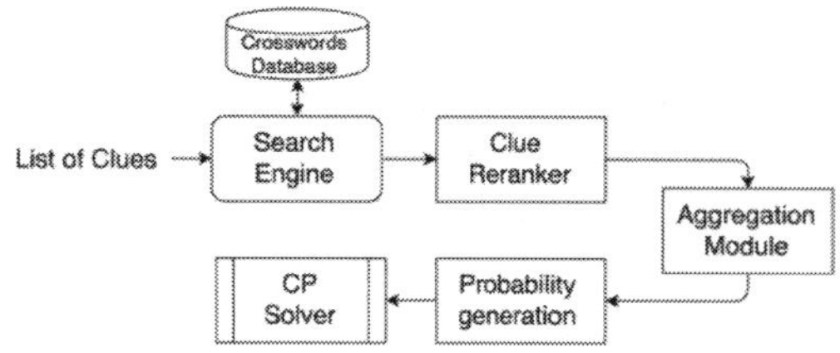

Figure 2: The architecture of our system

aim at aggregating clues associated with the same answer and building meaningful features for such groups. For this purpose, we train an SVM^{rank} with each candidate answer a_{c_i} represented with features derived from all the clues c_i associated with such answer, i.e., we aggregate them using standard operators such as average, min. and max.

We model an answer a using its set of clues $C_a = \{c_i : a_{c_i} = a\}$ in SVM^{rank}. The feature vector associated with a must contains information from all $c \in C_a$. Thus, we designed novel aggregated features that we call **AVG**: (i) we average the feature values used for each clue by the first reranker, i.e., those described in Sec. 3.1 as well as the scores produced by the clue reranker. More specifically, we compute their sum, average, maximum and minimum values. (ii) We also add the term frequency of the answer word in CPDB.

Additionally, we model the occurrences of the answer instance in the list by means of positional features: we use n features, where n is the size of our candidate list (e.g., 10). Each feature corresponds to the positions of each candidate and it is set to the reranker score if $c_i \in C_a$ (i.e., for the target answer candidate) and 0 otherwise. We call such features (**POS**). For example, if an answer candidate is associated with clues appearing at positions 1 and 3 of the list, Feature 1 and Feature 3 will be set to the score calculated from the reranker. We take into account the similarity between the answer candidate and the input clues using a set of features, derived from word embeddings (Mikolov et al., 2013). These features consider (i) the similarities between the clues in a pair, (ii) the target clue and the candidate answer and (iii) the candidate clue and the candidate answer. They are computed summing the embedding vectors of words and computing the cosine similarity. This way we produce some evidence of semantic relatedness. We call such features (**W2V**).

3.3 Generating probabilities for the solver

After the aggregation and reranking steps we have a set of unique candidate answers ordered by their reranking scores. Using the latter in WebCrow generally produces a decrease of its accuracy since it expects probabilities (or values ranging from 0 to 1). The summed votes or the scores produced by the reranker can have a wider range and can also be negative. Therefore, we apply logistic regression (**LGR**) to learn a mapping between the reranking scores and values ranging from 0 to 1.

4 Experiments

In our experiments we compare our approach with WebCrow both on ranking candidate answers and on the end-to-end CP resolution.

4.1 Database of previously resolved CPs

The most commonly used databases of clues contain both single clues taken from various crosswords (Ginsberg, 2011) and entire crossword puzzle (Ernandes et al., 2008). They refer to relatively clean pairs of clue/answer and other crossword related information such as date of the clue, name of the CP editor and difficulty of the clue (e.g., clues taken from the CPs published on *The Sunday* newspaper are the most difficult). Unfortunately, they are not publicly available.

Therefore, we compiled a crossword corpus combining (i) CP downloaded from the Web[3] and (ii) the clue database provided by Otsys[4]. We removed duplicates, fill-in-the-blank clues (which are better solved by using other strategies) and clues representing anagrams or linguistic games. We collected over 6.3 millions of clues, published by many different American editors. Although this is a very rich database, it contains many duplicates and non-standard clues, which introduce significant noise in the dataset. For this reason we created a compressed dataset of 2,131,034 unique and standard clues, with associated answers. It excludes the *fill-in-the-blank* clues mentioned above.

4.2 Experimental Setup

To train our models, we adopted SVM-light-TK[5], which enables the use of the Partial Tree Kernel (PTK) (Moschitti, 2006) in SVM-light (Joachims, 2002), with default parameters. We applied a polynomial kernel of degree 3 to the explicit feature vectors (FV). To measure the impact of the rerankers as well as the CWDB module, we used well-known metrics for assessing the accuracy of

[3]http://www.crosswordgiant.com

[4]http://www.otsys.com/clue

[5]`http://disi.unitn.it/moschitti/Tree-Kernel.htm`

QA and retrieval systems, i.e.: Recall at different ranks (R@1, 5, 20, 50, 100), Mean Reciprocal Rank (MRR) and Mean Average Precision (MAP). R@1 is the percentage of questions with a correct answer ranked at the first position. MRR is computed as follows: $MRR = \frac{1}{|Q|}\sum_{q=1}^{|Q|}\frac{1}{rank(q)}$, where *rank(q)* is the position of the first correct answer in the candidate list. For a set of queries Q, MAP is the mean over the average precision scores for each query: $\frac{1}{Q}\sum_{q=1}^{Q} AveP(q)$.

To measure the complete CP resolution task, we use the accuracy over the entire words filling a CP grid (one wrong letter causes the entire definition to be incorrect).

4.3 Clue reranking experiments

Given an input clue BM25 retrieves a list of 100 clues. On the latter, we tested our different models for clue reranking. For space constraints, we only report a short summary of our experiments: kernel-based rerankers combined with *traditional features* (PTK+FV) relatively improve standard IR by 16%. This is an interesting result as in (Barlacchi et al., 2014), the authors showed that standard IR greatly improves on the DB methods for clue retrieval, i.e., they showed that BM25 relatively improves on SQL by about 40% in MRR.

4.4 Answer aggregation and reranking

Reranking clues is just the first step as the solver must be fed with the list of unique answers. Thus, we first used our best model (i.e., PTK+FV) for clue reranking to score the answers of a separate set, i.e., our answer reranking training set. Then, we used these scores to train an additional reranker for aggregating identical answers. The aggregation module merges clues sharing the same answer into a single instance.

Tab. 1 shows the results for several answer reranking models tested on a development set: the first row shows the accuracy of the answer list produces by WebCrow. The second row reports the accuracy of our model using a simple voting strategy, i.e., the score of the clue reranker is used as a vote for the target candidate answer. The third row applies Logistic Regression (LGR) to transform the SVM reranking scores in probabilities. It uses Lucene score for the candidate answer as well as the max and min scores of the entire list. From the fourth column, the answer reranker is trained using SVM^{rank} using FV, AVG, POS, W2V and some of their combinations. We note that: (i) voting the answers using the raw score improves WebCrow but the probabilities computed by LGR perform much better, i.e., about 2 percent points better than Raw voting and 4.5 points better than WebCrow; (ii) the SVM^{rank} aggregation model can provide another additional point, when positional features and standard feature vectors are used along with aggregated and W2C features. (iii) The overall relative improvement of 14% over WebCrow is promising for improving the end-to-end CP resolution task.

Models	MRR	R@1	R@5	R@10	R@20	R@50	R@80
WebCrow	39.12	31.51	47.37	54.38	58.60	63.34	64.06
Raw voting	41.84	33.0	52.9	58.7	62.7	66.6	67.5
LGR voting	43.66	35	53.7	59.3	63.4	67.4	67.7
SVM^{rank}							
AVG	43.5	35.3	53.5	59.4	63.9	67.4	67.7
AVG+POS	44.1	36.3	53.6	58.9	63.9	67.4	67.6
AVG+W2V	43.2	35	53.3	58.8	63.9	67.4	67.7
AVG+POS+FV	44.4	36.7	54.2	60	64.3	67.4	67.7
AVG+FV+W2V	44.1	35.8	54.4	60	64.4	67.4	67.7
AVG+POS+ FV+W2V	**44.6**	**36.8**	**54.2**	**59.8**	**64.4**	**67.4**	**67.7**

Table 1: Answer reranking on the dev. set.

4.5 Evaluation of the CP resolution

In order to test the effectiveness of our method, we evaluated the resolution of full CP. We selected five crosswords from *The New York Times* newspaper and other five from the *Washington Post*. Fig. 3 shows the average resolution accuracy over the ten CP of the original WebCrow compared to WebCrow using our reranked lists. We ran the solver by providing it with lists of different size. We note that our model consistently outperforms WebCrow. This means that the lists of candidate answers generated by our models help the solver, which in turn fills the grid with higher accuracy. In particular, our CP system achieves an average accuracy of 99.17%, which makes it competitive with international CP resolution challenges.

Additionally, WebCrow achieves the highest accuracy when uses the largest candidate lists (both original or reranked) but a large list size negatively impacts on the speed of the solver, which in a CP competition is critical to beat the other competitors (if participants obtain the same score, the solving time decides who is ranked first). Thus, our approach also provide a speedup as the best accuracy is reached for just 50 candidates (in contrast with the 100 candidates needed by the original WebCrow).

5 Final Remarks

In this paper, we describe our system SACRY for automatic CP resolution. It is based on

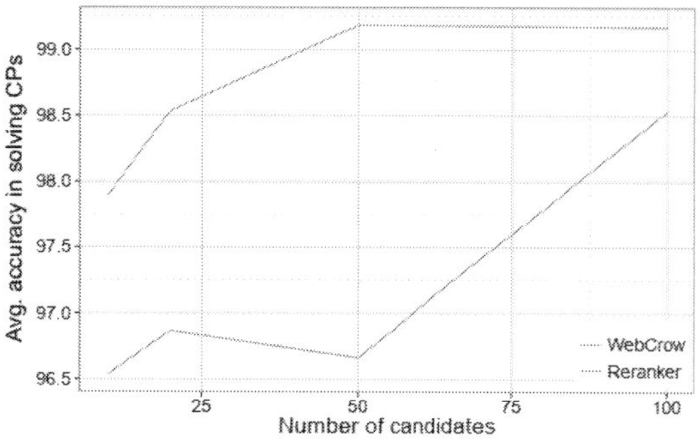

Figure 3: Average accuracy over 10 CPs.

modeling rerankers for clue retrieval from DBs. SACRY achieves a higher accuracy than WebCrow. SACRY uses rerankers based on SVMs and structural kernels, where the latter are applied to robust shallow syntactic structures. Our structural models applied to clue reranking enable us to learn clue paraphrasing by exploiting relational syntactic structures representing pairs of clues.

We collected the biggest clue dataset ever, which can be also used for QA tasks since it is composed by pairs of clue/answer. The dataset includes 2,131,034 unique pairs of clue/answers, which we are going to make available to the research community. The experiments show that our methods improve the quality of the lists generated by WebCrow by 14% in MRR. When used in WebCrow solver with its best setting, its resolution error relatively decreases by 50%, achieving almost a perfect resolution accuracy, i.e., 99.17%. In the future, we would like to release the solver to allow researchers to contribute to the project and make the system even more competitive.

Acknowledgments

This work has been supported by the EC project CogNet, 671625 (H2020-ICT-2014-2, Research and Innovation action). This research is part of the Interactive sYstems for Answer Search (IYAS) project, conducted by the Arabic Language Technologies (ALT) group at Qatar Computing Research Institute (QCRI) within the Hamad Bin Khalifa University and Qatar Foundation.

References

Daniel Bär, Torsten Zesch, and Iryna Gurevych. 2013. Dkpro similarity: An open source framework for text similarity. In *Proceedings of ACL (System Demonstrations)*.

Gianni Barlacchi, Massimo Nicosia, and Alessandro Moschitti. 2014. Learning to rank answer candidates for automatic resolution of crossword puzzles. In *Proceedings of CoNLL*.

Chris Biemann. 2013. Creating a system for lexical substitutions from scratch using crowdsourcing. *Lang. Resour. Eval.*, 47(1):97–122, March.

Marco Ernandes, Giovanni Angelini, and Marco Gori. 2005. Webcrow: A web-based system for crossword solving. In *In Proc. of AAAI 05*, pages 1412–1417. Menlo Park, Calif., AAAI Press.

Marco Ernandes, Giovanni Angelini, and Marco Gori. 2008. A web-based agent challenges human experts on crosswords. *AI Magazine*, 29(1).

David Ferrucci and Adam Lally. 2004. Uima: An architectural approach to unstructured information processing in the corporate research environment. *Nat. Lang. Eng.*, 10(3-4):327–348, September.

Evgeniy Gabrilovich and Shaul Markovitch. 2007. Computing semantic relatedness using wikipedia-based explicit semantic analysis. In *Proceedings of IJCAI*.

Matthew L. Ginsberg. 2011. Dr.fill: Crosswords and an implemented solver for singly weighted csps. *J. Artif. Int. Res.*, 42(1):851–886, September.

Thorsten Joachims. 2002. Optimizing search engines using clickthrough data. In *Proceedings of ACM SIGKDD*, New York, NY, USA. ACM.

Michael L. Littman, Greg A. Keim, and Noam Shazeer. 2002. A probabilistic approach to solving crossword puzzles. *Artificial Intelligence*, 134(12):23 – 55.

Michael McCandless, Erik Hatcher, and Otis Gospodnetic. 2010. *Lucene in Action, Second Edition: Covers Apache Lucene 3.0*. Manning Publications Co., Greenwich, CT, USA.

Rada Mihalcea, Courtney Corley, and Carlo Strapparava. 2006. Corpus-based and knowledge-based measures of text semantic similarity. In *Proceedings AAAI*.

Tomas Mikolov, Kai Chen, Greg Corrado, and Jeffrey Dean. 2013. Efficient estimation of word representations in vector space. *CoRR*, abs/1301.3781.

Alessandro Moschitti. 2006. Efficient convolution kernels for dependency and constituent syntactic trees. In *ECML*, pages 318–329.

Ira Pohl. 1970. Heuristic search viewed as path finding in a graph. *Artificial Intelligence*, 1(34):193 – 204.

Aliaksei Severyn and Alessandro Moschitti. 2012. Structural relationships for large-scale learning of answer re-ranking. In *Proceedings of ACM SIGIR*, New York, NY, USA.

LEXenstein: A Framework for Lexical Simplification

Gustavo Henrique Paetzold and **Lucia Specia**
Department of Computer Science
University of Sheffield, UK
{ghpaetzold1,l.specia}@sheffield.ac.uk

Abstract

Lexical Simplification consists in replacing complex words in a text with simpler alternatives. We introduce LEXenstein, the first open source framework for Lexical Simplification. It covers all major stages of the process and allows for easy benchmarking of various approaches. We test the tool's performance and report comparisons on different datasets against the state of the art approaches. The results show that combining the novel Substitution Selection and Substitution Ranking approaches introduced in LEXenstein is the most effective approach to Lexical Simplification.

1 Introduction

The goal of a Lexical Simplification (LS) approach is to replace complex words and expressions in a given text, often a sentence, with simpler alternatives of equivalent meaning in context. Although very intuitive, this is a challenging task since the substitutions must preserve both the original meaning and the grammaticality of the sentence being simplified.

The LS task has been gaining significant attention since the late 1990's, thanks to the positive influence of the early work presented by (Devlin and Tait, 1998) and (Carroll et al., 1999). More recently, the LS task at SemEval-2012 (Specia et al., 2012) has given LS wider visibility. Participants had the opportunity to compare their approaches in the task of ranking candidate substitutions, all of which were already known to fit the context, according to their "simplicity".

Despite its growth in popularity, the inexistence of tools to support the process and help researchers to build upon has been hampering progress in the area. We were only able to find one tool for LS: a set of scripts designed for the training and testing of ranking models provided by (Jauhar and Specia, 2012)[1]. However, they cover only one step of the process. In an effort to tackle this issue, we present LEXenstein: a framework for Lexical Simplification development and benchmarking.

LEXenstein is an easy-to-use framework that provides simplified access to many approaches for several sub-tasks of the LS pipeline, which is illustrated in Figure 1. Its current version includes methods for the three main sub-tasks in the pipeline: Substitution Generation, Substitution Selection and Substitution Ranking.

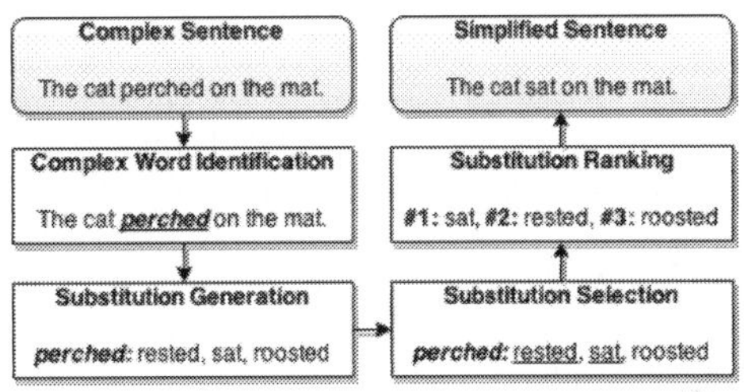

Figure 1: Lexical Simplification Pipeline

LEXenstein was devised to facilitate performance comparisons among various LS approaches, as well as the creation of new strategies for LS. In the following Sections we present LEXenstein's components (Section 2) and discuss the results of several experiments conducted with the tool (Section 3).

2 System Overview

LEXenstein is a Python library that provides several approaches for sub-tasks in LS. To increase its flexibility, the library is structured in six modules: Substitution Generation, Substitution Selection, Substitution Ranking, Feature Estimation, Evaluation and Text Adorning. In the following Sections, we describe them in more detail.

[1]https://github.com/sjauhar/simplex

Proceedings of ACL-IJCNLP 2015 System Demonstrations, pages 85–90,
Beijing, China, July 26-31, 2015.

2.1 Substitution Generation

We define Substitution Generation (SG) as the task of producing candidate substitutions for complex words, which is normally done regardless of the context of the complex word. Previous work commonly addresses this task by querying general domain thesauri such as WordNet (Fellbaum, 1998), or domain specific ones such as UMLS (Bodenreider, 2004). Examples of work resorting to this strategy are (Devlin and Tait, 1998) and (Carroll et al., 1999). Recent work focuses on learning substitutions from sentence-aligned parallel corpora of complex-simple texts (Paetzold and Specia, 2013; Horn et al., 2014).

LEXenstein's SG module offers support for five approaches. All approaches use LEXenstein's Text Adorning module to create substitutions for all possible inflections of verbs and nouns. Each approach is represented by one of the following Python classes:

KauchakGenerator (Horn et al., 2014) Automatically extracts substitutions from parallel corpora. It requires a set of tagged parallel sentences and the word alignments between them in Pharaoh format (Och and Ney, 2000). It produces a dictionary of complex-to-simple substitutions filtered by the criteria described in (Horn et al., 2014).

BiranGenerator (Biran et al., 2011) Filters substitutions based on the Cartesian product between vocabularies of complex and simple words. It requires vocabularies of complex and simple words, as well as two language models trained over complex and simple corpora. It produces a dictionary linking words to a set of synonyms and hypernyms filtered by the criteria described in (Biran et al., 2011).

YamamotoGenerator (Kajiwara et al., 2013) Extracts substitutions from dictionary definitions of complex words. It requires an API key for the Merriam Dictionary[2], which can be obtained for free. It produces a dictionary linking words in the Merriam Dictionary and WordNet to words with the same Part-of-Speech (POS) tag in its entries' definitions and examples of usage.

MerriamGenerator Extracts a dictionary linking words to their synonyms, as listed in the Merriam Thesaurus. It requires an API key.

WordnetGenerator Extracts a dictionary linking words to their synonyms, as listed in WordNet.

2.2 Substitution Selection

Substitution Selection (SS) is the task of selecting which substitutions – from a given list – can replace a complex word in a given sentence without altering its meaning. Most work addresses this task referring to the context of the complex word by employing Word Sense Disambiguation (WSD) approaches (Sedding and Kazakov, 2004; Nunes et al., 2013), or by discarding substitutions which do not share the same POS tag of the target complex word (Kajiwara et al., 2013; Paetzold and Specia, 2013).

LEXenstein's SS module provides access to three approaches. All approaches require as input a dictionary of substitutions generated by a given approach and a dataset in the VICTOR format (as in Victor Frankenstein (Shelley, 2007)). As output, they produce a set of selected substitutions for each entry in the VICTOR dataset. The VICTOR format is structured as illustrated in Example 1, where S_i is the ith sentence in the dataset, w_i a target complex word in the h_ith position of S_i, c_i^j a substitution candidate and r_i^j its simplicity ranking. Each bracketed component is separated by a tabulation marker.

$$\begin{bmatrix} \langle \mathrm{S}_1 \rangle & \langle \mathrm{w}_1 \rangle & \langle \mathrm{h}_1 \rangle & \langle \mathrm{r}_1^1\mathrm{:c}_1^1 \rangle \cdots \langle \mathrm{r}_1^n\mathrm{:c}_1^n \rangle \\ & & \vdots & \\ \langle \mathrm{S}_m \rangle & \langle \mathrm{w}_m \rangle & \langle \mathrm{h}_m \rangle & \langle \mathrm{r}_m^1\mathrm{:c}_m^1 \rangle \cdots \langle \mathrm{r}_m^n\mathrm{:c}_m^n \rangle \end{bmatrix} \quad (1)$$

LEXenstein includes two resources for training/testing in the VICTOR format: the LexMTurk (Horn et al., 2014) and the SemEval corpus (Specia et al., 2012). Each approach in the SS module is represented by one of the following Python classes:

WSDSelector Allows for the user to use one among various classic WSD approaches in SS. It requires the PyWSD (Tan, 2014) module to be installed, which includes the approaches presented by (Lesk, 1986) and (Wu and Palmer, 1994), as well as baselines such as random and first senses.

BiranSelector (Biran et al., 2011) Employs a strategy in which a word co-occurrence model is used to determine which substitutions have meaning similar to that of a target complex word. It requires a plain text file with each line in the format specified in Example 2, where $\langle w_i \rangle$ is a word,

[2] http://www.dictionaryapi.com/

$\langle c_i^j \rangle$ a co-occurring word and $\langle f_i^j \rangle$ its frequency of occurrence.

$$\langle w_i \rangle \ \langle c_i^0 \rangle : \langle f_i^0 \rangle \cdots \langle c_i^n \rangle : \langle f_i^n \rangle \tag{2}$$

Each component in the format in 2 must be separated by a tabulation marker. Given such a model, the approach filters all substitutions which are estimated to be more complex than the target word, and also those for which the distance between their co-occurrence vector and the target sentence's vector is higher than a threshold set by the user.

WordVectorSelector Employs a novel strategy, in which a word vector model is used to determine which substitutions have the closest meaning to that of the sentence being simplified. It requires a binary word vector model produced by Word2Vec[3], and can be configured in many ways. It retrieves a user-defined percentage of the substitutions, which are ranked with respect to the cosine distance between their word vector and the sum of some or all of the sentences' words, depending on the settings defined by the user.

2.3 Substitution Ranking

Substitution Ranking (SR) is the task of ranking a set of selected substitutions for a target complex word with respect to their simplicity. Approaches vary from simple word length and frequency-based measures (Devlin and Tait, 1998; Carroll et al., 1998; Carroll et al., 1999; Biran et al., 2011) to more sophisticated linear combinations of scoring functions (Jauhar and Specia, 2012), as well as machine learning-based approaches (Horn et al., 2014).

LEXenstein's SR module provides access to three approaches. All approaches receive as input datasets in the VICTOR format, which can be either training/testing datasets already containing only valid substitutions in context, or datasets generated with (potentially noisy) substitutions by a given SS approach. They also require as input a FeatureEstimator object to calculate feature values describing the candidate substitutes. More details on the FeatureEstimator class are provided in Section 2.4. Each approach in the SR module is represented by one of the following Python classes:

[3]https://code.google.com/p/word2vec/

MetricRanker Employs a simple ranking strategy based on the values of a single feature provided by the user. By configuring the input FeatureEstimator object, the user can calculate values of several features for the candidates in a given dataset and easily rank the candidates according to each of these features.

SVMRanker (Joachims, 2002) Use Support Vector Machines in a setup that minimises a loss function with respect to a ranking model. This strategy is the one employed in the LS experiments of (Horn et al., 2014), yielding promising results. The user needs to provide a path to their SVM-Rank installation, as well as SVM-related configurations, such as the kernel type and parameter values for C, $epsilon$, etc.

BoundaryRanker Employs a novel strategy, in which ranking is framed as a binary classification task. During training, this approach assigns the label 1 to all candidates of rank $1 \geq r \geq p$, where p is a range set by the user, and 0 to the remaining candidates. It then trains a stochastic descent linear classifier based on the features specified in the FeatureEstimator object. During testing, candidate substitutions are ranked based on how far from 0 they are. This ranker allows the user to provide several parameters during training, such as loss function and penalty type.

2.4 Feature Estimation

LEXenstein's Feature Estimation module allows the calculation of several features for LS-related tasks. Its class FeatureEstimator allows the user to select and configure many features commonly used by LS approaches.

The FeatureEstimator object can be used either for the creation of LEXenstein's rankers, or in stand-alone setups. For the latter, the class provides a function called *calculateFeatures*, which produces a matrix MxN containing M feature values for each of the N substitution candidates listed in the dataset. Each of the 11 features supported must be configured individually. They can be grouped in four categories:

Lexicon-oriented: Binary features which receive value 1 if a candidate appears in a given vocabulary, and 0 otherwise.

Morphological: Features that exploit morphological characteristics of substitutions, such as word length and number of syllables.

Collocational: N-gram probabilities of the form $P\left(S_{h-1}^{h-l}\, c\, S_{h+1}^{h+r}\right)$, where c is a candidate substitution in the hth position in sentence S, and S_{h-1}^{h-l} and S_{h+1}^{h+r} are n-grams of size l and r, respectively.

Sense-oriented: Several features which are related to the meaning of a candidate substitution such as number of senses, lemmas, synonyms, hypernyms, hyponyms and maximum and minimum distances among all of its senses.

2.5 Evaluation

Since one of the goals of LEXenstein is to facilitate the benchmarking LS approaches, it is crucial that it provides evaluation methods. This module includes functions for the evaluation of all subtasks, both individually and in combination. It contains four Python classes:

GeneratorEvaluator: Provides evaluation metrics for SG methods. It requires a gold-standard in the VICTOR format and a set of generated substitutions. It returns the Potential, Precision and F-measure, where Potential is the proportion of instances for which at least one of the substitutions generated is present in the gold-standard, Precision the proportion of generated instances which are present in the gold-standard, and F-measure their harmonic mean.

SelectorEvaluator: Provides evaluation metrics for SS methods. It requires a gold-standard in the VICTOR format and a set of selected substitutions. It returns the Potential, Precision and F-measure of the SS approach, as defined above.

RankerEvaluator: Provides evaluation metrics for SR methods. It requires a gold-standard in the VICTOR format and a set of ranked substitutions. It returns the TRank-at-1:3 and Recall-at-1:3 metrics (Specia et al., 2012), where Trank-at-i is the proportion of instances for which a candidate of gold-rank $r \leq i$ was ranked first, and Recall-at-i the proportion of candidates of gold-rank $r \leq i$ that are ranked in positions $p \leq i$.

PipelineEvaluator: Provides evaluation metrics for the entire LS pipeline. It requires as input a gold-standard in the VICTOR format and a set of ranked substitutions which have been generated and selected by a given set of approaches. It returns the approaches' Precision, Accuracy and Change Proportion, where Precision is the proportion of instances for which the highest ranking substitution is not the target complex word itself and is in the gold-standard, Accuracy is the proportion of instances for which the highest ranking substitution is in the gold-standard, and Change Proportion is the proportion of instances for which the highest ranking substitution is not the target complex word itself.

2.6 Text Adorning

This approach provides a Python interface to the Morph Adorner Toolkit (Paetzold, 2015), a set of Java tools that facilitates the access to Morph Adorner's functionalities. The class provides easy access to word lemmatisation, word stemming, syllable splitting, noun inflection, verb tensing and verb conjugation.

2.7 Resources

LEXenstein also provides a wide array of resources for the user to explore in benchmarking tasks. Among them are the aforementioned LexMturk and SemEval corpora in the VICTOR format, lists of stop and basic words, as well as language models and lexica built over Wikipedia and Simple Wikipedia.

3 Experiments

In this Section, we discuss the results obtained in four benchmarking experiments.

3.1 Substitution Generation

In this experiment we evaluate all SG approaches in LEXenstein. For the KauchakGenerator, we use the corpus provided by (Kauchak, 2013), composed of $150,569$ complex-to-simple parallel sentences, parsed by the Stanford Parser (Klein and Manning, 1965). From the the same corpus, we build the required vocabularies and language models for the BiranGenerator. We used the LexMturk dataset as the gold-standard (Horn et al., 2014), which is composed by 500 sentences, each with a single target complex word and 50 substitutions suggested by turkers. The results are presented in Table 1.

The results in Table 1 show that the method of (Horn et al., 2014) yields the best F-Measure results, although combining the output of all generation methods yields the highest Potential. This shows that using parallel corpora to generate substitution candidates for complex words can be a

Approach	Pot.	Prec.	F
Kauchak	0.830	**0.155**	**0.262**
Wordnet	0.608	0.109	0.184
Biran	0.630	0.102	0.175
Merriam	0.540	0.067	0.120
Yamamoto	0.504	0.054	0.098
All	**0.976**	0.066	0.124

Table 1: SG benchmarking results

more efficient strategy than querying dictionaries and databases. We must, however, keep in mind that the sentences that compose the LexMturk corpus were extracted from Wikipedia, which is the same corpus from which the KauchakGenerator learns substitutions.

3.2 Substitution Selection

Here we evaluate of all SS approaches in LEXenstein. For the BiranSelector, we trained a co-occurrence model over a corpus of 6+ billion words extracted from the various sources suggested in the Word2Vec documentation[4], the same sources over which the word vector model required by the WordVectorSelector was trained. In order to summarise the results, we present the scores obtained only with the best performing configurations of each approach. The LexMturk corpus is used as the gold-standard, and the initial set of substitutions is the one produced by all SG approaches combined. The results are presented in Table 2.

Approach	Pot.	Prec.	F	Size
Word Vec.	0.768	**0.219**	**0.341**	3,042
Biran	0.508	0.078	0.136	9,680
First	0.176	0.045	0.072	2,471
Lesk	0.246	0.041	0.070	4,716
Random	0.082	0.023	0.035	2,046
Wu-Pa	0.038	0.013	0.020	1,749
No Sel.	**0.976**	0.066	0.124	26,516

Table 2: SS benchmarking results

"Size" in Table 2 represents the total number of substitutions selected for all test instances. The results in Table 2 show that our novel word vector approach outperforms all others in F-Measure by a considerable margin, including the method of not performing selection at all. Note that not performing selection allows for Potential to be higher, but yields very poor Precision.

3.3 Substitution Ranking

In Table 3 we present the results of the evaluation of several SR approaches. We trained the SVMRanker with features similar to the ones used in (Horn et al., 2014), and the BoundaryRanker with a set of 10 features selected through univariate feature selection. We compare these approaches to three baseline Metric Rankers, which use the word's frequency in Simple Wikipedia, its length or its number of senses. The SemEval corpus is used as the gold-standard so that we can compare our results with the best one obtained at SemEval-2012 (Jauhar and Specia, 2012) (SemEval, in Table 3).

Approach	TR-1	Rec-1	Rec-2	Rec-3
Boundary	**0.655**	**0.608**	0.602	0.663
SVM	0.486	0.451	0.502	0.592
Freq.	0.226	0.220	0.236	0.300
Length	0.180	0.175	0.200	0.261
Senses	0.130	0.126	0.161	0.223
SemEval	0.602	0.575	**0.689**	**0.769**

Table 3: SR benchmarking results

The novel Boundary ranking approach outperforms all other approaches in both TRank-at-1 and Recall-at-1 by a considerable margin, but it is worse than the best SemEval-2012 approach in terms of Recall-at-2 and 3. This however reveals not a limitation but a strength of our approach: since the Boundary ranker focuses on placing the best substitution in the highest rank, it becomes more effective at doing so as opposed to at producing a full ranking for all candidates.

3.4 Round-Trip Evaluation

In this experiment we evaluate the performance of different combinations of SS and SR approaches in selecting suitable substitutions for complex words from the ones produced by all generators combined. Rankers and selectors are configured in the same way as they were in the experiments in Sections 3.3 and 3.2. The gold-standard used is LexMturk, and the performance metric used is the combination's Precision: the proportion of times in which the candidate ranked highest is not the target complex word itself and belongs to the gold-standard list. Results are shown in Table 4.

The results show that combining the WordVectorSelector with the BoundaryRanker yields

[4]https://code.google.com/p/word2vec/

	No Sel.	Word Vector	Biran
Boundary	0.342	**0.550**	0.197
SVM	0.108	0.219	0.003
Freq.	0.114	0.501	0.096
Length	0.120	0.408	0.092
Senses	0.214	0.448	0.122

Table 4: Round-trip benchmarking results

the highest performance in the pipeline evaluation. Interestingly, the SVMRanker, which performed very well in the individual evaluation of Section 3.3, was outperformed by all three baselines in this experiment.

4 Final Remarks

We have presented LEXenstein, a framework for Lexical Simplification distributed under the permissive BSD license. It provides a wide arrange of useful resources and tools for the task, such as feature estimators, text adorners, and various approaches for Substitution Generation, Selection and Ranking. These include methods from previous work, as well as novel approaches. LEXenstein's modular structure also allows for one to easily add new approaches to it.

We have conducted evaluation experiments including various LS approaches in the literature. Our results show that the novel approaches introduced in this paper outperform those from previous work. In the future, we intend to incorporate in LEXenstein approaches for Complex Word Identification, as well as more approaches for the remaining tasks of the usual LS pipeline.

The tool can be downloaded from: `http://ghpaetzold.github.io/LEXenstein/`.

References

O. Biran, S. Brody, and N. Elhadad. 2011. Putting it Simply: a Context-Aware Approach to Lexical Simplification. *The 49th Annual Meeting of the ACL.*

O. Bodenreider. 2004. The unified medical language system (umls): integrating biomedical terminology. *Nucleic acids research.*

J. Carroll, G. Minnen, Y. Canning, S. Devlin, and J. Tait. 1998. Practical simplification of english newspaper text to assist aphasic readers. In *The 15th AAAI.*

J. Carroll, G. Minnen, D. Pearce, Y. Canning, S. Devlin, and J. Tait. 1999. Simplifying Text for Language Impaired Readers. *The 9th EACL.*

S. Devlin and J. Tait. 1998. The use of a psycholinguistic database in the simplification of text for aphasic readers. *Linguistic Databases.*

C. Fellbaum. 1998. *WordNet: An Electronic Lexical Database.* Bradford Books.

C. Horn, C. Manduca, and D. Kauchak. 2014. Learning a Lexical Simplifier Using Wikipedia. *The 52nd Annual Meeting of the ACL.*

S.K. Jauhar and L. Specia. 2012. UOW-SHEF: SimpLex–lexical simplicity ranking based on contextual and psycholinguistic features. *The 1st *SEM.*

T. Joachims. 2002. Optimizing search engines using clickthrough data. In *The 8th ACM.*

T. Kajiwara, H. Matsumoto, and K. Yamamoto. 2013. Selecting Proper Lexical Paraphrase for Children.

D. Kauchak. 2013. Improving Text Simplification Language Modeling Using Unsimplified Text Data. *The 51st Annual Meeting of the ACL.*

D. Klein and C.D. Manning. 1965. Accurate Unlexicalized Parsing. In *The 41st Annual Meeting of ACL.*

M. Lesk. 1986. Automatic sense disambiguation using machine readable dictionaries: how to tell a pine cone from an ice cream cone. In *The 5th SIGDOC.*

B.P. Nunes, R. Kawase, P. Siehndel, M.A. Casanova, and S. Dietze. 2013. As Simple as It Gets - A Sentence Simplifier for Different Learning Levels and Contexts. *IEEE 13th ICALT.*

F.J. Och and H. Ney. 2000. Improved statistical alignment models. In *The 38th Annual Meeting of the ACL.*

G.H. Paetzold and L. Specia. 2013. Text simplification as tree transduction. In *The 9th STIL.*

G.H. Paetzold. 2015. Morph adorner toolkit: Morph adorner made simple. http://ghpaetzold.github.io/MorphAdornerToolkit/.

J. Sedding and D. Kazakov. 2004. Wordnet-based text document clustering. In *The 3rd ROMAND.*

M. Shelley. 2007. *Frankenstein.* Pearson Education.

L. Specia, S.K. Jauhar, and R. Mihalcea. 2012. Semeval-2012 task 1: English lexical simplification. In *The 1st *SEM.*

L. Tan. 2014. Pywsd: Python implementations of word sense disambiguation technologies. https://github.com/alvations/pywsd.

Z. Wu and M. Palmer. 1994. Verbs semantics and lexical selection. In *The 32nd Annual Meeting of ACL.*

Sharing annotations better: RESTful Open Annotation

Sampo Pyysalo[1] **Jorge Campos**[2] **Juan Miguel Cejuela**[2] **Filip Ginter**[1]
Kai Hakala[1] **Chen Li**[3] **Pontus Stenetorp**[4] **Lars Juhl Jensen**[5]
[1] University of Turku, Finland, [2] tagtog, Germany,
[3] Massachusetts Institute of Technology, United States,
[4] University of Tokyo, Japan, [5] University of Copenhagen, Denmark
sampo@pyysalo.net jorge@tagtog.net juanmi@tagtog.net
filip.ginter@utu.fi kai.hakala@utu.fi cli@csail.mit.edu
p.stenetorp@cs.ucl.ac.uk lars.juhl.jensen@cpr.ku.dk

Abstract

Annotations are increasingly created and shared online and connected with web resources such as databases of real-world entities. Recent collaborative efforts to provide interoperability between online annotation tools and resources have introduced the Open Annotation (OA) model, a general framework for representing annotations based on web standards. Building on the OA model, we propose to share annotations over a minimal web interface that conforms to the Representational State Transfer architectural style and uses the JSON for Linking Data representation (JSON-LD). We introduce tools supporting this approach and apply it to several existing annotation clients and servers, demonstrating direct interoperability between tools and resources that were previously unable to exchange information. The specification and tools are available from http://restoa.github.io/.

1 Introduction

Annotation is an important task in many fields ranging from historical and literary study to experimental sciences including biology. The value of annotations is closely associated with the ability to share them. The web has become instrumental to information sharing, and there has thus been much interest in web-based tools and repositories for the creation, collaborative editing and sharing of annotations. Unfortunately, design and implementation differences have resulted in poor interoperability, raising barriers to communication and introducing costs from the need to convert between data models, formats, and protocols to bridge different systems.

To fully interoperate, annotation tools and resources must agree at least on a way to name and refer to things, an abstract data model, a format capturing that model, and a communication protocol. Here, we suggest a web application programming interface (API) that resolves these questions by building upon web standards and best practices, namely Linked Data principles (Bizer et al., 2009), the Open Annotation data model (Bradshaw et al., 2013) and its serialization as JSON-LD (Sporny et al., 2014), and a minimal HTTP-based protocol adhering to the Representational State Transfer (REST) architectural style (Fielding and Taylor, 2002). By implementing support for the API in a variety of independently developed annotation tools and resources, we demonstrate that this approach enables interoperability and novel ways of combining previously isolated methods.

2 Design

We aim to define a minimal web API for sharing annotations that conforms closely to relevant standards and best practices. This should reduce implementation effort and ensure generality and compatibility with related efforts (Section 5). We next briefly discuss the components of our design.

Linked Data. We use representations based on the Resource Description Framework (RDF) standards for modeling data on the web, following the best practice of using HTTP uniform resource identifiers (URIs), which provide useful information when dereferenced (Bizer et al., 2009).

Open Annotation. We describe text annotations according to the OA draft W3C standard[1], which

[1]http://www.openannotation.org/

Proceedings of ACL-IJCNLP 2015 System Demonstrations, pages 91–96,
Beijing, China, July 26-31, 2015. ©2015 ACL and AFNLP

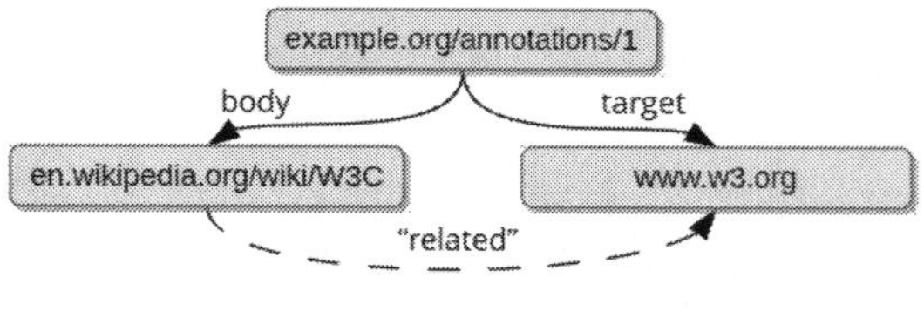

Figure 1: OA model example. The annotation expresses that the W3C Wikipedia article is related to the W3C homepage. The three resources are all in different domains, and the *"related"* relation is not represented explicitly.

is an RDF-based graph representation compatible with linguistic annotation formalisms such as LAF/GrAF (Ide and Suderman, 2007; Verspoor and Livingston, 2012). At its most basic level, the OA model differentiates between three key components: *annotation*, *body*, and *target*, where the annotation expresses that the body is related to the target of the annotation (Figure 1). The body can carry arbitrarily complex embedded data.

JSON-LD was recently accepted as a standard RDF serialization format (Sporny et al., 2014) and is the recommended serialization of OA. Every JSON-LD document is both a JSON document and a representation of RDF data. Figure 2 shows an example of a simple annotation using the OA JSON-LD representation.[2]

```
{
   "@id":      "/annotations/1",
   "@type":    "oa:Annotation",
   "target":   "/documents/1#char=0,10",
   "body":     "Person"
}
```

Figure 2: Example annotation in JSON-LD format.

RESTful architecture We define a resource-oriented API that uses HTTP verbs to manipulate resources (Table 1). The API provides hypermedia controls in data using JSON-LD and established link relations, in conformance with best practices for RESTful APIs (Fielding and Taylor, 2002).

The API defines just two types of resources: an annotation and a collection of annotations. The former is defined according to the core OA specification. While there are no formal standards for the representation of collections in RESTful APIs, the basic collection pattern is well established. We specify a simple implementation, drawing on relevant draft standards such as Collection+JSON[3] and Hydra[4].

[2]The OA JSON-LD `@context` is understood to be active. Relative URLs are interpreted with respect to the HTTP request base.

Verb	Resource	Action
`GET`	Annotation	Read annotation
`GET`	Collection	Read all annotations
`PUT`	Annotation	Update annotation
`DELETE`	Annotation	Delete annotation
`POST`	Collection	Create annotation

Table 1: HTTP verbs, resources, and actions. Read-only services support only the two `GET` requests.

3 Reference Implementation

To support the development, testing and integration of RESTful OA API implementations, we have created a reference server and client as well as tools for format conversion and validation.

3.1 OA Store

The OA Store is a reference implementation of persistent, server-side annotation storage that allows clients to create, read, update and delete annotations using the API. The store uses MongoDB, which is well suited to the task as it is a document-oriented, schema-free database that natively supports JSON for communication. The API is implemented using the Python Eve framework, which is specifically oriented towards RESTful web APIs using JSON and is thus easily adapted to support OA JSON-LD.

3.2 OA Explorer

The OA Explorer is a reference client that provides an HTML interface for navigating and visualizing the contents of any compatible store (Figure 3). The service first prompts the user for a store URL and then provides the user with a dynamically generated view of the contents of the store, which it discovers using the API. OA Explorer is implemented in Python using the Flask microframework for web development.

[3]`http://amundsen.com/media-types/collection/`

[4]`http://www.hydra-cg.com/spec/latest/core/`

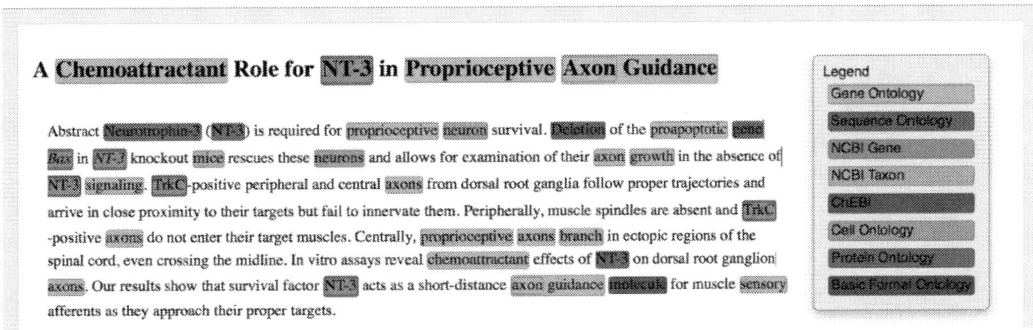

Figure 3: OA Explorer shown visualizing annotations from the CRAFT corpus (Bada et al., 2012) converted to OA and served from the OA Store.

3.3 Format conversion

The OA Adapter is middleware that we created for sharing Open Annotation data. The software implements both the client and server sides of the API and a variety of conversions to and from different serializations of the OA model and related formats using the OA JSON-LD serialization as the pivot format. This allows the OA Adapter to operate transparently between a client and a server, providing on-the-fly conversions of client requests from representations favored by the client into ones favored by the server, and vice versa for server responses. Standard HTTP content negotiation is used to select the best supported representations. The adapter implements full support for all standard RDF serializations: JSON-LD, N-Triples and N-Quads, Notation3, RDF/XML, TriG, TriX, and Turtle. With the exception of named graphs for serializations that do not support them, conversion between these representations is guaranteed to preserve all information.

In addition to the general, reversible format translation services provided by the OA Adapter, we provide scripts for offline conversion of various annotation file formats into the OA JSON-LD format to allow existing datasets to be imported into OA stores. The following are currently supported: Penn Treebank format (including PTB II PAS) (Marcus et al., 1994), a number of variants of CoNLL formats, including CoNLL-U,[5] Knowtator XML (Ogren, 2006), and the standoff format used by the BRAT annotation tool (Stenetorp et al., 2012). We also provide supporting tools for importing files with OA JSON-LD data to a store and exporting to files over the RESTful OA API.

[5]http://universaldependencies.github.io/docs/

3.4 Validation

OA JSON-LD data can be validated on three levels: 1) whether the data is syntactically well-formed JSON, 2) whether it conforms to the JSON-LD specification, and 3) whether the abstract information content fulfills the OA data model. The first two can be accomplished using any one of the available libraries that implement the full JSON-LD syntax and API specifications.[6] To facilitate also validation of conformity to the OA data model, we define the core model of the OA standard using JSON Schema (Galiegue and Zyp, 2013). The JSON Schema community has provided tools in various programming languages for validating JSON against a JSON Schema. The schema we defined is capable of validating data for compliance against JSON-LD and OA Core at the same time. Complementing this support for data validation, we are also developing a standalone tool for testing web services for conformance to the RESTful OA API specification.

4 Adaptation of Existing Tools

In addition to creating reference implementations, we have adapted two previously introduced web-based annotation tools to support the API. We further demonstrate the scope and scalability of the framework on several publicly available mass-scale datasets from the biomedical domain, showing how annotations on millions of documents can be transparently linked across well-established database services and to non-textual resources such as gene and protein databases.

[6]http://json-ld.org

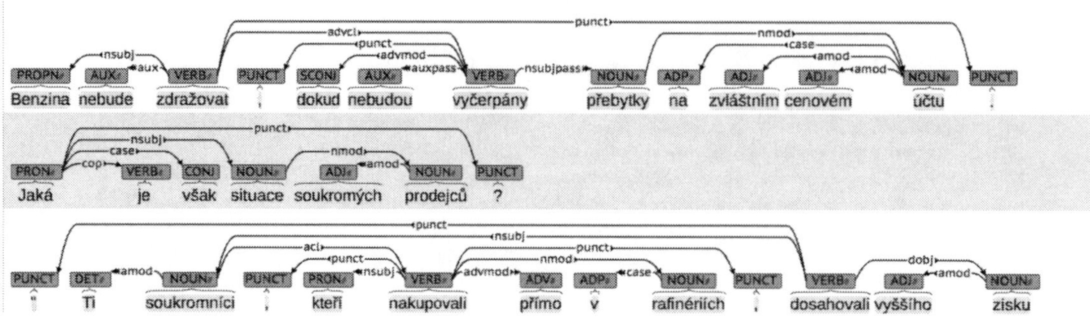

Figure 4: BRAT showing Czech dependency annotations from the Universal Dependencies corpus (`http://universaldependencies.github.io/docs/`).

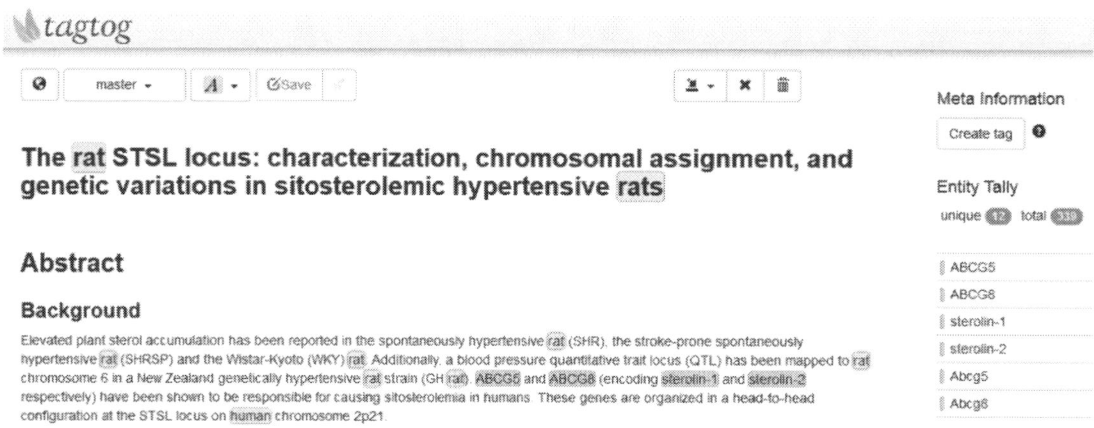

Figure 5: tagtog showing entity annotations for a full-text document from PubMed Central.

4.1 BRAT

The brat rapid annotation tool (BRAT) is an open-source web-based annotation tool that supports a wide range of text annotation tasks (Stenetorp et al., 2012). It provides intuitive visualization of text-bound and relational annotations and allows for annotations to be created and edited using a drag-and-drop interface (Figure 4). The server is a web service implemented in Python, whereas the client is a browser-based application written in JavaScript. For annotation storage, the server uses a file-based back-end with a stand-off file format[7].

The original client and server implement a custom communication protocol, leading to tight coupling between the two. We rewrote the client and server communication components to use OA JSON-LD and the RESTful API as an alternative to the native format and protocol, thus enabling both components to communicate also with other clients and servers.

[7] `http://brat.nlplab.org/standoff.html`

4.2 tagtog

The tagtog web-based annotation system is designed to combine manual and automatic annotations to accurately and efficiently mark up full-text articles (Cejuela et al., 2014). The system was originally developed with a focus on annotating biological entities and concepts such as genes and Gene Ontology terms. The web interface is implemented in JavaScript using the Play framework with Scala. The system is centered on the concept of user projects, each of which holds a corpus of annotated documents.

To make tagtog interoperable with other RESTful OA clients and servers, we made two major implementation changes. First, the server can now serve annotations in OA JSON-LD format, thus allowing them to be viewed by other clients. Second, the tagtog interface can visualize and edit OA JSON annotations from other OA stores, without a backing tagtog project. Figure 5 shows a sample document annotated in tagtog.

4.3 Biomedical entity recognition resources

We implemented the API for four large-scale databases of biomedical entity mentions. The COMPARTMENTS database integrates evidence on protein subcellular localization (Binder et al., 2014), and TISSUES and DISEASES similarly integrate evidence on tissue expression and disease-associations of human genes, respectively (Santos et al., 2015; Pletscher-Frankild et al., 2015). All three resources include a text mining component based on the highly efficient NER engine used also for detection of species names and names of other taxa in the ORGANISMS database (Pafilis et al., 2014). Together, these databases contain over 123M mentions of genes/proteins, cellular components, tissues and cell lines, disease terms and taxonomic identifiers. This dataset is regularly precomputed for the entire Medline corpus, which currently consists of more than 24M abstracts and 3B tokens.

To make this large collection of automatic annotations available as OA JSON-LD, we defined the annotations of each abstract to be a separate (sub)collection of a document resource, accessible using URL patterns of the form `http://.../document/{docid}/annotations/`. The web services were implemented as part of the Python framework common to all four databases. They query a PostgreSQL back-end for text and annotations, which are formatted as OA JSON-LD using the standard Python `json` module.

4.4 EVEX

The EVEX database is a collection of events from the molecular biology domain obtained by processing the entire collection of PubMed articles and PubMed Central Open Access full-text articles (Van Landeghem et al., 2013), together constituting a corpus of nearly 6B tokens. In total, EVEX contains 40M individual events among 77M entity mentions. The events are of 24 different types (e.g. POSITIVE REGULATION, PHOSPHORYLATION) and the participants are primarily genes and proteins. Where possible, the entity mentions are grounded to their corresponding Entrez Gene database identifiers.

The event structures consist of entity mentions, *trigger phrases* expressing events, and typed relations identifying the roles that the entities play in the events. All of this data is accessible through a newly implemented EVEX API compliant with the OA JSON-LD format. Every document is defined as a separate annotation collection following the approach described in Section 4.3. The EVEX web service is written in Python using the Django web framework. Data are stored in a MySQL database and the OA JSON-LD interface uses the standard Python `json` module for formatting.

5 Related work

Our approach builds directly on the OA data model (Bradshaw et al., 2013), which harmonizes the earlier Open Annotation Collaboration (Haslhofer et al., 2011) and Annotation Ontology Initiative (Ciccarese et al., 2011) efforts and is currently developed further under the auspices of the W3C Web Annotation WG.[8] Approaches building on RESTful architectures and JSON-LD are also being pursued by the Linguistic Data Consortium (Wright, 2014) and the Language Application Grid (Ide et al., 2014), among others. A number of annotation stores following similar protocols have also been released recently, including Lorestore (Hunter and Gerber, 2012), PubAnnotation (Kim and Wang, 2012), the Annotator.js store[9], and NYU annotations[10].

6 Conclusions and future work

We have proposed to share annotations using a minimal RESTful interface for Open Annotation data in JSON-LD. We introduced reference implementations of a server, client, validation and conversion tools, and demonstrated the integration of several independently developed annotation tools and resources using the API. In future work, we will continue to develop the API specification further in collaboration with the relevant standardization efforts and interested parties using a fully open process. We will focus in particular on modular extensions to the specification for supporting search, tagging, and bulk modifications. We will also continue to develop and extend the tools, with emphasis on reversible conversions between OA JSON-LD and major related formats. Except for tagtog, a commercial tool, all of the tools and resources introduced in this study are available under open licenses from `http://restoa.github.io/`.

[8] `http://www.w3.org/annotation/`
[9] `http://annotateit.org/`
[10] `http://annotations.dlib.nyu.edu/home/`

Acknowledgments

This work was in part funded by the Novo Nordisk Foundation Center for Protein Research [NNF14CC0001], by the National Institutes of Health [U54 CA189205-01], by JSPS KAKENHI [13F03041], and by Quanta Computer Inc.

References

Michael Bada, Miriam Eckert, Donald Evans, Kristin Garcia, Krista Shipley, Dmitry Sitnikov, William A Baumgartner, K Bretonnel Cohen, Karin Verspoor, Judith A Blake, et al. 2012. Concept annotation in the craft corpus. *BMC bioinformatics*, 13(1):161.

Janos X Binder, Sune Pletscher-Frankild, Kalliopi Tsafou, Christian Stolte, Sean I O'Donoghue, Reinhard Schneider, and Lars Juhl Jensen. 2014. COMPARTMENTS: unification and visualization of protein subcellular localization evidence. *Database*, 2014:bau012.

Christian Bizer, Tom Heath, and Tim BernersLee. 2009. Linked Data the story so far. *International Journal on Semantic Web & Information Systems*.

Shannon Bradshaw, Dan Brickley, Leyla Jael Garca Castro, Timothy Clark, Timothy Cole, Phil Desenne, Anna Gerber, Antoine Isaac, Jacob Jett, Thomas Habing, et al. 2013. Open annotation data model (community draft).

Juan Miguel Cejuela, Peter McQuilton, Laura Ponting, Steven J Marygold, Raymund Stefancsik, Gillian H Millburn, Burkhard Rost, et al. 2014. tagtog: interactive and text-mining-assisted annotation of gene mentions in PLOS full-text articles. *Database*, 2014:bau033.

Paolo Ciccarese, Marco Ocana, Leyla Jael Garcia-Castro, Sudeshna Das, and Tim Clark. 2011. An open annotation ontology for science on web 3.0. *J. Biomedical Semantics*, 2(S-2):S4.

Roy T Fielding and Richard N Taylor. 2002. Principled design of the modern web architecture. *ACM Transactions on Internet Technology (TOIT)*, 2(2):115–150.

Francis Galiegue and Kris Zyp. 2013. JSON Schema: Core definitions and terminology. *Internet Engineering Task Force (IETF)*.

Bernhard Haslhofer, Rainer Simon, Robert Sanderson, and Herbert Van de Sompel. 2011. The open annotation collaboration (oac) model. In *Proc. MMWeb'11*, pages 5–9.

Jane Hunter and Anna Gerber. 2012. Towards annotopiaenabling the semantic interoperability of web-based annotations. *Future Internet*, 4(3):788–806.

Nancy Ide and Keith Suderman. 2007. Graf: A graph-based format for linguistic annotations. In *Proc. LAW'07*, pages 1–8.

Nancy Ide, James Pustejovsky, Christopher Cieri, Eric Nyberg, Denise DiPersio, Chunqi Shi, Keith Suderman, Marc Verhagen, Di Wang, and Jonathan Wright. 2014. The language application grid. *Proc. LREC'14*.

Jin-Dong Kim and Yue Wang. 2012. Pubannotation: a persistent and sharable corpus and annotation repository. In *Proc. BioNLP'12*, pages 202–205.

Mitchell Marcus, Grace Kim, Mary Ann Marcinkiewicz, Robert MacIntyre, Ann Bies, Mark Ferguson, Karen Katz, and Britta Schasberger. 1994. The penn treebank: annotating predicate argument structure. In *Proc. HLT*, pages 114–119.

Philip V Ogren. 2006. Knowtator: a protégé plug-in for annotated corpus construction. In *Proc. HLT-NAACL'06 demos*, pages 273–275.

Evangelos Pafilis, Sune Pletscher-Frankild, Lucia Fanini, Sarah Faulwetter, Christina Pavloudi, Aikaterini Vasileiadou, Christos Arvanitidis, and Lars Juhl Jensen. 2014. The SPECIES and ORGANISMS resources for fast and accurate identification of taxonomic names in text. *PLoS ONE*, 8:e65390.

Sune Pletscher-Frankild, Albert Palleja, Kalliopi Tsafou, Janos X Binder, and Lars Juhl Jensen. 2015. DISEASES: Text mining and data integration of disease-gene associations. *Methods*, 74:83–89.

Alberto Santos, Kalliopi Tsafou, Christian Stolte, Sune Pletscher-Frankild, Sean I O'Donoghue, and Lars Juhl Jensen. 2015. Comprehensive comparison of large-scale tissue expression datasets. *PeerJ*.

Manu Sporny, Dave Longley, Gregg Kellogg, Markus Lanthaler, and Niklas Lindström. 2014. JSON-LD 1.0: A JSON-based serialization for linked data.

Pontus Stenetorp, Sampo Pyysalo, Goran Topić, Tomoko Ohta, Sophia Ananiadou, and Jun'ichi Tsujii. 2012. Brat: a web-based tool for nlp-assisted text annotation. In *Proc. ACL'12 demos*, pages 102–107.

Sofie Van Landeghem, Jari Björne, Chih-Hsuan Wei, Kai Hakala, Sampo Pyysalo, Sophia Ananiadou, Hung-Yu Kao, Zhiyong Lu, Tapio Salakoski, Yves Van de Peer, et al. 2013. Large-scale event extraction from literature with multi-level gene normalization. *PLoS ONE*, 8(4):e55814.

Karin Verspoor and Kevin Livingston. 2012. Towards adaptation of linguistic annotations to scholarly annotation formalisms on the semantic web. In *Proc. LAW'12*, pages 75–84.

Jonathan Wright. 2014. Restful annotation and efficient collaboration. In *Proc. LREC'14*.

A Data Sharing and Annotation Service Infrastructure

Stelios Piperidis, Dimitrios Galanis, Juli Bakagianni, Sokratis Sofianopoulos
Institute for Language and Speech Processing, Athena R.C., Athens, Greece
{spip, galanisd, julibak, s_sofian}@ilsp.gr

Abstract

This paper reports on and demonstrates META-SHARE/QT21, a prototype implementation of a data sharing and annotation service platform, which was based on the META-SHARE infrastructure. META-SHARE, which has been designed for sharing datasets and tools, is enhanced with a processing layer for annotating textual content with appropriate NLP services that are documented with the appropriate metadata. In META-SHARE/QT21 pre-defined processing workflows are offered to the users; each workflow is a pipeline of atomic NLP services/tools (e.g. sentence splitting, part-of-speech tagging). Currently, workflows for annotating monolingual and bilingual resources of various formats are provided (e.g. XCES, TXT, TMX). From the legal framework point of view, a simple operational model is adopted by which only openly licensed datasets can be processed by openly licensed services.

1 Introduction

Language technology research and development relies on the deployment of appropriate resources and processing services more than ever before. However, the resources and services landscape is unorganized and highly fragmented (Soria et al., 2012). Recently, initiatives like CLARIN (Wittenburg et al., 2010), Language Grid (Ishida, 2011), Panacea (Poch and Bel, 2011), LAPPS Grid (Ide et al., 2014) have been launched aiming at improving discoverability and accessibility of resources and services, as well as their lawful re-use and direct deployment in modern computational environments. In this paper, we present META-SHARE/QT21, a prototype implementation of a linguistic data infrastructure enhanced with linguistic processing services, thus bringing language datasets and processing services together in a unified platform. META-SHARE/QT21 builds upon and extends META-SHARE (Piperidis, 2012). Section 2 briefly introduces the basics of META-SHARE, the underlying data model and the supporting software implementation. Section 3 elaborates on the operations of the new language processing layer and Section 4 presents the assumptions of the current implementation. Finally, in section 5 we conclude and present directions of future work.

2 META-SHARE design and repository

META-SHARE is designed as a network of distributed repositories of language data, tools and web services, documented with high-quality metadata, aggregated in central inventories allowing for uniform search and access to resources and services. Language resources and services are documented with the META-SHARE metadata schema (Gavrilidou et al., 2012)[1] which builds upon previous initiatives (Broeder et al., 2010), including elements, most of which are linked to ISOCat Data Categories[1], as well as relations (e.g. is_part_of, is_annotation_of) used to describe and link resources that are included in the META-SHARE repository.

Every resource in META-SHARE is primarily assigned to one of the network's repositories, implementing the notion of a master copy of a resource, with the member maintaining the repository undertaking its curation. Metadata records are harvested and stored in the META-SHARE central servers, which maintain an inventory including metadata of all resources available in the distributed network. META-SHARE users, depending on their role, are able to create a user profile, log-in, browse and search

[1] ISO 12620, http://www.isocat.org.

Proceedings of ACL-IJCNLP 2015 System Demonstrations, pages 97–102,
Beijing, China, July 26-31, 2015. ©2015 ACL and AFNLP

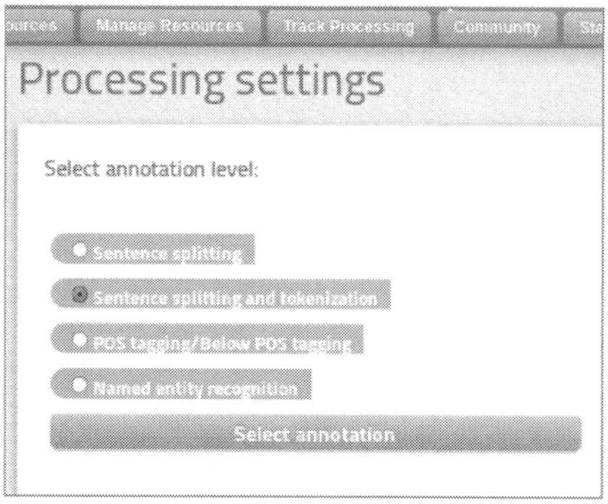

Figure 1: Dynamically generating annotation levels relevant to a dataset.

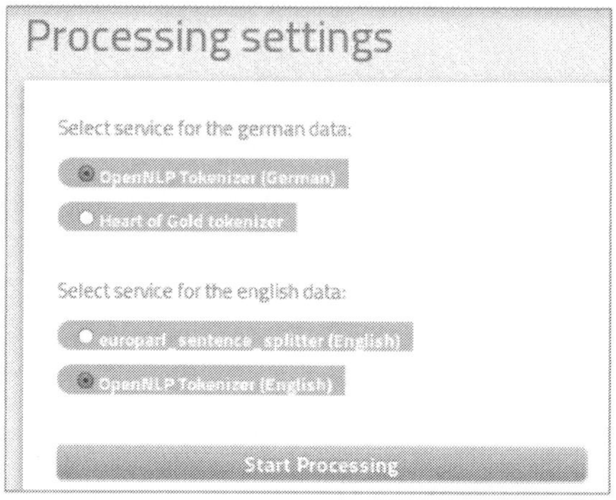

Figure 2: Presenting the processing services relevant to the annotation level chosen by the user.

the repository, download resources, upload and document resources etc. All META-SHARE software is open source[2], released under a BSD licence and available at the GitHub repository[3].

3 Enhancing META-SHARE with annotation services

For the purposes of infrastructural projects where META-SHARE was to be used as the language resource sharing platform, notably the CLARIN EL national language infrastructure[4], its functionalities have been extended by providing a mechanism for processing language datasets with appropriate natural language services. The motivation behind this extension is twofold: a) to make language processing services accessible to and usable by a wide range of users (e.g. linguists, lexicographers, social sciences and digital humanities researchers), relieving them from the burden of the technical details of running the tools or services, and b) to bring these tools and services together in a unified platform and facilitate their combination with language datasets, thus paving the way towards the organic growth of the data infrastructure.

Language processing tools are documented with the appropriate metadata in the enhanced repository version (META-SHARE/QT21)[5], and are provided as web services through the language processing (LP) layer. The LP layer has been implemented in Java, based on the Apache Camel framework[6], an open-source project that provides libraries, which enable the easy integration of different technologies and the creation of data processing workflows[7]. For example, Camel offers ready-to-use components/connectors for a) reading the files of a directory b) splitting/aggregating their contents (e.g. txt or XML) into chunks c) forwarding the chunks to data processors d) writing final results to disk.

In the typical scenario that we propose to demonstrate, when a registered META-SHARE/QT21 user selects to process a resource, a list of all available annotation levels (Figure 1) is provided. Then all the available tools/services that correspond to the chosen level are presented (Figure 2). Annotation services can be atomic or composite (a.k.a. workflows) and include: tokenization, sentence splitting, POS tagging, lemmatization, dependency parsing, named entity recognition, and parallel text alignment. As soon as the user selects a service (Figure 2), the META-SHARE/QT21 application consults its database. If the user requests to process a dataset with a specific service, and this dataset has already been processed by the specific service, then the system will forward the user to the processed dataset that has been created and stored in the repository.

[2] The META-SHARE software has been developed using the Django framework, a Python-based web framework, PostgreSQL database and Apache web server. META-SHARE comes with a pre-configured Apache Solr server used to index the META-SHARE database for browsing and searching.
[3] https://github.com/metashare/META-SHARE
[4] http://www.clarin.gr/, http://inventory.clarin.gr
[5] http://qt21.metashare.ilsp.gr/
[6] http://camel.apache.org/
[7] The implemented LP layer is bundled as a web application and can be deployed in a standard java-based web container.

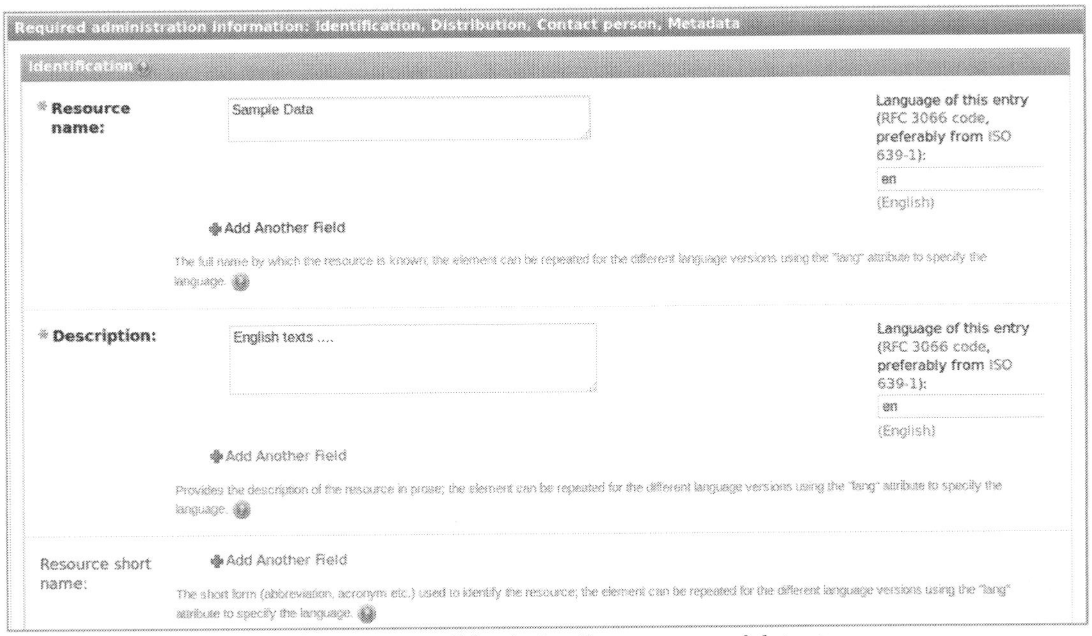

Figure 3: Describing/uploading user-owned datasets

Otherwise, META-SHARE/QT21 sends the user request to the LP layer. When the LP gets the request, it starts to process the specified resource by invoking the appropriate tools; when it finishes it notifies the META-SHARE/QT21 application so that the result of the processing is added to the META-SHARE/QT21 repository along with appropriate metadata. Finally, the META-SHARE/QT21 application sends the user an email with the link to the newly created resource. LP's workflows are implemented based on a variety of natural language processing services. These services run either within the LP application environment (loc), or they are accessed via services (rmt). Currently, OpenNLP[8] services (loc) are deployed for English, German and Portuguese, Panacea-DCU[9] services (rmt) for English, LX-Center/University of Lisbon[10] services (rmt) for Portuguese, Heart of Gold (HoG) services[11] (rmt) for German, ILSP NLP[12] services (loc) for Greek, and HunAlign (Varga et al., 2005) text alignment services for aligning parallel corpora at sentence level (loc).

Each set of workflows forms an acyclic directed graph (tree) where each node corresponds to a processing service/tool (e.g. Figure 4). The processing of a data chunk is performed by following a path in such a workflow tree. For example, in case the input is raw text the starting point is the root of the tree. However, LP is also capable of processing already annotated resources thus saving processing time and resources; i.e., if the user requests to process a dataset at a level L (e.g. OpenNLP chunking), and the resource has already been processed at a level A that is a prerequisite for L (e.g. Open NLP Tokenization), then the process will start from the already existing level A annotated resource. Also, the system is aware of what annotation levels make sense and therefore are available for an already processed resource and presents the corresponding choices (e.g. a POS-tagged corpus can be parsed or chunked, but not tokenised) to the user via the web interface (as in Figure 1).

Currently, LP implements services and workflows that can process a) monolingual resources in raw text as well as XCES format and b) bilingual resources in TMX, MOSES, and XCES formats. Bilingual resources, essentially parallel corpora, are split into their language specific parts and monolingual processing services are invoked for each language side.

The resources are stored in the META-SHARE/QT21 repository in a compressed format (e.g. .zip, tar.gz, .gz). Before processing starts, META-SHARE/QT21 decompresses the speci-

[8] https://opennlp.apache.org/
[9] http://www.panacea-lr.eu
[10] http://lxcenter.di.fc.ul.pt/tools/en/
[11] http://heartofgold.dfki.de/
[12] http://nlp.ilsp.gr

fied resource file and then uses an appropriate reader that splits the content of the extracted files in smaller text (data) chunks, so that any file size constraints that a service might have can be met. These chunks are then forwarded to the appropriate processing service/workflow. As soon as the META-SHARE/QT21 has completed the data processing a symmetric procedure collects the resulting (annotated) data chunks and merges them in a single compressed resource.

Additional features of the implemented infrastructure include: a) mechanisms for automatically creating the metadata records of the newly generated datasets, as a result of processing using an annotation service or workflow, b) discoverability of processing services for a particular language and annotation level by simple or faceted search, c) describing and uploading of user-owned datasets up to a size limit (in compressed format) depending on the user's status (Figure 3), d) temporarily storing user-owned processed datasets for 48 hours and deleting them afterwards, unless the user decides to publicly share them, e) checking processed resources for potential errors (e.g. number of files processed as expected), f) monitoring progress of all processing requests and using mechanisms to prevent the application from hanging when waiting for a service response, g) automatically cancelling processing requests that either hang for a long period (e.g. due to network connectivity problems) or are not executed correctly (e.g. when the encoding or the format is not compatible with a service/tool) h) concurrently executing several workflows or parts of a workflow.

3.1 META-SHARE/QT21 user evaluation and scalability tests.

Initially, we conducted a set of user tests which aimed at spotting bugs; then we assessed the stability and usability of META-SHARE/QT21 by asking 15 users to complete a list of 8 annotation tasks for resources of various formats and languages. All testers were researchers and they managed to locate or create the needed resources, submit their requests and receive the annotation results within a few hours without problems. Completion times varied depending on the requested task.

In addition, we assessed the performance and scalability of the LP application by testing it with resources of various lengths depending on the workflow.

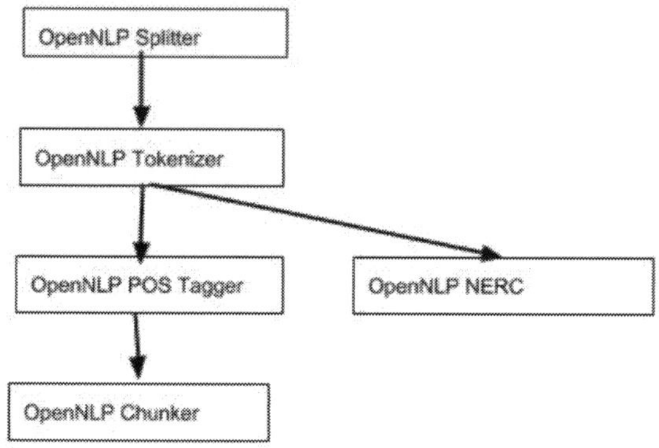

Figure 4: Workflow tree for the English OpenNLP tools.

Locally running services (tools that run within our application) were tested with resources of 1MB, 10MB and 50MB. Remote services were tested with smaller resources of 500KB, 5MB and 10MB. First, each tool/service was tested separately (not concurrently) so as to assess its processing efficiency. Then, we initiated concurrent workflows. All performed tests, concurrent or not, were completed successfully generating the expected output, with the processing times of all growing linearly with resource size; (Figure 5). The tests have also shown that LP application can handle in parallel at least 4 workflows that process ~200MB of data. We plan to handle the processing overload that can be generated by multiple user request for large datasets by using multiple instances of the Camel-based LP in a distributed environment (e.g. Hadoop) in which processing will be carried out in parallel.

4 Assumptions and limitations

Currently, each META-SHARE/QT21 workflow chains together components or services of the same suite of tools, e.g. OpenNLP or the Panacea/DCU services. To accommodate cases where the services deployed belong to different suites, we have developed the appropriate converters. For example, in a UIMA-based tree, where a GATE-based Named Entity Recogniser (NER) is integrated in the respective NER workflow, the UIMA output of the processing services preceding named entity recognition is converted to the GATE format and is fed to the GATE-compatible NER (e.g. Tokenizer → Splitter → POS-Tagger → UIMA-GATE Converter → NER).

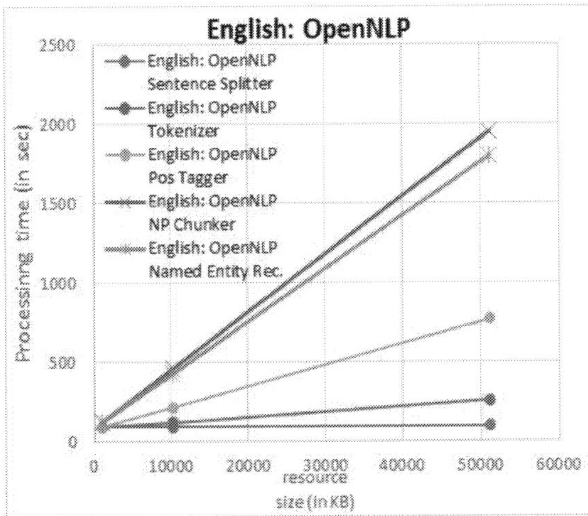

Figure 5: Plot of processing times over resource size for all local English services

Enabling the user to define and deploy custom workflows, cross-suite or not, is on our agenda for the immediate future. The implementation of cross-suite workflows requires the development of several data format converters for each pair of different technologies (e.g. UIMA-GATE, OpenNLP-Panacea/DCU). There are several performance, compatibility and interoperability issues that arise in such cases and have to be investigated and addressed, especially in the light of Language Grid and LAPPS Grid developments (Ide et al., 2014).

Last, but not least, considering the experimental META-SHARE/QT21 repository operations from the legal framework point of view, we have adopted a rather simple operational model by which only openly licensed, with no no-derivatives restriction, datasets can be processed by openly licensed services and workflows. In future versions, in collaboration with other infrastructure providers, we intend to elaborate on a business logic that will allow processing of otherwise licensed datasets and services supporting the appropriate business models.

5 Conclusions and Future Work

The demonstration presented META-SHARE/QT21, a data sharing and annotation service infrastructure. META-SHARE/QT21 is based on META-SHARE, an open-source data infrastructure platform and a language processing layer. The latter is implemented using a widely used integration framework which enables easy creation of data workflows by providing appropriate mechanisms and components for gluing different technologies, services and data sources (XML, txt, TMX). This capability is very useful in a data processing platform, since there is a) an abundance of NLP and machine learning tools implemented (or offered) using different technologies and libraries (e.g. UIMA, GATE, SOAP services, etc.) and b) a variety of data formats (e.g. XCES, TMX). The user evaluation that we conducted has shown that META-SHARE/QT21 can be easily used by NLP researchers for obtaining annotations on a set of resources of various formats. Also a set of stress tests that we conducted revealed that the LP layer can process concurrently a significant amount of data. We are now investigating how data annotation can run on multiple machines in a distributed environment (e.g. Hadoop clusters), thus enabling the processing of large volumes of data.

Acknowledgments

This paper presents work done in the framework of the projects T4ME (GA no. 249119), QTLaunchPad project (GA no. 296347), funded by DG INFSO of the European Commission through the FP7 and ICT-PSP Programmes, and maintained as well as further extended in the framework of the Greek CLARIN Attiki project (MIS 441451), Support for ESFRI/2006 Research Infrastructures, of the Greek Government.

We are grateful to the NLX-Natural Language and Speech Group of the University of Lisbon and its head, Antonio Branco, for kindly providing access to the LX-Center services.

References

Soria, C., Bel, N., Choukri, K., Mariani, J., Monachini, M., Odijk, J., Piperidis, S., Quochi, V., Calzolari, N. (2012). The FLaReNet Strategic Language Resource Agenda. Proceedings of the 8th Language Resources and Evaluation Conference (LREC'12), ELRA.

Gavrilidou, M.; Labropoulou, P.; Desypri, E.; Piperidis, S.; Papageorgiou, H.; Monachini, M.; Frontini, F.; Declerck, T.; Francopoulo, G.; Arranz, V. and Mapelli, V. (2012). The META-SHARE Metadata Schema for the Description of Language Resources. In Nicoletta Calzolari, Khalid Choukri, Thierry Declerck, Mehmet Uğur Doğan, Bente Maegaard, Joseph Mariani, Jan Odijk, Stelios Piperidis (Eds), Proceedings of the Eighth International Conference on Language Resources and Evaluation (LREC'12), 23-25 May, Istanbul, Turkey. European Language Resources Association (ELRA).

Wittenburg, P., Bel, N., Borin, L., Budin, G., Calzolari, N. Hajicova, E. Koskenniemi, K., Lemnitzer, L., Maegaard B., Piasecki, M., Pierrel, J.M., Piperidis, S., Skadina, I., Tufis, D., Veenendaal, R.v ., Váradi, T., Wynne, M. (2010). Resource and Service Centres as the Backbone for a Sustainable Service Infrastructure. Proceedings of the 7th Language Resources and Evaluation Conference (LREC'10), ELRA.

Ishida, T. (Ed) (2011). The Language Grid. Service-Oriented Collective Intelligence for Language Resource Interoperability, Springer

Poch, M., Bel, N. (2011) Interoperability and technology for a language resources factory Workshop on Language Resources, Technology and Services in the Sharing Paradigm – IJCNLP 2011.

Piperidis, S. (2012). The META-SHARE language resources sharing infrastructure: Principles, challenges, solutions. In Proceedings of LREC-2012, pages 36–42, Istanbul, Turkey.

Ide, N., Pustejovsky, J., Cieri, C., Nyberg, E., Wang, D., Suderman, K., Verhagen, M., and Wright, J. (2014) The Language Application Grid. Proceedings of the 9th Language Resources and Evaluation Conference (LREC'14), ELRA

Broeder, D., Kemps-Snijders, M., Van Uytvanck, D., Windhouwer, M., Withers, P., Wittenburg, P. and Zinn, C. (2010). A Data Category Registry- and Component-based Metadata Framework. Proceedings of the 7th Language Resources and Evaluation Conference (LREC'10), ELRA.

Varga, D., Németh, L., Halácsy, A., Kornai,, P., Trón, V., Nagy, V. (2005). Parallel corpora for medium density languages. In Proceedings of the RANLP 2005, pages 590-596.

JoBimViz: A Web-based Visualization for Graph-based Distributional Semantic Models

Eugen Ruppert and **Manuel Kaufmann** and **Martin Riedl** and **Chris Biemann**
FG Language Technology
Computer Science Department, Technische Universität Darmstadt,
Hochschulsstrasse 10, D-62489 Darmstadt, Germany
{eugen.ruppert, riedl, biem}@cs.tu-darmstadt.de, mtk@kisad.de

Abstract

This paper introduces a web-based visualization framework for graph-based distributional semantic models. The visualization supports a wide range of data structures, including term similarities, similarities of contexts, support of multiword expressions, sense clusters for terms and sense labels. In contrast to other browsers of semantic resources, our visualization accepts input sentences, which are subsequently processed with language-independent or language-dependent ways to compute term-context representations. Our web demonstrator currently contains models for multiple languages, based on different preprocessing such as dependency parsing and n-gram context representations. These models can be accessed from a database, the web interface and via a RESTful API. The latter facilitates the quick integration of such models in research prototypes.

1 Introduction

Statistical semantics has emerged as a field of computational linguistics, aiming at automatically computing semantic representations for words, sentences and phrases from (large) corpora. While early approaches to distributional semantics were split into symbolic, graph-based approaches (Lin, 1998) and vector-based approaches (Schütze, 1993), recent trends have mainly concentrated on optimizing the representation of word meanings in vector spaces and how these account for compositionality (cf. Baroni and Lenci (2010); Turney and Pantel (2010)).

While dense vector representations, obtained by singular value decomposition (cf. Rapp (2002)) or neural embeddings (Mikolov et al., 2010), have gained popularity due to successes in modelling semantic and relational similarity, we propose to revisit graph-based approaches to distributional semantics in the tradition of Lin (1998), Curran (2002) and Biemann and Riedl (2013) – at least as an additional alternative – for the following reasons:

- (dense) vector representations are not interpretable, thus it cannot be traced why two terms are similar
- vectors do not make word senses explicit, but represent ambiguous words as a mix of their senses
- graph-based models can be straightforwardly structured and extended, e.g. to represent taxonomic or other relationships

In this demonstration paper, we describe JoBimViz, a visualization and interactive demonstrator for graph-based models of distributional semantics. Our models comprise similarities between terms (a.k.a. distributional thesaurus) and multiword units, similarities between context features, clustered word senses and their labeling with taxonomic is-a relations. The demonstrator transforms input sentences into a term-context representation and allows to browse parts of the underlying model relevant to the sentence at hand. Requests are handled through a RESTful API, which allows to use all available information in custom prototypes via HTTP requests. The demonstrator, as well as the computation of the models, is fully available open source under a permissive license.

Proceedings of ACL-IJCNLP 2015 System Demonstrations, pages 103–108,
Beijing, China, July 26-31, 2015.

2 Related Work

Aside from providing a convenient lookup for human users, the visualization of semantic models provides an important tool for debugging models visually. Additionally, prototyping of semantic applications based on these models is substantially accelerated.

VISUALSYNONYMS[1] and THESAURUS.COM[2] offer lookup possibilities to retrieve various information for input words. Users can view information, like WordNet or Wikipedia definitions and related words (synonyms, hypernyms, etc.). BABELNET[3] (Navigli and Ponzetto, 2012) uses such information to compile multilingual definitions and translations for input words. Here, the words are differentiated by senses, with taxonomical labels. BABELNET offers a SPARQL endpoint and APIs for web access.

SERELEX[4] (Panchenko et al., 2013) is a graphical thesaurus viewer. Users can enter a term for different languages and retrieve related words. The similarity graph displays the similarity links between similar items ('secondary links'). The items can be expanded for a denser graph. The input terms map to nominal phrases, allowing the interface to display short definitions and disambiguations from Wikipedia. An API with JSON output for similar words is provided.

SKETCH ENGINE[5] (Kilgarriff et al., 2004) offers access to pre-processed corpora. For each corpus, the user can view concordances and similar terms (thesaurus) for a given term. SKETCH ENGINE also features statistical information, like word frequency and co-occurrence counts. Furthermore it shows meta information for a corpus. One drawback of the SKETCH ENGINE is that the tools and the models are not freely available.

NETSPEAK[6] (Stein et al., 2010) is a search engine for words in context. Access is possible via a graphical UI, a RESTful interface and a Java API. Users can enter wildcards and other meta symbols into the input phrases and thus retrieve all the words and phrases that occur in a given context. The information is displayed with corpus statistics.

A novel aspect of JOBIMVIZ is that it incorporates several different aspects of symbolic methods (distributional thesaurus, context feature scores, sense clusters), and all of these methods are derived from the input corpus alone, without relying on external resources, which are not available for every language/domain. Furthermore, we provide domain-based sense clusterings with is-a labels (cf. Figure 4), which is not performed by the other discussed tools.

Our interface features a generic interactive visualization that is adaptable to different kinds of parses and also handles multiword units in the visualization. All of this information is made freely available by the API, enabling rapid prototyping techniques. To our knowledge, the presented demonstrator is the only online tool that combines technical accessibility (open source project, open API) with rich, flexible preprocessing options (cf. Section 3) and graph-based, structured semantic models that contain context similarities.

3 Computation of distributional models

The visualization is based on distributional models computed with the JoBimText framework (Biemann and Riedl, 2013)[7]; however it can also be used for other semantic models of similar structure. One of the major components of the framework is a method for the computation of distributional thesauri. This method consists of two steps: a holing operation and a similarity computation.

The holing operation processes text and yields a representation consisting of jos and bims. Jos and bims are normally instantiated by a term (jo) and its context features (bims), but the definition extends to arbitrary splits of the input perception that mutually characterize each other distributionally. The holing operation executes a preprocessing pipeline that can be as simple as text segmentation or complex like POS tagging and dependency parsing, depending on the complexity of the context features. As the preprocessing is defined in UIMA (Ferrucci and Lally, 2004) pipeline descriptors, it is straightforward to exchange components or define new preprocessing operations. Using this processed and annotated text, the holing annotator generates the term–feature representation of the input text, e.g. by using the neighboring words ('trigram holing') or dependency paths

[1]http://www.visualsynonyms.com
[2]http://www.thesaurus.com
[3]http://babelnet.org/
[4]http://serelex.org/
[5]http://www.sketchengine.co.uk/
[6]http://www.netspeak.org/

[7]The framework is available under the permissive ASL 2.0 license at http://sf.net/p/jobimtext.

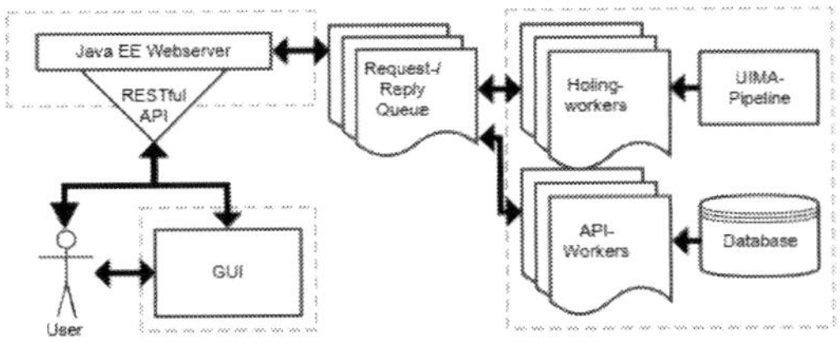

Figure 1: Architecture of JoBimViz, with the three components GUI, Web Server and Workers.

between terms ('dependency holing'). A graphical example is given in Figure 5, where the holing operation yields four context features for the term `example#NN`. Different term representations are possible, like surface text, lemma, lemma+POS and also multiword expressions. This flexibility allows, on the one hand, domain- and language-independent similarity computations using general holing operations, while on the other hand allowing complex, language-specific processing in the holing operations for higher quality models (e.g. using parsing and lemmatization).

The second part consists of the similarity computation, which relies on MapReduce (Dean and Ghemawat, 2004) for scalability and employs efficient pruning strategies to keep runtime feasible even for very large corpora. After the computation of similarities, sense clusters for each term are computed using Chinese Whispers graph clustering (Biemann, 2006), as described in Biemann et al. (2013). Furthermore, the sense clusters are also labeled with hypernyms (is-a relations) derived from Hearst patterns (Hearst, 1992), implemented using the UIMA Ruta (Kluegl et al., 2014) pattern matching engine[8].

4 Web-based Demonstrator

4.1 Architecture and Technology

The architecture of JoBimViz consists of three main components (see Figure 1). The central element is a Java EE based web server, which provides a RESTful interface (Fielding, 2000) for accessing API resources, such as sentence holing operations and the distributional models.

To handle many parallel requests for long running holing operations like dependency parsing, we use an Apache ActiveMQ[9] based request/reply queue. All requests to the web server are stored in the queue and processed by one of the worker processes, which can be distributed on different machines and handle the requests in parallel. These workers form the second component of our system. The holing workers execute the UIMA pipelines that define the holing operations. Usage of UIMA descriptors provides great flexibility, since one type of workers can run every holing operation. Every model defines a custom UIMA pipeline to ensure the same holing operation for the input and the model. To speed up the holing operation we cache frequently queried holing outputs into the in-memory database Redis[10]. Requests to the API are processed by another type of workers, which retrieve the relevant data from the models database.

The third component of the software is a HTML5-based GUI with an overall layout based on the Bootstrap[11] framework. The front-end uses Ajax requests to connect to the RESTful interface of the web server and retrieves responses in the JSON format. The received data is processed by a Javascript application, which uses D3.js (Bostock et al., 2011) to visualize the graphs.

4.2 Visualization

In the demonstrator, users can enter sentences or phrases, run different holing operations on the input and browse distributional models. The demonstrator can be accessed online[12].

Figure 2 shows the application layout. First, the user can decide on the model, which consists of a corpus and a holing operation, and select it via the dropdown holing operation selector (3). Then, the user enters a sentence in the text field (1) and activates the processing by clicking the *Parse* button (2). The holing output is presented as a graph (4) with marked terms and context features. Other views are available in tab bar at the top (5). To retrieve term similarities, a term in the displayed sentence can be selected (4a), activating the information boxes (6, 7, 8, 9). Context similarities can be viewed by selecting the corresponding feature arc (4b). The frequency of the selected term/feature is presented on the top right (6). Similar items are displayed in the first box in the lower pane (7). Similarity scores between

[8] `https://uima.apache.org/ruta.html`
[9] `http://activemq.apache.org/`
[10] `http://redis.io`
[11] `http://www.getbootstrap.com/`
[12] `http://goo.gl/V2ZEly`

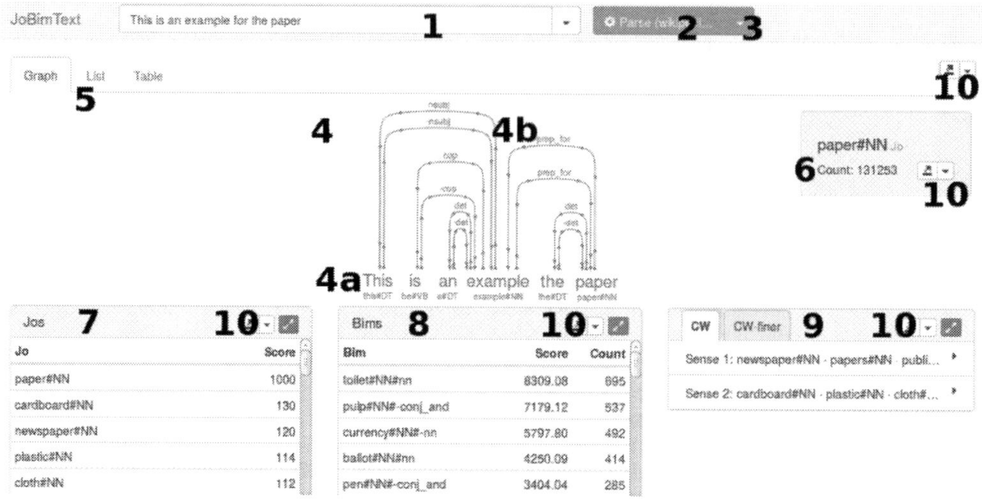

Figure 2: Overview of the visualization with a collapsed dependency parse of the input sentence *This is an example for the paper*; the selected term is *paper#NN*.

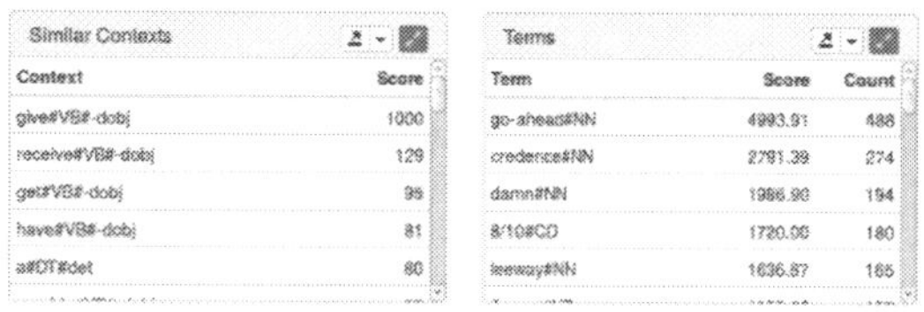

Figure 3: Similar bims (left) and most significant jos (right) for the dependency parse context `give#VB-dobj` (direct object of *give*).

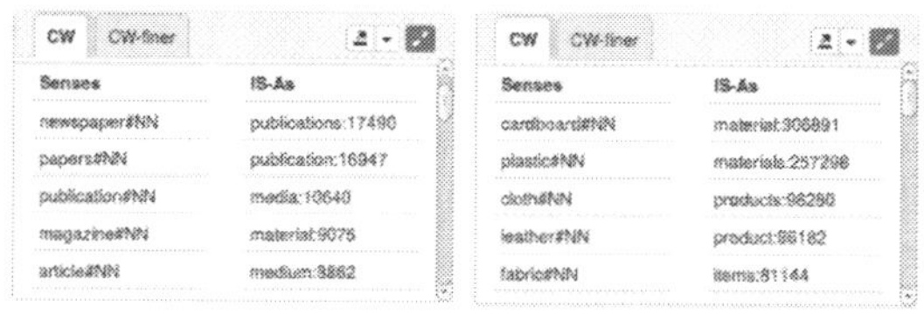

Figure 4: Different word senses for *paper*, with hypernym terms (sense 1 *paper:publication*, sense 2 *paper:material*), as accessed from field (9) in Figure 2. The tabs "CW/CW-finer" provide access to different sense clustering inventories, e.g. with a different granularity.

the selected and similar terms are shown, including self-similarities as an upper limit for similarity of the selected item.

The most relevant context features for the term are displayed with the significance score and their term-feature count in the corpus (8). When selecting a context feature, the most relevant terms for a context feature are shown (cf. Figure 3). For terms, there is a box displaying sense clusters (9). These are often available in different granularities to match the application requirements (e.g. 'CW' or 'CW-finer')[13]. When a user selects a sense cluster, a list of related terms for the selected cluster and a list of hypernyms (is-a relations) with frequency scores are displayed (cf. Figure 4). Buttons for API calls are displayed for all data display in the GUI (10). This enables users to get comfortable with the models and the API before deploying it in an application. The buttons feature selectors for different output data format options, i.e. TSV, XML, JSON and RDF. For the boxes with list content, there is a 'maximize' button next to the API button that brings up a screen-filling overlay.

4.2.1 Sentence Holing Operations

For the graphical representation of holing operations, the web demo offers views for single terms (Figure 5 and 6) as well as support for n-grams (Figure 7). Figure 5 shows the tree representation for a dependency parser using collapsed dependencies. Figure 6 exemplifies a holing operation considering the left and right neighboring words as one context feature ('trigram holing'). Figure 7 shows the result of the same holing operation, applied for n-grams, where several different possible left and right multiword items can be selected as context. Here, the demonstrator identified mul-

[13]Here, 'CW' is referring to sense clusters computed with Chinese Whispers (Biemann, 2006).

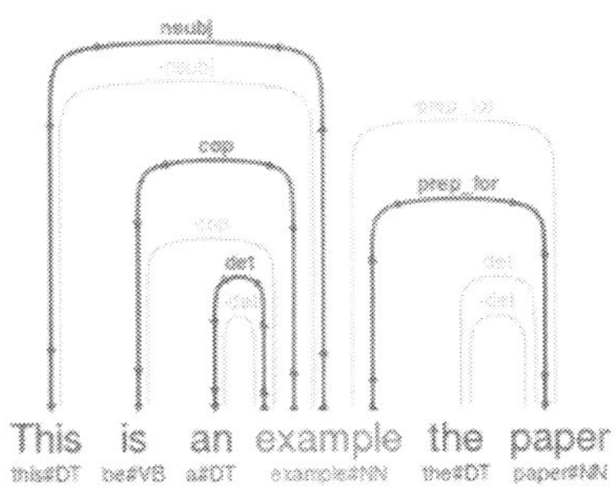

Figure 5: Collapsed dependency (de Marneffe et al., 2006) holing result for *This is an example for the paper*; the preposition *for* is collapsed into the `prep_for` dependency.

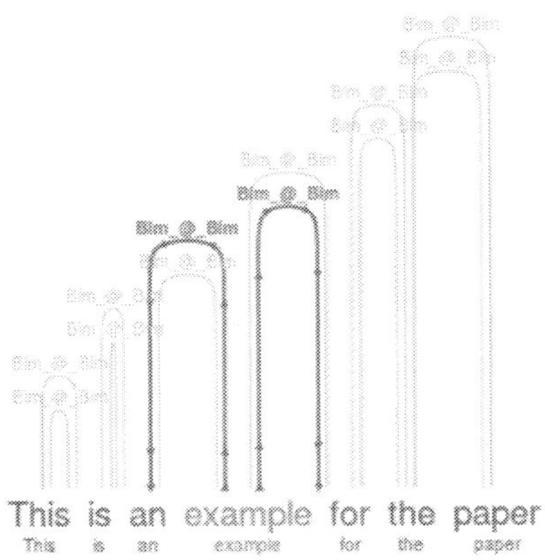

Figure 6: Trigram holing (unigram) result for *This is an example for the paper*.

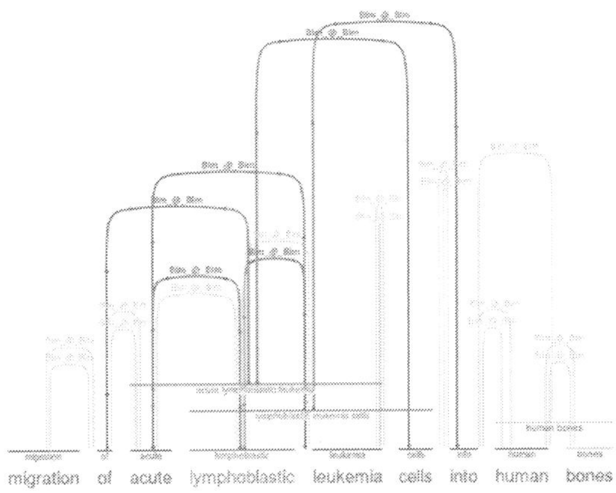

Figure 7: Trigram holing (n-gram) result for *migration of acute lymphoblastic leukemia cells into human bones* with display of multiwords that are part of the model.

tiword expressions that are present in the corresponding distributional model (*acute lymphoblastic leukemia, lymphoblastic leukemia cells* and *human bones*). These expressions can be selected like single word items. Furthermore, there is a filtering function for n-grams, where users can refine the display of n-grams by selecting the desired n-gram lengths.

4.2.2 Model Access

The demonstrator features a selection of models for different languages (currently: German, English, Hindi, Bengali) and different domains, like news, encyclopedia or medical domain. Besides term similarities, typical context features and sense clusters are also part of these models. Distributional similarities for context features can be viewed as well. By selecting an arc that represents the feature relation, the user can view similar features in the GUI. In Figure 3, the context features that are most similar to `give#VB#-dobj` (direct object of verb *give*) are displayed. Here, the most significant words for a feature are shown. To our knowledge, we are the first ones to explicitly provide similarities of contexts in distributional semantic models.

Holing operations and models can be accessed via an open RESTful API. The access URIs contain the model identifier (consisting of dataset and holing operation), the desired method, like sentence holing or similar terms, and the input sentence, term or context feature. The distributional project also features a Java API to access models via the web-based API[14].

5 Conclusion and Future Work

In this paper we have introduced a new web-based tool that can be used to browse and to access graph-based semantic models based on distributional semantics. In its current form, it can display data from a distributional thesaurus, similarities of context features, sense clusters labeled with taxonomic relations, and provides the display of multiword expressions. Additionally, it provides the functionality to transform sentences into term–context representations. The web demo can give a first impression for people who are interested in the JoBimText framework for distributional semantics. Providing a RESTful interface for accessing all information with state-

[14]For an overview of available API methods, see `http://goo.gl/16K6Gu`.

less requests allows for an easy integration into prototypes. The RESTful API can also be accessed using our Java API, which also can access other back-ends such as on-disk and in-memory databases. The complete project is available under the permissive Apache ASL 2.0 license and models for several languages are available for download[15].

Whereas at the moment similar terms are globally ranked, we will add visualization support for a contextualization method, in order to rank similar terms regarding their context within the sentence. Furthermore, we are working on incorporating more complex pre-processing for the holing operation in the visualization, e.g. aggregating context features over co-reference chains, as well as relation extraction and frame-semantic parsing for term–context representations.

Acknowledgments

This work has been supported by the German Federal Ministry of Education and Research (BMBF) within the context of the Software Campus project *LiCoRes* under grant No. 01IS12054 and by an IBM Shared University Research award.

References

Marco Baroni and Alessandro Lenci. 2010. Distributional memory: A general framework for corpus-based semantics. *Computational Linguistics*, 36(4):673–721.

Chris Biemann and Martin Riedl. 2013. Text: Now in 2D! a framework for lexical expansion with contextual similarity. *Journal of Language Modelling*, 1(1):55–95.

Chris Biemann, Bonaventura Coppola, Michael R. Glass, Alfio Gliozzo, Matthew Hatem, and Martin Riedl. 2013. JoBimText Visualizer: A graph-based approach to contextualizing distributional similarity. In *Proc. TextGraphs 2013*, pages 6–10, Seattle, Washington, USA.

Chris Biemann. 2006. Chinese Whispers – an efficient graph clustering algorithm and its application to natural language processing problems. In *Proc. TextGraphs 2006*, pages 73–80, New York City, NY, USA.

Michael Bostock, Vadim Ogievetsky, and Jeffrey Heer. 2011. D3: Data-driven documents. *IEEE Transactions on Visualization & Computer Graphics*, 17(12):2301–2309.

James R. Curran. 2002. Ensemble methods for automatic thesaurus extraction. In *Proc. EMNLP'02/ACL-2002*, pages 222–229, Philadelphia, PA, USA.

[15]Selection of models available under `http://sf.net/projects/jobimtext/files/data/models/`.

Marie-Catherine de Marneffe, Bill MacCartney, and Christopher D. Manning. 2006. Generating typed dependency parses from phrase structure parses. In *Proc. LREC-2006*, pages 449–454, Genova, Italy.

Jeffrey Dean and Sanjay Ghemawat. 2004. MapReduce: Simplified Data Processing on Large Clusters. In *Proc. OSDI '04*, pages 137–150, San Francisco, CA, USA.

David Ferrucci and Adam Lally. 2004. UIMA: An Architectural Approach to Unstructured Information Processing in the Corporate Research Environment. *Natural Language Engineering*, 10(3-4):327–348.

Roy Thomas Fielding. 2000. *Architectural Styles and the Design of Network-based Software Architectures*. Doctoral dissertation, University of California, Irivne.

Marti A. Hearst. 1992. Automatic acquisition of hyponyms from large text corpora. In *Proc. COLING-1992*, pages 539–545, Nantes, France.

Adam Kilgarriff, Pavel Rychlý, Pavel Smrž, and David Tugwell. 2004. The Sketch Engine. In *Proc. EURALEX 2004*, pages 105–116, Lorient, France.

Peter Kluegl, Martin Toepfer, Philip-Daniel Beck, Georg Fette, and Frank Puppe. 2014. UIMA Ruta: Rapid development of rule-based information extraction applications. *Natural Language Engineering*.

Dekang Lin. 1998. Automatic retrieval and clustering of similar words. In *Proc. COLING-98*, pages 768–774, Montréal, Quebec, Canada.

Tomas Mikolov, Martin Karafiát, Lukas Burget, Jan Cernockỳ, and Sanjeev Khudanpur. 2010. Recurrent neural network based language model. In *Proc. INTERSPEECH 2010*, pages 1045–1048, Makuhari, Chiba, Japan.

Roberto Navigli and Simone P. Ponzetto. 2012. BabelNet: The automatic construction, evaluation and application of a wide-coverage multilingual semantic network. *Artificial Intelligence*, 193:217–250.

Alexander Panchenko, Pavel Romanov, Olga Morozova, Hubert Naets, Andrey Philippovich, Alexey Romanov, and Fairon Cédrick. 2013. Serelex: Search and visualization of semantically related words. In *Proc. ECIR 2013*, pages 837–840, Moscow, Russia.

Reinhard Rapp. 2002. The computation of word associations: Comparing syntagmatic and paradigmatic approaches. In *Proc. COLING '02*, pages 1–7, Taipei, Taiwan.

Hinrich Schütze. 1993. Word space. In *Advances in Neural Information Processing Systems 5*, pages 895–902, Denver, Colorado, USA.

Benno Stein, Martin Potthast, and Martin Trenkmann. 2010. Retrieving Customary Web Language to Assist Writers. In *Advances in Information Retrieval, ECIR 10*, pages 631–635, Milton Keynes, UK.

Peter D. Turney and Patrick Pantel. 2010. From frequency to meaning: Vector space models of semantics. *Journal of artificial intelligence research*, 37(1):141–188.

End-to-end Argument Generation System in Debating

Misa Sato Kohsuke Yanai Toshihiko Yanase
Toshinori Miyoshi Makoto Iwayama Qinghua Sun Yoshiki Niwa
Hitachi Ltd. Research & Development Group
1-280, Higashi-koigakubo, Kokubunji-shi, Tokyo 185-8601 Japan
{misa.sato.mw, kohsuke.yanai.cs, toshihiko.yanase.gm,
toshinori.miyoshi.pd, makoto.iwayama.nw,
qinghua.sun.ap, yoshiki.niwa.tx}@hitachi.com

Abstract

We introduce an argument generation system in debating, one that is based on sentence retrieval. Users can specify a motion such as *This house should ban gambling*, and a stance on whether the system *agrees* or *disagrees* with the motion. Then the system outputs three argument paragraphs based on "values" automatically decided by the system. The "value" indicates a topic that is considered as a positive or negative for people or communities, such as *health* and *education*. Each paragraph is related to one value and composed of about seven sentences. An evaluation over 50 motions from a popular debate website showed that the generated arguments are understandable in 64 paragraphs out of 150.

1 Introduction

This paper describes our end-to-end argument generation system, developed to participate in English debating games as an AI debater. When users give a "motion" like *This house should ban gambling* and a "stance" on whether the system should *agree* or *disagree* with the motion, the system generates argument scripts in the first constructive round of a debate.

Among NLP communities, interest is growing in argumentation, such as argumentation mining and claim detection (Levy et al., 2014; Mizuno et al., 2012; Park et al., 2014). However, argument generation is still as hard a task as other text generation tasks; no standard methods or systems exist, as far as we know.

We assume that argument generation systems are helpful in a variety of decision-making situations such as business, law, politics and medical care. This is because people usually investigate existing arguments on the Internet, newspapers, or research papers before reaching conclusions. In this research, we focus on debating game style because there is similarity in argument construction between debating games and actual decision-making.

The difficulty in argument generation is that argument scripts have to be *persuasive*. We explain this need by comparing argument generation with multi-document summarization. In the two tasks, one practical approach is combining partial texts retrieved from multiple documents. Generated scripts in both tasks should be natural and have sufficient content. Because the summarization task is to generate summary scripts of multiple documents, the essential basis of its evaluation is coverage, that is, how much content in the original documents is included in the generated scripts. However, as the role of argument scripts is to persuade people, *persuasiveness* is more important than coverage.

We believe that the following three points are required to generate persuasive argument scripts:

1. Consistency with a given stance
2. Cause and effect relationships
3. Relevance to people's values

For example, when debaters focus on an *agree* stance with a motion of *This house should ban gambling*, one persuasive argument would discuss the negative effects of *gambling*. To reach a discussion about the negative effects under this condition, we need to consider the three points.

1. Consistency means that the stance of argument scripts must be equal to the given stance and consistent in the overall arguments. For example, because the gambling motion implies the claim that *gambling is negative*, the generated argument should include only negative aspects of gambling.

2. Causality makes argumentation persuasive. To capture causality, we focus on promoting/suppressing relationships. Hashimoto et

Proceedings of ACL-IJCNLP 2015 System Demonstrations, pages 109–114,
Beijing, China, July 26-31, 2015.

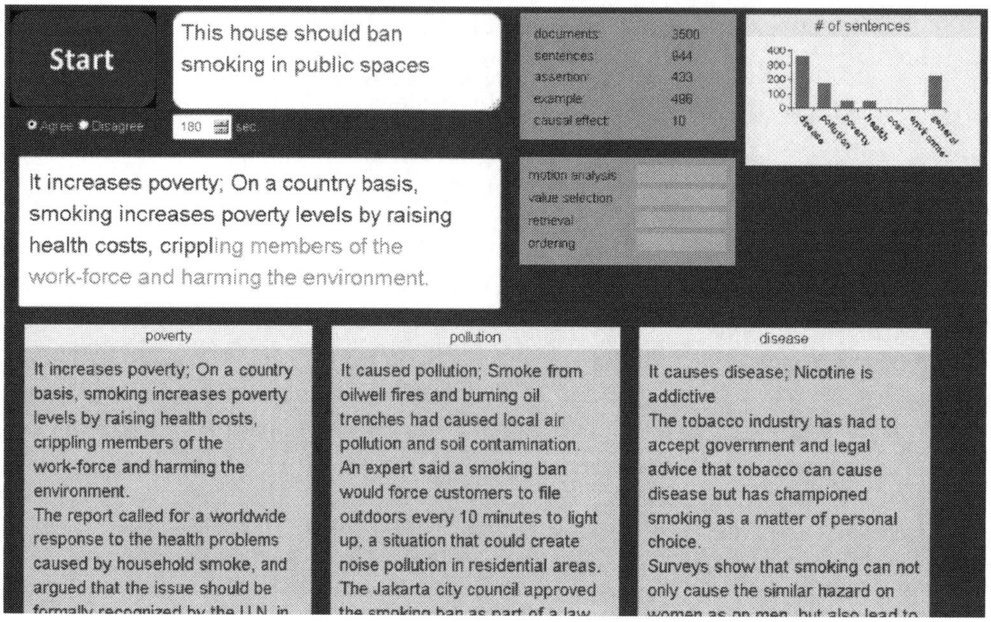

Figure 1: Screenshot and Sample Input & Output Script

al. (2012) also showed that the relationships are useful for causality extractions. The claim *gambling promotes negative issues* would be persuasive in an argumentation that agrees with a ban on gambling.

3. Values There are topics obviously considered to be positive or negative and highly relevant to people's values. For instance, *health*, *education* and *natural environment* are considered to be positive values, while *crime*, *pollution* and *high cost* are considered to be negative. It is possible to generate scripts about negative effects by collecting partial texts describing negative values linked to *gambling*, such as *crime*.

2 Overview

2.1 Demo Description

Visitors will have the opportunity to select a motion and a stance and to run the system to generate argument scripts automatically.

Each argument script generated by the system consists of three topics corresponding to values, such as *health*, *education* and *revenue*. This approach comes from our observations that persuasive arguments would be related to multiple values. Figure 1 shows the interface of the system and an example of generated argument scripts. First, users give text scripts about the "motion" and select the "stance" whether *agree* or *disagree*. In the figure, the given motion is *This house should ban smoking in public spaces*, and the given stance is an *agree* side. When users click the start button, the system begins processing. Users can see how many sentences or documents are processed and how many sentences belong to each value in the graphs in the upper right corner. Finally, the system provides three generated paragraphs with their value titles such as *poverty*, *pollution*, and *disease* while the generated argument scripts are read aloud by our text-to-speech system.

2.2 System Overview

Figure 2 shows the overview of the system.

As discussed above, the key of constructing arguments is to find positive/negative effects of a target in the motion. In this paper, we call the target "a motion keyphrase".

Positive/negative effects appear in the form of *affect* relationships like *something affects something*. Main elements of arguments are sentences that contain *affect* relationships whose subject is a motion keyphrase and whose object represents a value.

We have two types of affect predicates: *affect+* and *affect−*. *Affect+* means a promoting predicate such as *create, enhance, expand, improve, increase*. On the other hand, *affect−* means a sup-

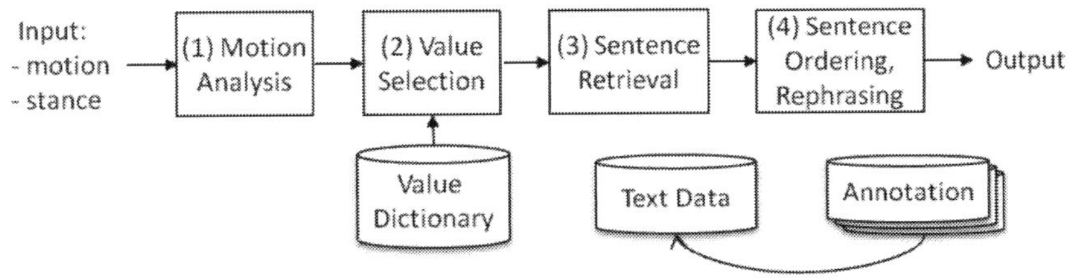

Figure 2: System Overview

pressing predicate such as *decrease, discourage, eliminate, limit, threaten*. The system stored the affect relationships in text data as automatically added annotations described in Section 4.

Though the system consists of 21 algorithms, we describe four main components in this paper:

(1) A motion analysis component decides a motion keyphrase and a polarity of arguments to be generated.

(2) A value selection component decides multiple values relevant to the given motion by retrieving sentences that contain *affect* relationships.

(3) A sentence retrieval component retrieves sentences relevant to each value from the stored text data.

(4) A sentence ordering and rephrasing component combines and arranges the retrieved sentences to construct natural argument scripts.

They are processed in a pipeline and some of the algorithms are processed in parallel on a cluster of 10 machines. We describe key functions of the components in Section 3.

The system uses large text data from Gigaword corpus (Napoles et al., 2012) and the annotations to the text data. The annotations are added automatically in a preprocessing step. Section 4 describes what kinds of annotations exploited in the system. The text and annotation data are stored using Cassandra[1], which is an open-source database management system designed for handling large amounts of data across commodity servers. They are indexed into Solr[2], open source enterprise search platform, that enables full-text search.

2.3 Evaluation

We evaluated the generated argument scripts on the basis of subjective evaluations.

[1]Cassandra: http://cassandra.apache.org

[2]Apache Solr: http://lucene.apache.org/solr

Table 1: Evaluation Results

Evaluation Score	Num of paragraphs
0: make-no-sense	86
1: understandable	38
2: +clear	16
3: +persuasive	10
4: +natural	0

We used 50 motions from a popular debate website *Debatabase* [3] as inputs to the system. The system outputs three paragraphs per motion, and each paragraph is composed of seven sentences, totaling 150 paragraphs for 50 motions. The paragraphs are rated by authors on a five point scale ranging from 0 to 4. Each evaluator judges 30 paragraphs in 10 motions. The paragraphs that do not include any claims or supporting evidence related to the motion, are given a rating of 0 points. A 1 point rating is given when the argument is understood by the evaluator, despite a number of irrelevant sentences. If more than four of the seven sentences in the paragraph are relevant to the given motion and consistent to the stance, it is given a 2 point rating. If the evaluator feels it is persuasive, it is given a 3 point rating. When it satisfies the above conditions and is presented as a natural argument, it is given a 4 point rating.

Table 1 shows the results. We found that the argumentations are understandable in 64 paragraphs (= 38+16+10+0) out of 150.

3 Pipeline Components

3.1 Motion Analysis Component

In the beginning of processing, the system analyzes the given motion text, and extracts a keyphrase, a motion polarity, a predicate, an attitude, and contexts. A predicate is a phrase which gives positive/negative sign to a keyphrase, and an

[3]Debatabase: http://idebate.org/debatabase

Table 2: Motion Analysis Results

motion	keyphrase	pol.	predicate	attitude	contexts
This house believes that casino is harmful for the city	*casino*	-1	*harmful*	*believe*	*the city*
This house would create a single EU army	*a single EU army*	$+1$	–	*create*	–
This house should ban gambling	*gambling*	-1	–	*ban*	–
This house believes that assisted suicide should be legalized	*assisted suicide*	$+1$	–	*legalize*	–

Table 3: Motion Analysis Rules. K = motion keyphrase, C = contexts.

priority	rule	predicate instances
1	K be **modify**-ed for C	**modify**: *good*$(+1)$, *honor*$(+1)$, *popular*$(+1)$, *harmful*(-1), *negative*(-1), *weak*(-1)
2	**affect** K	**affect**: *create*$(+1)$, *enhance*$(+1)$, *increase*$(+1)$, *cut*(-1), *discourage*(-1), *eliminate*(-1)
3	**believe** K	**believe**: *allow*$(+1)$, *legalize*$(+1)$, *permit*$(+1)$, *support*$(+1)$, *ban*(-1), *oppose*(-1)
4	K be **believe**-ed	**believe**: *allow*$(+1)$, *legalize*$(+1)$, *permit*$(+1)$, *support*$(+1)$, *ban*(-1), *oppose*(-1)
...	...	...

attitude is a predicate of *this house*. Table 2 shows results of motion analysis.

To analyze a motion, the system has 22 rules with their priority. Table 3 shows a part of the rules. The rules are applied in the order by their priority, until a motion keyphrase is extracted.

Suppose that the given motion is *This house believes that casino is harmful for the city* and the given stance is *agree*$(+1)$ (corresponding to the first line of Table 2). The first rule "K be **modify**-ed for C" in Table 3 matches the motion. As *harmful* is a *modifying* predicate, *casinos* is K and *the city* is C. An attitude of *this house* is *believe*. A motion polarity is -1 because of the negative predicate *harmful*(-1). In the same way, from the second to the fourth rules in Table 3 can analyze the other three motion examples in Table 2.

The system calculates an argument polarity by multiplying the sign of the given stance and the motion polarity. The system constructs arguments that discuss the motion keyphrase, in accordance with the argument polarity. For example, if the given stance is *agree*$(+1)$ and the motion polarity is *negative*(-1), then the system decides an argument polarity is -1 and constructs arguments that claim "the motion keyphrase is negative(-1)".

3.2 Value Selection Component

The value selection component decides multiple values relevant to the given motion by using a value dictionary. The value dictionary formulates a set of values that represents what is important in human's life, what is harmful in communities, etc. Each value is regarded as a viewpoint of the generated argument.

Table 4 describes an example of the value dictionary. As shown in Table 4, each value (e.g., disease, investment) belongs to a field (e.g., health, economy, respectively), and has three attributes: a value polarity, representative phrases, and context phrases. The value polarity $+1(-1)$ means that the value is something good(bad). The representative phrases are linguistic expressions of the values, and the numbers are their weights calculated by IDF in Gigaword corpus. The context phrases are phrases that are likely to appear in neighbor of the value in text documents. They are used to solve ambiguity of the linguistic expressions. The value dictionary of the current system contains 16 fields and 61 values.

The procedure of the value selection is below:

Step 1 Retrieves sentences that contain affect relationships between the motion keyphrase and one of representative phrases in the value dictionary. For instance, it retrieves *Gambling increases the number of crimes*.

Step 2 Calculates a polarity to the keyphrase in each sentence, and filters out the sentences where the polarity is not equivalent to the argument polarity. For instance, the polarity for *Gambling increases the number of crimes* is -1 by multiplying $+1$ (*increase* in the affect dictionary) and -1 (*crime* in the value dictionary), which equals to the argument polarity.

Step 3 Sums weights of found values and selects the top five values.

The value dictionary was created manually. First, fields of the dictionary were determined by the authors in reference to the roles of government agencies, and then value entries related to each field were chosen manually from Debatabase. Second, a rule-based extractor that extracts values discussed in a document was constructed using the dictionary, and the extractor applied to each docu-

Table 4: Value Dictionary

field	value	polarity	representative phrases	context phrases
economy	investment	$+1$	investment:27.8, development_aid:48.2	asset, bank, capital, fund, profit, stock, ...
finance	cost	-1	expense:35.9, expenditure:55.7	budget, dollar, fuel, lower, price, share, ...
finance	income	$+1$	revenue:35.4, wage:39.8	budget, company, earnings, higher, gain, ...
health	disease	-1	disease:36.6, complication:40.1	AIDS, Alzheimer, blood, cancer, death, ...
safety	crime	-1	crime:31.5, prostitution:56.2	arrest, gun, jail, kidnapping, victim, ...
...	...	...	...	...

ment in Debatabase. Third, we manually added new entries to the dictionary. If a value is extracted from a document, we extracted representative/context phrases corresponding to the value from the document. If no value is extracted, we extracted new values that were contained in the document. We continued these steps of classifying documents and adding entries to the dictionary like a Bootstrapping method.

3.3 Sentence Retrieval Component

This component retrieves sentences relevant to each value from the stored text data.

It first retrieves documents using a query composed of weighted phrases. The retrieved documents should contain both the motion keyphrase and more than one representative phrases of the decided values. While the motion keyphrases can be replaced with their synonyms or hyponyms, their weights are smaller than the original keyphrases; those of synonyms are 0.75 and those of hyponyms are 0.5. The synonyms and hyponyms are acquired by WordNet (Miller, 1995). Because short documents don't usually contains informative scripts, the length of retrieved documents are limited to more than 200 words.

For example, when the motion keyphrase is *gambling*, a search query for a *health* value is

```
(gambling#49.53 OR gaming#22.87)
AND (health#27.48 OR disease#36.60
  OR addiction#52.39
  OR hospital#29.76)
AND (length:[200 TO *]).
```

The real numbers following sharp signs are weights of the former phrases, calculated by multiplying the IDF of the phrase and a synonym or hyponym reduction rate.

The retrieval step prefers sentences that contain promote/suppress relationships. The polarities of the retrieved sentences must be equal to the argument polarity. The polarity of each sentence is calculated by the product of the signs of related phrases, such as the predicate of the keyphrase, the promote/suppress verb, and the representative value phrase. In the example of *gambling ban*(-1) *decrease*(-1) *the number of crimes*(-1), the polarity of the sentence is -1.

The system uses about 10,000,000 newswire documents and retrieves 500 per value in this step.

3.4 Sentence Ordering and Rephrasing Component

This component processes the sentence set of each value separately.

The sentence ordering step orders the retrieved sentences in the natural order in debating by the method reported in (Yanase et al., 2015). The method employs an assumpsion that a constructive speech item in debating consists of a claim sentence and one or more supporting sentences, and that the claim sentence lies in the first position of the paragraph. The assumption is implemented as two machine learning problems: claim sentence selection and supporting sentence ordering. The claim sentence selection problem is formulated as a binary-classification problem where a given sentence is a claim or not. In the supporting sentence ordering problem, the method orders the other sentences on the basis of connectivity of pairs of sentences. This problem is formulated as a ranking problem, similarly to (Tan et al., 2013). Features for machine learning models in both problems are extracted not only from the sentences to be ordered but also from the motion text.

Finally, the rephrasing step trims or replaces surplus phrases referring to too many details for argument scripts, such as dates and people's names. Several simple rules are used.

4 Data Preprocessing: Annotations

The system adds annotations automatically in preprocessing into the stored text data by using dictionaries and syntax information by Stanford Core NLP (Manning et al., 2014). In the current system, about 250 million annotations are stored. Users can add the annotations manually. A list of main semantic annotations is below:

affect: promoting/suppressing relationships. For example, it adds an annotation of "affect+: *casino* → *the number of crimes*" into a text *casino increases the number of crimes*. The affect dictionary, which is manually created, contains 608 positive phrases and 371 negative phrases.

modify: phrases which gives positive/negative sign to words governed by them. For example, it adds an annotation of "modify−: *environment*" into a text *harmful environment*. The modification dictionary contains 79 positive phrases and 134 negative phrases.

believe: relationships which represents attitudes of a subject to its object. For example, it adds an annotation of "believe−: *smoking*" into a text *The government bans smoking in public spaces* because of a negative believe phrase *ban*. The believe dictionary contains 30 positive phrases, 47 negative phrases and 15 neutral phrases.

5 Error Analysis

We describe three major problems of the system here: (1) identification errors, (2) polarity errors, (3) motion format limitation.

(1) Identification errors occur on recognizing a motion keyphrase in text data on sentence retrieval step. The system can incorrectly retrieve sentences including mentions whose expressions are the same as or similar to the motion keyphrase but different in their meanings. In the screenshot of Figure 1, for example, although "smoking" in the motion refers to "tobacco smoking," the first sentence in the *pollution* paragraph argues about "smoking caused by a fire."

The identification problem is especially obvious in the case a motion keyphrase forms a compound noun. For instance, on the motion of *This House should ban cosmetic surgery*, it is not clear if *surgery* in some text is equal to *cosmetic surgery* or not. The errors would show requirements of more precise word sense disambiguation or coreference resolution among multiple documents.

(2) Polarity errors are not so rare. Regarding the *disease* paragraph in Figure 1, the second sentence would contain an argument on the opposite stance in error.

(3) Motion format limitation is that the system can process only motions in formats which ask people if its motion keyphrase should be banned or permitted. Representative examples of unacceptable motions are comparison like *This house believes that capitalism is better than socialism* and questions of an adequate degree like *This House should lower the drinking age.*

6 Conclusion

We described a demonstration of our argument generation system. Our system can generate understandable arguments on a given motion for a given stance. Our next work is to generate counterarguments, which argue against the opponents.

Acknowledgments

We would like to thank Prof. Kentaro Inui from Tohoku University for valuable discussion.

References

Chikara Hashimoto, Kentaro Torisawa and Stijn De Saeger. 2012. *Excitatory or Inhibitory: A New Semantic Orientation Extracts Contradiction and Causality from the Web*, In *Proceedings of EMNLP-CoNLL 2012*, pages 619–630.

Christopher D. Manning, Mihai Surdeanu, John Bauer, Jenny Finkel, Steven J. Bethard and David McClosky. 2014. *The Stanford CoreNLP Natural Language Processing Toolkit*, In *Proceedings of ACL 2014 System Demonstrations*, pages 55–60.

George A. Miller. 1995. *WordNet: A Lexical Database for English* In *Communications of the ACM*, 38(11): pages 39–41.

Joonsuk Park and Claire Cardie. 2014. *Identifying Appropriate Support for Propositions in Online User Comments* In *Proceedings of the First Workshop on Argumentation Mining*, pages 29–38.

Junta Mizuno, Eric Nichols, Yotaro Watanabe and Kentaro Inui. 2012. *Organizing Information on the Web through Agreement-Conflict Relation Classification* In *Proceedings of the Eighth Asia Information Retrieval Societies Conference* , pages 126–137.

Napoles, Courtney, Matthew Gormley and Benjamin Van Durme. 2012. *Annotated English Gigaword LDC2012T21*. Web Download, Philadelphia: Linguistic Data Consortium.

Ran Levy, Yonatan Bilu, Daniel Hershcovich, Ehud Aharoni and Noam Slonim. 2014. *Context Dependent Claim Detection* In *Proceedings of COLING 2014: Technical Papers*, pages 1489–1500.

Jiwei Tan, XiaojunWan and Jianguo Xiao 2013. *Learning to order natural language texts* In *Proceedings of the 51st Annual Meeting of the Association for Computational Linguistics*, pages 87-91.

Toshihiko Yanase, Toshinori Miyoshi, Kohsuke Yanai, Misa Sato, Makoto Iwayama, Yoshiki Niwa, Paul Reisert and Kentaro Inui 2015. *Learning Sentence Ordering for Opinion Generation of Debate* In *Proceedings of the 2nd Workshop on Argumentation Mining*, pages 94–103.

Multi-level Translation Quality Prediction with QuEst++

Lucia Specia, Gustavo Henrique Paetzold and **Carolina Scarton**
Department of Computer Science
University of Sheffield, UK
{l.specia,ghpaetzold1,c.scarton}@sheffield.ac.uk

Abstract

This paper presents QuEst++ , an open source tool for quality estimation which can predict quality for texts at word, sentence and document level. It also provides pipelined processing, whereby predictions made at a lower level (e.g. for words) can be used as input to build models for predictions at a higher level (e.g. sentences). QuEst++ allows the extraction of a variety of features, and provides machine learning algorithms to build and test quality estimation models. Results on recent datasets show that QuEst++ achieves state-of-the-art performance.

1 Introduction

Quality Estimation (QE) of Machine Translation (MT) have become increasingly popular over the last decade. With the goal of providing a prediction on the quality of a machine translated text, QE systems have the potential to make MT more useful in a number of scenarios, for example, improving post-editing efficiency (Specia, 2011), selecting high quality segments (Soricut and Echihabi, 2010), selecting the best translation (Shah and Specia, 2014), and highlighting words or phrases that need revision (Bach et al., 2011).

Most recent work focuses on sentence-level QE. This variant is addressed as a supervised machine learning task using a variety of algorithms to induce models from examples of sentence translations annotated with quality labels (e.g. 1-5 *likert* scores). Sentence-level QE has been covered in shared tasks organised by the Workshop on Statistical Machine Translation (WMT) annually since 2012. While standard algorithms can be used to build prediction models, key to this task is work of feature engineering. Two open source feature extraction toolkits are available for that: Asiya[1] and QuEst[2] (Specia et al., 2013). The latter has been used as the official baseline for the WMT shared tasks and extended by a number of participants, leading to improved results over the years (Callison-Burch et al., 2012; Bojar et al., 2013; Bojar et al., 2014).

QE at other textual levels have received much less attention. Word-level QE (Blatz et al., 2004; Luong et al., 2014) is seemingly a more challenging task where a quality label is to be produced for each target word. An additional challenge is the acquisition of sizable training sets. Although significant efforts have been made, there is considerable room for improvement. In fact, most WMT13-14 QE shared task submissions were unable to beat a trivial baseline.

Document-level QE consists in predicting a single label for entire documents, be it an absolute score (Scarton and Specia, 2014) or a relative ranking of translations by one or more MT systems (Soricut and Echihabi, 2010). While certain sentences are perfect in isolation, their combination in context may lead to an incoherent document. Conversely, while a sentence can be poor in isolation, when put in context, it may benefit from information in surrounding sentences, leading to a good quality document. Feature engineering is a challenge given the little availability of tools to extract discourse-wide information. In addition, no datasets with human-created labels are available and thus scores produced by automatic metrics have to be used as approximation (Scarton et al., 2015).

Some applications require fine-grained, word-level information on quality. For example, one may want to highlight words that need fixing. Document-level QE is needed particularly for gisting purposes where post-editing is not an option.

[1] http://nlp.lsi.upc.edu/asiya/
[2] http://www.quest.dcs.shef.ac.uk/

Proceedings of ACL-IJCNLP 2015 System Demonstrations, pages 115–120,
Beijing, China, July 26-31, 2015.

For example, for predictions on translations of product reviews in order to decide whether or not they are understandable by readers. We believe that the limited progress in word and document-level QE research is partially due to lack of a basic framework that one can be build upon and extend.

QUEST++ is a significantly refactored and expanded version of an existing open source sentence-level toolkit, QUEST. Feature extraction modules for both word and document-level QE were added and the three levels of prediction were unified into a single pipeline, allowing for interactions between word, sentence and document-level QE. For example, word-level predictions can be used as features for sentence-level QE. Finally, sequence-labelling learning algorithms for word-level QE were added. QUEST++ can be easily extended with new features at any textual level. The architecture of the system is described in Section 2. Its main component, the feature extractor, is presented in Section 3. Section 4 presents experiments using the framework with various datasets.

2 Architecture

QUEST++ has two main modules: a feature extraction module and a machine learning module. The first module is implemented in Java and provides a number of feature extractors, as well as abstract classes for features, resources and pre-processing steps so that extractors for new features can be easily added. The basic functioning of the feature extraction module requires raw text files with the source and translation texts, and a few resources (where available) such as the MT source training corpus and source and target language models (LMs). Configuration files are used to indicate paths for resources and the features that should be extracted. For its main resources (e.g. LMs), if a resource is missing, QUEST++ can generate it automatically.

Figure 1 depicts the architecture of QUEST++ . *Document* and *Paragraph* classes are used for document-level feature extraction. A *Document* is a group of *Paragraphs*, which in turn is a group of *Sentences*. *Sentence* is used for both word- and sentence-level feature extraction. A *Feature Processing Module* was created for each level. Each processing level is independent and can deal with the peculiarities of its type of feature.

Machine learning QUEST++ provides scripts to interface the Python toolkit `scikit-learn`[3] (Pedregosa et al.,). This module is independent from the feature extraction code and uses the extracted feature sets to build and test QE models. The module can be configured to run different regression and classification algorithms, feature selection methods and grid search for hyper-parameter optimisation. Algorithms from `scikit-learn` can be easily integrated by modifying existing scripts.

For word-level prediction, QUEST++ provides an interface for `CRFSuite` (Okazaki, 2007), a sequence labelling C++ library for Conditional Random Fields (CRF). One can configure CRFSuite training settings, produce models and test them.

3 Features

Features in QUEST++ can be extracted from either source or target (or both) sides of the corpus at a given textual level. In order describe the features supported, we denote:

- S and T the source and target *documents*,
- **s** and **t** for source and target *sentences*, and
- s and t for source and target *words*.

We concentrate on MT system-independent (*black-box*) features, which are extracted based on the output of the MT system rather than any of its internal representations. These allow for more flexible experiments and comparisons across MT systems. System-dependent features can be extracted as long they are represented using a predefined XML scheme. Most of the existing features are either language-independent or depend on linguistic resources such as POS taggers. The latter can be extracted for any language, as long as the resource is available. For a pipelined approach, predictions at a given level can become features for higher level model, e.g. features based on word-level predictions for sentence-level QE.

3.1 Word level

We explore a range of features from recent work (Bicici and Way, 2014; Camargo de Souza et al., 2014; Luong et al., 2014; Wisniewski et al., 2014), totalling 40 features of seven types:

Target context These are features that explore the context of the target word. Given a word t_i in position i of a target sentence, we extract: t_i,

[3] `http://scikit-learn.org/`

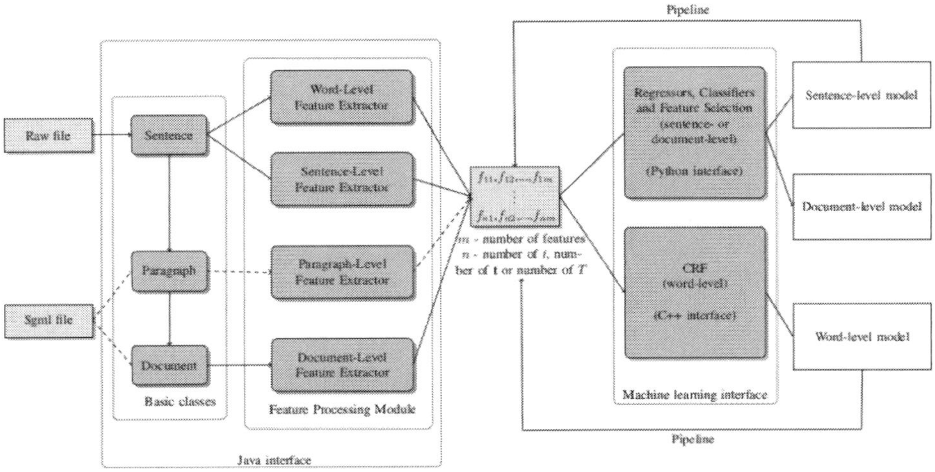

Figure 1: Architecture of QuEst++

i.e., the word itself, bigrams $t_{i-1}t_i$ and t_it_{i+1}, and trigrams $t_{i-2}t_{i-1}t_i$, $t_{i-1}t_it_{i+1}$ and $t_it_{i+1}t_{i+2}$.

Alignment context These features explore the word alignment between source and target sentences. They require the 1-to-N alignment between source and target sentences to be provided. Given a word t_i in position i of a target sentence and a word s_j aligned to it in position j of a source sentence, the features are: the aligned word s_j itself, target-source bigrams $s_{j-1}t_i$ and t_is_{j+1}, and source-target bigrams $t_{i-2}s_j$, $t_{i-1}s_j$, s_jt_{i+1} and s_jt_{i+2}.

Lexical These features explore POS information on the source and target words. Given the POS tag Pt_i of word t_i in position i of a target sentence and the POS tag Ps_j of word s_j aligned to it in position j of a source sentence, we extract: the POS tags Pt_i and Ps_j themselves, the bigrams $Pt_{i-1}Pt_i$ and Pt_iPt_{i+1} and trigrams $Pt_{i-2}Pt_{i-1}Pt_i$, $Pt_{i-1}Pt_iPt_{i+1}$ and $Pt_iPt_{i+1}Pt_{i+2}$. Four binary features are also extracted with value 1 if t_i is a stop word, punctuation symbol, proper noun or numeral.

LM These features are related to the n-gram frequencies of a word's context with respect to an LM (Raybaud et al., 2011). Six features are extracted: lexical and syntactic backoff behavior, as well as lexical and syntactic longest preceding n-gram for both a target word and an aligned source word. Given a word t_i in position i of a target sentence, the lexical backoff behavior is calculated as:

$$f(t_i) = \begin{cases} 7 & \text{if } t_{i-2}, t_{i-1}, t_i \text{ exists} \\ 6 & \text{if } t_{i-2}, t_{i-1} \text{ and } t_{i-1}, t_i \text{ exist} \\ 5 & \text{if only } t_{i-1}, t_i \text{ exists} \\ 4 & \text{if } t_{i-2}, t_{i-1} \text{ and } t_i \text{ exist} \\ 3 & \text{if } t_{i-1} \text{ and } t_i \text{ exist} \\ 2 & \text{if } t_i \text{ exists} \\ 1 & \text{if } t_i \text{ is out of the vocabulary} \end{cases}$$

The syntactic backoff behavior is calculated in an analogous fashion: it verifies for the existence of n-grams of POS tags in a POS-tagged LM. The POS tags of target sentence are produced by the Stanford Parser[4] (integrated in QuEst++).

Syntactic QuEst++ provides one syntactic feature that proved very promising in previous work: the Null Link (Xiong et al., 2010). It is a binary feature that receives value 1 if a given word t_i in a target sentence has at least one dependency link with another word t_j, and 0 otherwise. The Stanford Parser is used for dependency parsing.

Semantic These features explore the polysemy of target and source words, i.e. the number of senses existing as entries in a WordNet for a given target word t_i or a source word s_i. We employ the Universal WordNet,[5] which provides access to WordNets of various languages.

[4] http://nlp.stanford.edu/software/lex-parser.shtml

[5] http://www.lexvo.org/uwn/

Pseudo-reference This binary feature explores the similarity between the target sentence and a translation for the source sentence produced by another MT system. The feature is 1 if the given word t_i in position i of a target sentence S is also present in a pseudo-reference translation R. In our experiments, the pseudo-reference is produced by Moses systems trained over parallel corpora.

3.2 Sentence level

Sentence-level QE features have been extensively explored and described in previous work. The number of QUEST++ features varies from 80 to 123 depending on the language pair. The complete list is given as part of QUEST++ 's documentation. Some examples are:

- number of tokens in **s** & **t** and their ratio,
- LM probability of **s** & **t**,
- ratio of punctuation symbols in **s** & **t**,
- ratio of percentage of numbers, content-/non-content words, nouns/verbs/etc in **s** & **t**,
- proportion of dependency relations between (aligned) constituents in **s** & **t**,
- difference in depth of syntactic trees of **s** & **t**.

In our experiments, we use the set of 80 features, as these can be extracted for all language pairs of our datasets.

3.3 Document level

Our document-level features follow from those in the work of (Wong and Kit, 2012) on MT evaluation and (Scarton and Specia, 2014) for document-level QE. Nine features are extracted, in addition to aggregated values of sentence-level features for the entire document:

- content words/lemmas/nouns repetition in S/T,
- ratio of content words/lemmas/nouns in S/T,

4 Experiments

In what follows, we evaluate QUEST++'s performance for the three prediction levels and various datasets.

4.1 Word-level QE

Datasets We use five word-level QE datasets: the WMT14 English-Spanish, Spanish-English, English-German and German-English datasets, and the WMT15 English-Spanish dataset.

Metrics For the WMT14 data, we evaluate performance in the three official classification tasks:

- **Binary:** A Good/Bad label, where Bad indicates the need for editing the token.
- **Level 1:** A Good/Accuracy/Fluency label, specifying the coarser level categories of errors for each token, or Good for tokens with no error.
- **Multi-Class:** One of 16 labels specifying the error type for the token (mistranslation, missing word, etc.).

The evaluation metric is the average F-1 of all but the Good class. For the WMT15 dataset, we consider only the Binary classification task, since the dataset does not provide other annotations.

Settings For all datasets, the models were trained with the CRF module in QUEST++ . While for the WMT14 German-English dataset we use the Passive Aggressive learning algorithm, for the remaining datasets, we use the Adaptive Regularization of Weight Vector (AROW) learning. Through experimentation, we found that this setup to be the most effective. The hyper-parameters for each model were optimised through 10-fold cross validation. The baseline is the majority class in the training data, i.e. a system that always predicts "Unintelligible" for Multi-Class, "Fluency" for Level 1, and "Bad" for the Binary setup.

Results The F-1 scores for the WMT14 datasets are given in Tables 1–4, for QUEST++ and systems that oficially participated in the task. The results show that QUEST++ was able to outperform all participating systems in WMT14 except for the English-Spanish baseline in the Binary and Level 1 tasks. The results in Table 5 also highlight the importance of selecting an adequate learning algorithm in CRF models.

System	Binary	Level 1	Multiclass
QUEST++	0.502	0.392	**0.227**
Baseline	**0.525**	**0.404**	0.222
LIG/BL	0.441	0.317	0.204
LIG/FS	0.444	0.317	0.204
FBK-1	0.487	0.372	0.170
FBK-2	0.426	0.385	0.230
LIMSI	0.473	–	–
RTM-1	0.350	0.299	0.268
RTM-2	0.328	0.266	0.032

Table 1: F-1 for the WMT14 English-Spanish task

4.2 Pipeline for sentence-level QE

Here we evaluate the pipeline of using word-level predictions as features for sentence-level QE.

System	Binary	Level 1	Multiclass
QuEst++	**0.386**	**0.267**	**0.161**
Baseline	0.299	0.151	0.019
RTM-1	0.269	0.219	0.087
RTM-2	0.291	0.239	0.081

Table 2: F-1 for the WMT14 Spanish-English task

System	Binary	Level 1	Multiclass
QuEst++	**0.507**	**0.287**	**0.161**
Baseline	0.445	0.117	0.086
RTM-1	0.452	0.211	0.150
RTM-2	0.369	0.219	0.124

Table 3: F-1 for the WMT14 English-German task

Dataset We use the WMT15 dataset for word-level QE. The split between training and test sets was modified to allow for more sentences for training the sentence-level QE model. The 2000 last sentences of the original training set were used as test along with the original 1000 dev set sentences. Therefore, word predictions were generated for 3000 sentences, which were later split in 2000 sentences for training and 1000 sentences for testing the sentence-level model.

Features The 17 QuEst++ baseline features are used alone (Baseline) and in combination with four word-level prediction features:

- count & proportion of Good words,
- count & proportion of Bad words.

Oracle word level labels, as given in the original dataset, are also used in a separate experiment to study the potential of this pipelined approach.

Settings For learning sentence-level models, the SVR algorithm with RBF kernel and hyperparameters optimised via grid search in QuEst++ is used. Evaluation is done using **MAE** (Mean Absolute Error) as metric.

Results As shown in Table 6, the use of word-level predictions as features led to no improvement. However, the use of the oracle word-level labels as features substantially improved the results, lowering the baseline error by half. We note that the method used in this experiments is the same as that in Section 4.1, but with fewer instances for training the word-level models. Improving word-level prediction could thus lead to better results in the pipeline for sentence-level QE.

System	Binary	Level 1	Multiclass
QuEst++	**0.401**	**0.230**	**0.079**
Baseline	0.365	0.149	0.069
RTM-1	0.261	0.082	0.023
RTM-2	0.229	0.085	0.030

Table 4: F-1 for the WMT14 German-English task

Algorithm	Binary
AROW	**0.379**
PA	0.352
LBFGS	0.001
L2SGD	0.000
AP	0.000

Table 5: F-1 for the WMT15 English-Spanish task

	MAE
Baseline	0.159
Baseline+Predicted	0.158
Baseline+Oracle	**0.07**

Table 6: MAE values for sentence-level QE

4.3 Pipeline for document-level QE

Here we evaluate the pipeline of using sentence-level predictions as features for QE of documents.

Dataset For training the sentence-level model, we use the English-Spanish WMT13 training set for sentence-level QE. For the document-level model, we use English-Spanish WMT13 data from the translation shared task. We mixed the outputs of all MT systems, leading to 934 translated documents. 560 randomly selected documents were used for training and 374 for testing. As quality labels, for sentence-level training we consider both the HTER and the Likert labels available. For document-level prediction, BLEU, TER and METEOR are used as quality labels (not as features), given the lack of human-target quality labels for document-level prediction.

Features The 17 QuEst++ baseline features are aggregated to produce document-level features (Baseline). These are then combined with document-level features (Section 3.3) and finally with features from sentence-level predictions:

- maximum/minimum predicted HTER or Likert score,
- average predicted HTER or Likert score,
- Median, first quartile and third quartile predicted HTER or Likert score.

Oracle sentence labels are not possible as they do not exist for the test set documents.

Settings For training and evaluation, we use the same settings as for sentence-level.

Results Table 7 shows the results in terms of MAE. The best result was achieved with the baseline plus HTER features, but no significant improvements over the baseline were observed. Document-level prediction is a very challenging task: automatic metric scores used as labels do not seem to reliably distinguish translations of different source documents, since they were primarily designed to compare alternative translations for the *same* source document.

	BLEU	TER	METEOR
Baseline	0.049	0.050	0.055
Baseline+Doc-level	0.053	0.057	0.055
Baseline+HTER	0.053	**0.048**	0.054
Baseline+Likert	0.054	0.056	0.054
Baseline+Doc-level+HTER	0.053	0.054	0.054
Baseline+Doc-level+Likert	0.053	0.056	0.054

Table 7: MAE values for document-level QE

5 Remarks

The source code for the framework, the datasets and extra resources can be downloaded from `https://github.com/ghpaetzold/questplusplus`.

The license for the Java code, Python and shell scripts is BSD, a permissive license with no restrictions on the use or extensions of the software for any purposes, including commercial. For pre-existing code and resources, e.g., `scikit-learn`, their licenses apply.

Acknowledgments

This work was supported by the European Association for Machine Translation, the QT21 project (H2020 No. 645452) and the EXPERT project (EU Marie Curie ITN No. 317471).

References

N. Bach, F. Huang, and Y. Al-Onaizan. 2011. Goodness: a method for measuring MT confidence. In *ACL11*.

E. Bicici and A. Way. 2014. Referential Translation Machines for Predicting Translation Quality. In *WMT14*.

J. Blatz, E. Fitzgerald, G. Foster, S. Gandrabur, C. Goutte, A. Kulesza, A. Sanchis, and N. Ueffing. 2004. Confidence Estimation for Machine Translation. In *COLING04*.

O. Bojar, C. Buck, C. Callison-Burch, C. Federmann, B. Haddow, P. Koehn, C. Monz, M. Post, R. Soricut, and L. Specia. 2013. Findings of the 2013 Workshop on SMT. In *WMT13*.

O. Bojar, C. Buck, C. Federmann, B. Haddow, P. Koehn, J. Leveling, C. Monz, P. Pecina, M. Post, H. Saint-Amand, R. Soricut, L. Specia, and A. Tamchyna. 2014. Findings of the 2014 Workshop on SMT. In *WMT14*.

C. Callison-Burch, P. Koehn, C. Monz, M. Post, R. Soricut, and L. Specia. 2012. Findings of the 2012 Workshop on SMT. In *WMT12*.

J. G. Camargo de Souza, J. González-Rubio, C. Buck, M. Turchi, and M. Negri. 2014. FBK-UPV-UEdin participation in the WMT14 Quality Estimation shared-task. In *WMT14*.

N. Q. Luong, L. Besacier, and B. Lecouteux. 2014. LIG System for Word Level QE task. In *WMT14*.

N. Okazaki. 2007. CRFsuite: a fast implementation of Conditional Random Fields. `http://www.chokkan.org/software/crfsuite/`.

F. Pedregosa, G. Varoquaux, A. Gramfort, V. Michel, B. Thirion, O. Grisel, M. Blondel, P. Prettenhofer, R. Weiss, V. Dubourg, J. Vanderplas, A. Passos, D. Cournapeau, M. Brucher, M. Perrot, and E. Duchesnay. Scikit-learn: Machine learning in Python. *Journal of Machine Learning Research*, 12.

S. Raybaud, D. Langlois, and K. Smali. 2011. This sentence is wrong. Detecting errors in machine-translated sentences. *Machine Translation*, 25(1).

C. Scarton and L. Specia. 2014. Document-level translation quality estimation: exploring discourse and pseudo-references. In *EAMT14*.

C. Scarton, M. Zampieri, M. Vela, J. van Genabith, and L. Specia. 2015. Searching for Context: a Study on Document-Level Labels for Translation Quality Estimation. In *EAMT15*.

K. Shah and L. Specia. 2014. Quality estimation for translation selection. In *EAMT14*.

R. Soricut and A. Echihabi. 2010. Trustrank: Inducing trust in automatic translations via ranking. In *ACL10*.

L. Specia, K. Shah, J. G. C. de Souza, and T. Cohn. 2013. Quest - a translation quality estimation framework. In *ACL13*.

L. Specia. 2011. Exploiting objective annotations for measuring translation post-editing effort. In *EAMT11*.

G. Wisniewski, N. Pcheux, A. Allauzen, and F. Yvon. 2014. LIMSI Submission for WMT'14 QE Task. In *WMT14*.

B. T. M. Wong and C. Kit. 2012. Extending machine translation evaluation metrics with lexical cohesion to document level. In *EMNLP/CONLL*.

D. Xiong, M. Zhang, and H. Li. 2010. Error detection for SMT using linguistic features. In *ACL10*.

WA-Continuum: Visualising Word Alignments across Multiple Parallel Sentences Simultaneously

David Steele
Department of Computer Science
The University of Sheffield
Sheffield, UK
dbsteele1@sheffield.ac.uk

Lucia Specia
Department of Computer Science
The University of Sheffield
Sheffield, UK
l.specia@sheffield.ac.uk

Abstract

Word alignment (WA) between a pair of sentences in the same or different languages is a key component of many natural language processing tasks. It is commonly used for identifying the translation relationships between words and phrases in parallel sentences from two different languages. WA-Continuum is a tool designed for the visualisation of WAs. It was initially built to aid research studying WAs and ways to improve them. The tool relies on the automated mark-up of WAs, as typically produced by WA tools. Different from most previous work, it presents the alignment information graphically in a WA matrix that can be easily understood by users, as opposed to text connected by lines. The key features of the tool are the ability to visualise WA matrices for multiple parallel aligned sentences simultaneously in a single place, coupled with powerful search and selection components to find and inspect particular sentences as required.

1 Introduction

Automatically generated WA of parallel sentences, as introduced by the IBM models (Brown et al., 1990), is a mapping between source words and target words. It plays a vital role in Statistical Machine Translation (SMT) as the initial step to generate translation rules in most state of the art SMT approaches. It is also widely classed as a valuable linguistic resource for multilingual text processing in general.

Accurate WAs form the basis for constructing probabilistic word or phrase-based translation dictionaries, as well as the generation of more elaborate translation rules, such as hierarchical or syntax-based rules. As WAs improve, it is expected that the translation rules also improve, which, in turn, should lead to better Machine Translation (MT).

Our research involves a careful study and evaluation of the WA process and aims to develop ways to improve its performance. A substantial part of evaluating WAs often includes human intervention where candidate WAs produced by various software are examined. Consequently, tools to display the alignment information are very important for humans to analyse and readily digest such information.

Various tools have been developed in previous work that enable the visualisation and, in some cases, direct manipulation of WAs. However, none of these tools meet important requirements in our research such as being able to quickly examine WAs for tens and even hundreds of sentences simultaneously in a very clear format and indeed being able to search, shuffle, and filter those alignments according to desired specific criteria. The WA-Continuum tool was developed to fulfil this need. It is implemented in Python and outputs to standard HTML files, utilising the powerful properties provided by CSS and JavaScript. As the output file is saved as regular HTML it works with modern web browsers and thus users can make use of many of the features they provide, such as 'search and find'.

The remainder of the paper is organised as follows: Section 2 gives a brief overview of existing WA visualisation tools. Section 3 highlights the technical specification of the WA-Continuum software as well as a number of useful features. Section 4 presents the conclusion along with a brief overview of future development plans.

2 Visualising Word Alignments

With the continuing attention given to SMT and the overarching importance of WAs, various tools

Proceedings of ACL-IJCNLP 2015 System Demonstrations, pages 121–126,
Beijing, China, July 26-31, 2015.

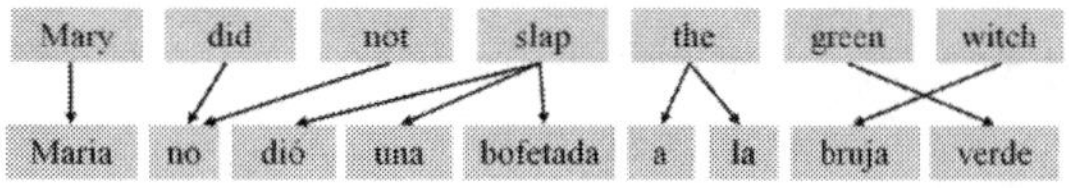

Figure 1: A simple graphical visualisation of WAs for an English-Spanish parallel sentence (Jurafsky and Martin, 2009).

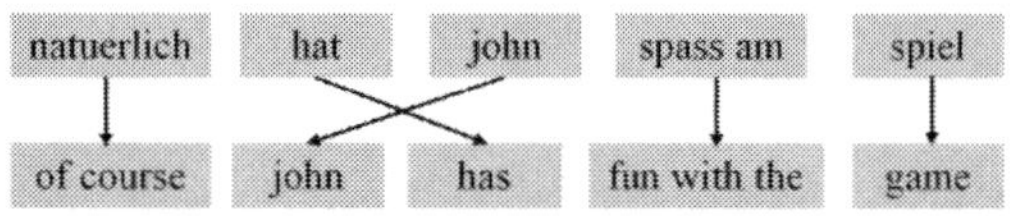

Figure 2: A simple graphical visualisation of WAs for a German-English parallel sentence. The input has been segmented into phrases (Koehn, 2013).

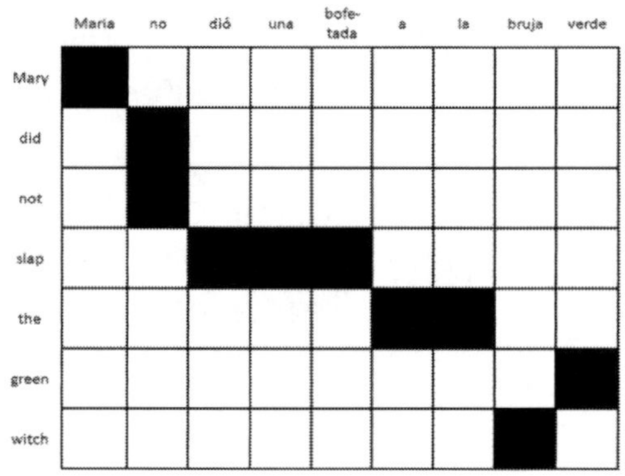

Figure 3: A graphical visualisation of WAs for the given Spanish-English parallel sentence using the matrix format. The columns represent Spanish words whilst the rows represent English words (Jurafsky and Martin, 2009).

have been developed that help evaluate and visualise such alignments by going beyond using text alone. To understand the limitations of text-only visualisation, consider the following Chinese-English example, where the alignments are given in terms of the positions of source-target tokens: 我 爱 你 ! ||| i love you ! ||| 0-0 1-1 2-2 3-3. For short and simple sentences with numerous 1-to-1 monotone alignments this visualisation style can be sufficient. However, it is certainly not suitable for longer and more complex sentences that may contain more intricate alignments.

Previous tools include Cairo (Smith et al., 2000) and VisualLIHLA (Caseli et al., 2008) and have different implementations serving different purposes, but they are usually presented in one of two main visual styles. The earlier styles show alignments by matching words in text boxes, across two sentences, using arrows or lines to make the connections. Figure 1 shows an example of this style, where the words in a parallel English and Spanish sentence have been aligned. From the example it can be seen clearly which words map to each other, where reordering occurs (arrows cross), and where phrases are mapped to single words (e.g. 'did not' is mapped to 'no'). Figure 2 shows a similar mapping, but this time it places whole phrases within a single text box and shows both word and phrase alignments. Again, the place where the arrows cross shows some reordering has occurred. The accuracy of the alignments shown in both figures is not a concern, as the tools are purely designed for visualisation purposes. The clarity in how the information is presented, on the other hand, is critical.

The second and perhaps more sophisticated style displays the alignments in a matrix type grid, where the individual columns of the grid map to single elements (words or punctuation marks) in one language and the rows do likewise for single elements in the other language. Figure 3 shows the same parallel sentences as those in Figure 1, but in the grid style. Single blocks show mappings between individual elements (e.g. 'Mary' and 'Maria') whereas multiple blocks appearing in the same row or column tend to show phrases mapping to single words or other phrases (e.g. 'did not' maps to 'no'). As can be seen from Figures 1, 2 and 3 the same information is clearly presented in two different formats, both of which are more intuitive than showing text and word position numbers only.

The tools described so far are static and only show visual representations of WAs. Tools such as Yawat (Yet Another Word Alignment Tool) (Germann, 2008) and the SWIFT Aligner (Gilmanov et al., 2014), however, allow the direct manipulation and editing of WAs via graphical interfaces. Picaro – a simple command-line alignment visualisation tool (Riesa, 2011) – uses the grid style to display information. It also has an online demo web page[1] that allows for the demonstration of the tool within a browser for a single parallel sentence. Although Picaro is a relatively simple tool, the visual presentation of the grid format on the demonstration web page is clear and is ideal for

[1]http://nlg.isi.edu/demos/picaro/

quickly understanding WAs. Our research in SMT requires the use of this type of presentation style using the grid format, but with a few more powerful features. Consequently, we had to develop a new tool that had extra features, but maintained the visual appeal and simplicity of the grid format.

3 Software Features

This section provides an overview of our software including input format and technical specification, as well as a number of the pertinent and powerful features that we have been using.

3.1 Input and Technical Specification

WA-Continuum is written in Python (version 2.7). The input commands can be typed directly into the command-line on Mac, Linux and Windows computers or laptops. They can also be passed as arguments in a number of integrated development environments (IDEs) such as Eclipse[2] or Spyder[3].

The input for the tool should include at least one aligned parallel sentence arranged in the following format:

SOURCE ||| TARGET ||| WAs.

For example:

我 爱 你 ||| i love you ||| 0-0 1-1 2-2

Typically though the input will be a text file containing a list of many such aligned parallel sentences, one per line. The file is read along with an optional user selected keyword or key-phrase (e.g. -k 'hello' or -k 'as soon as'), which then only returns sentence pairs containing that given word or phrase. Once these commands have been provided, the output is returned as an HTML page, which uses a mixture of HTML, CSS and JavaScript. The page is then automatically opened in the default web browser. This implementation has been successfully tested with a number of modern web browsers including Mozilla Firefox, Internet Explorer 11, Google Chrome and Opera.

A single web page can show thousands of alignment grids (it has been tested for 10000+ sentences), but despite the fact that the program produces the HTML for the output very quickly, it takes the browser a while to render the page when thousands of grids are involved. We have found through testing that up to 1000 grids can be loaded and rendered fairly quickly (under four seconds on an Intel dual core i3-3220 (3GHZ) computer with 12GB of RAM running Windows 8.1), and so, for performance, we have set the current maximum number of grids to 512 as this is usually enough per search for inspection and evaluation purposes.

A short video showing a demonstration of the WA-Continuum software is available online at: `http://wa-continuum.vidmeup.com/` The software itself will be made available for download at: `http://staffwww.dcs.shef.ac.uk/people/D.Steele/`

3.2 Features

This section provides an overview of the pertinent features that have been developed and used in our research including: keyword search, phrase search, simple regular expression searches, viewing phrase pairs (minimal bi-phrases), and utilising useful browser features.

For all the given figures in this section exemplifying the WA-continuum software, the individual coordinates for each square in the matrices should be read as row number first, followed by the column number. For Figure 4, the alignment point mapping '因为' to 'because' (as highlighted at the top and right hand side) should be read as alignment point 3-5. The three lines of text below each grid show the source language, target language and WAs as they appear in the input file.

Keyword Searching

As the main aim of the WA-Continuum software is to be able to display clearly WAs for many sentences (possibly the whole corpus), a keyword search was implemented to enable users to select sentences to visualise from the input file, for example, for the analysis of particular constructions such as those using discourse markers.

Figure 4 shows a typical alignment grid returned from using the keyword search 'because'. The '14' in the top left of the figure is an indication that it is the 15th[4] grid for 'because' that appears in the output page. Scrolling up the page will show previous sentences featuring 'because', while scrolling down will show subsequent sentences.

[2]https://eclipse.org/

[3]https://github.com/spyder-ide/spyder/releases

[4]The sentence count starts at 0 to keep it consistent with the alignment point numbering, which also starts at 0.

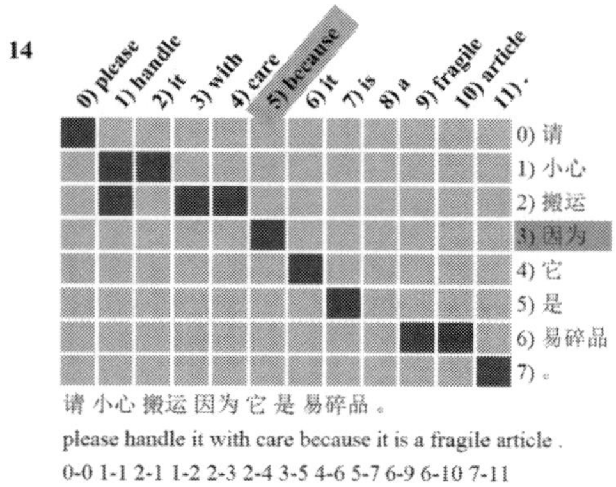

Figure 4: An example of a WA grid returned using the keyword search term 'because'. The cursor was placed over the alignment point for 'because' and '因为' (point 3-5) so the tokens involved in the alignment are highlighted.

Phrase Searching

This is simply an extension of the keyword search, but by enclosing the search term in quotes it enables the user to input a phrase. For example, a user could easily run the program with the search term 'as soon as' and only results containing that complete phrase will be returned. If the 'as soon as' was typed without the quotes, the tool will return results for the keyword 'as'.

It is worth noting here that the keyword/phrase searches also apply to other alphabets/languages in the input file. For example, a user could do a search using either 'china' (lower case) or '中国'.

Support for Simple Regular Expressions

While keyword and phrase searches are useful tools, if the user is looking for more specific sentences then they can use searches combined with basic regular expressions (RE). Figure 5 is an example of WAs returned using the RE search term 'if.*, then' which is being used to examine sentences containing the if/then conditional. Using the RE search term 'if.*, then' matches any sentence that contains: 'if' followed by any number of characters (.*) followed by a comma and space and finally a 'then'. Being able to use REs makes the search very flexible and helps to pinpoint specific examples.

Using Browser Features

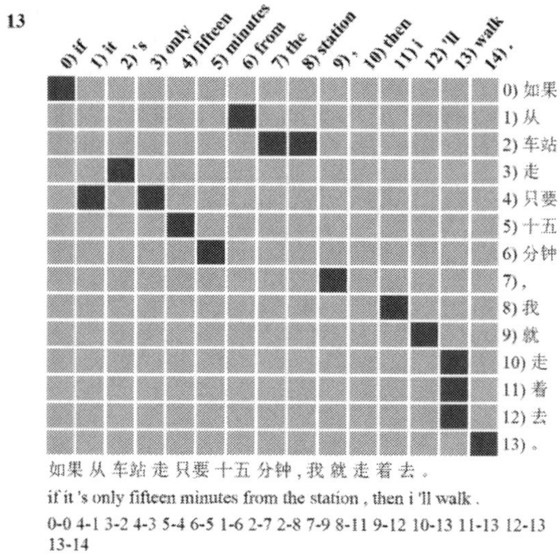

Figure 5: A WA grid returned by using the regular expression search term 'if.*, then'.

Web browsers often contain many powerful features, but one that is particularly useful for searching the output of tens or hundreds of grids is the 'search and find' function. Figure 6 shows a browser search for 'go to the airport' being performed on all alignment grids returned by the original command-line keyword search term 'the'. The figure shows that the sentence being examined is the fifty-fifth one on the page as well as it being the second out of eleven containing matches for 'go to the airport'. The up and down arrows next to the search term enables the user to quickly jump through the matches on the page. Finally, the small yellow/orange lines on the right hand side show where the other grids containing a match appear on the page.

Phrase Pairs (Minimal Bi-phrases)

Koehn (2013) describes the idea of extracting phrase pairs from word alignments for phrase-based SMT. The reasoning is that if a phrase pair has been identified, it can then be used as evidence for the translation of future occurrences of the phrase. Figure 7 shows an example where 'assumes that' has been mapped to 'geht davon aus , dass'. Using this idea we enabled our software to highlight phrase pairs in order to better evaluate the WAs not just for single words, but also for entire phrases. The input file remains the same, but when the optional

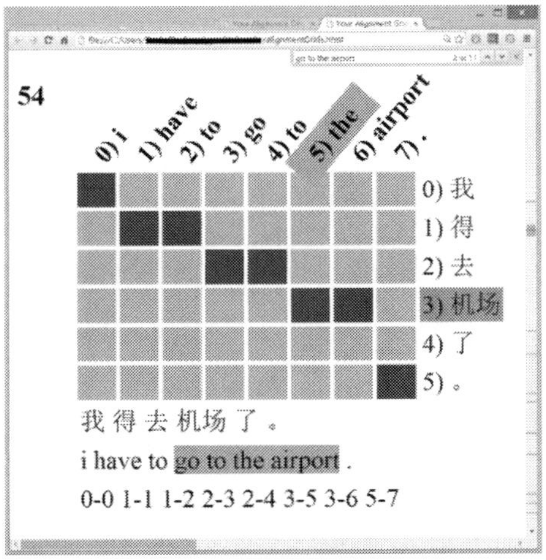

Figure 6: Using the web browser features to search the results. In this case, matches for 'go to the airport' are sought.

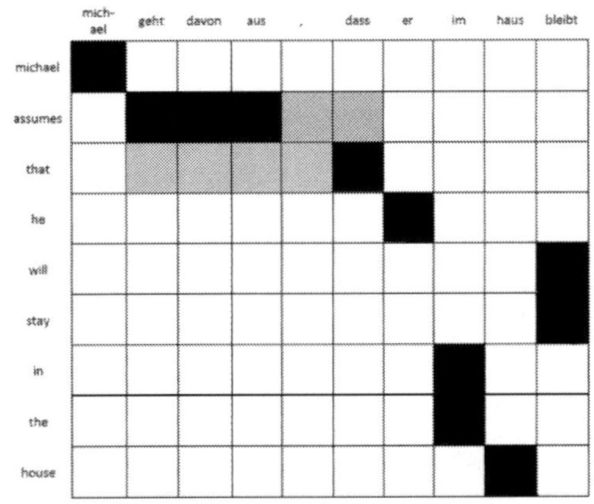

Figure 7: A WA grid showing a phrase pair mapping of 'assumes that' to 'geht davon aus , dass' (Koehn, 2013).

'-b' switch, for bi-phrases on, is used in the command-line then the tool recursively extracts the phrase pairs at runtime and displays them in the relevant matrices.

Figure 8 shows the first result returned using the phrase search 'as soon as' plus the command-line flag '-b', which highlights phrase pairs. Each single block containing the hash symbol represents the actual word alignment points, whereas the large block represents phrase alignments. Phrase alignments will always appear as rectangles and may include blocks that were not originally aligned (coloured, but no hash symbol). In the context of Figure 8, the English words 'to call you' have been mapped as a phrase to '给你打电话' (literally: 'give you make phone [call]). In this case, quite a good translation. The process to establish a phrase pair works as follows. If column 5 ('call') is examined it is clear that it contains three mappings to rows 7, 9 and 10 respectively. This means that in order to use column 5 in a phrase we must include every alignment point that occurs in the column and by extension those that appear in each of the rows 7, 9 and 10. However, to get from row 7 to row 9 we must also include everything in row 8, and so it goes on in a recursive process.

The phrase 'to call you' uses columns 4, 5 and 6. Column 4 has an alignment point at row 9 (9-4). Row 9 in turn also has an alignment point with column 5 (9-5), which then encompasses the other alignment points in column 5 (7-5 and 10-5). As moving through column 5 includes using row 8 then we must also include all alignment points for that row as well, which in this case is in column 6 (8-6). After this, as there are no more alignment points to consider outside of that block, then the phrase is complete. A similar process is applied in Figure 7, which is why the ' , ' in column 4 must be included as part of the phrase 'geht davon aus , dass'.

Another point worth noting in Figure 8 is that the alignment at point 8-6 (highlighted) mapping '你' to 'you' is in a different colour. The reason for this is that the software has been developed to show possible phrases/words that may occur within a larger phrase (nested phrases), as well as being a phrase or single aligned word in its own right. That is, in this case no other item appears in column 6 or row 8 and so the word alignment could be extracted in its own right as a mapping between '你' and 'you'. None of the other elements that appear in the phrase 'to call you' have the same property.

Finally columns 7, 8, 9, and row 2 have no alignment points in them at all. This means that the alignment software has not found suitable alignments for these elements. Using the grid format enables one to spot this issue right away. Based on knowledge of Chinese, we can also quickly spot that the word 'returns' (column 11) should be mapped to '回来' (row 2) and 'as soon as' (columns 7, 8 and 9) should be mapped to '一' (row 1). These errors would be much harder to spot when examining the alignments in a text only format.

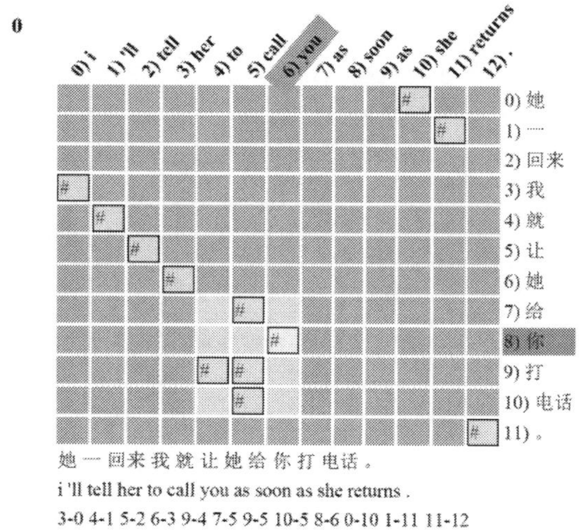

Figure 8: A WA grid showing a phrase pair mapping of 'to call you' to '给 你 打 电话'.

Other Features

A number of other features are available to the user, including the ability to shuffle the results, select a range of matrices, and filter the results to include sentences under a certain length. Extra features such as these are continually being incorporated into the software as the need arises. Furthermore, as the software is open source and well documented, its modular design will enable others to develop and extend the tool to easily add further features as required.

4 Conclusion and Future Work

WA-Continuum was designed with one main specific purpose in mind, which is visualising WAs for a large number of sentences at once, making it possible to evaluate them more efficiently. Software that enables the visualisation of WAs has been developed in previous work and they offer a myriad of features including manual editing of WAs and text highlighting. However, none of the tools that we found appeared to offer the full set of functionalities that were required. WA-Continuum builds on the idea of displaying WAs in an intuitive matrix style, but makes accessing and searching large volumes of data a fairly straightforward task.

In the future we aim to further enhance the software by making a number of additions:

- Extra interactivity will be added to enable manual editing of WAs.
- Phrase pairs could be shown on a separate page or alongside the main grids, which is useful where nested phrase pairs occur.
- Results that return a larger number of grids (e.g. over 1000) will be spread over multiple pages, with a main master page containing links to each of the sub pages.
- The option to output a small number of grids to PDF may also be added as it is a useful format, which could be used consistently in numerous ways across many devices.

Acknowledgements The authors wish to thank W Aziz for his valued input (including code snippets), ideas and suggestions.

References

Peter F. Brown, John Cocke, Stephen A. Della, Vincent J. Della Pietra, Fredrick Jelinek, John D. Lafferty, Robert L. Mercer, and Paul S. Roosin. 1990. *A Statistical Approach to Machine Translation.* Computational Linguistics, 16(2):76-85.

Helena Caseli, Felipe T. Gomes, Thiago A.S. Pardo, and Maria das Gracas V. Nunes. 2008. *Visual-LIHLA: The Visual Online Tool for Lexical Alignment.* In XIV Brazilian Symposium on Multimedia and the Web, pages 378-380. Vila Velha, Brazil.

Ulrich Germann. 2008. *Yawat: Yet Another Word Alignment Tool.* ACL-08: HLT Demo Session, pages 20-23. Columbus, Ohio.

Timur Gilmanov, Olga Scrivner, and Sandra Kubler. 2014. *SWIFT Aligner, A Multifunctional Tool for Parallel Corpora: Visualization, Word Alignment, and (Morpho)-Syntactic Cross-Language Transfer.* LREC, pages 2913-2919. Reykjavik, Iceland.

Daniel Jurafsky and James H. Martin. 2009. *Speech and Language Proecessing (2nd ed.).* Pearson Prentice Hall, London.

Philipp Koehn. 2013. *Statistical Machine Translation.* Cambridge University Press, Cambridge.

Patrick Lambert. 2004. *Alignment set toolkit.* http://gps-tsc.upc.es/veu/personal/lambert/software/AlignmentSet.html.

Jason Riesa. 2011. *Picaro: A simple Command-Line Alignment Visualisation Tool.* http://nlg.isi.edu/demos/picaro/.

Noah A. Smith and Michael E. Jahr. 2000. *Cairo: An Alignment Visualisation Tool.* In LREC. Athens, Greece.

Jörg Tiedemann. 2006. *ISA and ICA —Two web interfaces for interactive alignment of bitexts.* In LREC. Genoa, Italy.

A Domain-independent Rule-based Framework for Event Extraction

Marco A. Valenzuela-Escárcega **Gus Hahn-Powell** **Thomas Hicks** **Mihai Surdeanu**
University of Arizona, Tucson, AZ, USA
{marcov,hahnpowell,msurdeanu,hickst}@email.arizona.edu

Abstract

We describe the design, development, and API of ODIN (Open Domain INformer), a domain-independent, rule-based event extraction (EE) framework. The proposed EE approach is: *simple* (most events are captured with simple lexico-syntactic patterns), *powerful* (the language can capture complex constructs, such as events taking other events as arguments, and regular expressions over syntactic graphs), *robust* (to recover from syntactic parsing errors, syntactic patterns can be freely mixed with surface, token-based patterns), and *fast* (the runtime environment processes 110 sentences/second in a real-world domain with a grammar of over 200 rules). We used this framework to develop a grammar for the biochemical domain, which approached human performance. Our EE framework is accompanied by a web-based user interface for the rapid development of event grammars and visualization of matches. The ODIN framework and the domain-specific grammars are available as open-source code.

1 Introduction

Rule-based information extraction (IE) has long enjoyed wide adoption throughout industry, though it has remained largely ignored in academia, in favor of machine learning (ML) methods (Chiticariu et al., 2013). However, rule-based systems have several advantages over pure ML systems, including: (a) the rules are interpretable and thus suitable for rapid development and domain transfer; and (b) humans and machines can contribute to the same model. Why then have such systems failed to hold the attention of the academic community? One argument raised by Chiticariu et al. is that, despite notable efforts (Appelt and Onyshkevych, 1998; Levy and Andrew, 2006; Hunter et al., 2008; Cunningham et al., 2011; Chang and Manning, 2014), there is not a standard language for this task, or a "standard way to express rules", which raises the entry cost for new rule-based systems.

Here we aim to address this issue with a novel event extraction (EE) language and framework called ODIN (Open Domain INformer). We follow the simplicity principles promoted by other natural language processing toolkits, such as Stanford's CoreNLP, which aim to "avoid over-design", "do one thing well", and have a user "up and running in ten minutes or less" (Manning et al., 2014). In particular, our approach is:

Simple: Taking advantage of a syntactic dependency[1] representation (de Marneffe and Manning, 2008), our EE language has a simple, declarative syntax (see Examples 1 & 2) for *n*-ary events, which captures single or multi-word event predicates (`trigger`) with lexical and morphological constraints, and event arguments (e.g., `theme`) with (generally) simple syntactic patterns and semantic constraints.

Powerful: Despite its simplicity, our EE framework can capture complex constructs when necessary, such as: (a) recursive events[2], (b) complex regular expressions over syntactic patterns for event arguments. Inspired by Stanford's Semgrex[3], we have extended a standard regular expression language to describe patterns over directed graphs[4], e.g., we introduce new < and > operators to specify the direction of edge traversal in the dependency graph. Finally, we allow for (c) optional arguments[5] and multiple arguments with the same name.

Robust: To recover from unavoidable syntactic errors, SD patterns (such as the ones in Examples 1 and 2) can be can be freely mixed with surface, token-based patterns, using a language inspired by the Allen Insti-

[1] Hereafter abbreviated as SD.

[2] Events that take other events as arguments (see Figure 1 and the corresponding Example (2) for such an event in the biochemical domain. The `Positive_Regulation` takes a `Phosphorylation` event as the `Controlled` argument)

[3] `nlp.stanford.edu/software/tregex.shtml`

[4] Here we use syntactic dependencies.

[5] `cause` in Example 1.

Proceedings of ACL-IJCNLP 2015 System Demonstrations, pages 127–132,
Beijing, China, July 26-31, 2015. ©2015 ACL and AFNLP

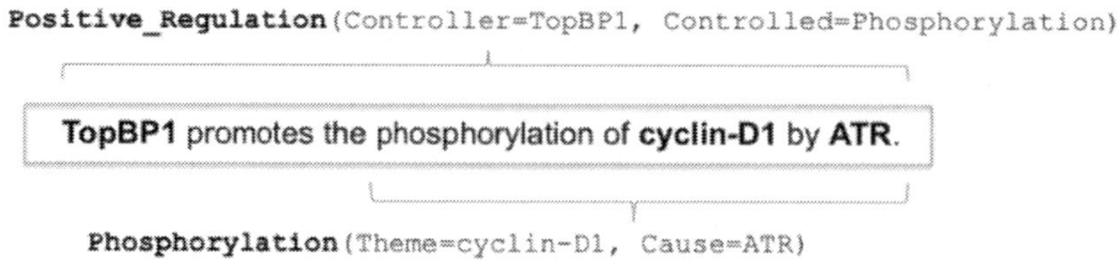

Figure 1: An example sentence containing a recursive event.

tute of Artificial Intelligence's Tagger[6]. These patterns match against information extracted in our text processing pipeline[7] , namely a token's part of speech, lemmatized form, named entity label, and the immediate incoming and outgoing edges in the SD graph. Example 3 shows an equivalent rule to the one in Example 1 using surface patterns (i.e. a pattern that is independent of a token sequence's underlying syntactic structure).

Fast: Our EE runtime is fast because our rules use event trigger phrases, captured with shallow lexico-morphological patterns, as starting points. Only when event triggers are detected is the matching of more complex syntactic patterns for arguments attempted. This guarantees quick executions. For example, in the biochemical domain (discussed in Section 2), our framework processes an average of 110 sentences/second[8] with a grammar of 211 rules on a laptop with an i7 CPU and 16GB of RAM.

2 Building a Domain from Scratch

We next describe how to use the proposed framework to build an event extractor for the biochemical domain (Ohta et al., 2013) from scratch.

Rule-based systems have been shown to perform at the state-of-the-art for event extraction in the biology domain (Peng et al., 2014; Bui et al., 2013). The domain, however, is not without its challenges. For example, it is not uncommon for biochemical events to contain other events as arguments. Consider the example sentence in Figure 1. The sentence contains two events, one event referring to the biochemical process known as phosphorylation, and a recursive event describing a biochemical regulation that controls the mentioned phosphorylation. We will introduce a minimal set of rules that capture these two events. Here, we will assume the simple entities (denoted in bold in Figure 1) have already been detected through a named entity recognizer.[9]

When a rule matches, the extracted token spans for trigger and arguments, together with the corresponding event and argument labels (here the event

```
1  - name: Phosphorylation_1
2    priority: 2
3    label: [Phosphorylation, Event]
4    pattern: |
5      trigger = [lemma="phosphorylation"]
6      theme:PhysicalEntity = prep_of
7          (nn|conj|cc)*
8      cause:PhysicalEntity? = prep_by
9          (nn|conj|cc)*
```

Example 1: An example of a rule using syntactic structure. For the phosphorylation event, our selected event `trigger` (LINE 5) is a nominal predicate with the lemma *phosphorylation*. This trigger serves as the starting point for the syntactic patterns that extract event arguments. When searching for a `theme` to the Phosphorylation event, we begin at the specified `trigger` and look for an incoming dependent that is the object of the preposition *of*. The pattern fragment `(nn|conj_and|cc)*` targets entities that appear as modifiers in noun phrases (e.g., ... *of the* **cyclin-D1** *protein*), or a series of arguments in a coordinated phrase. The entity mention associated with our `theme` must be a named entity with the label `PhysicalEntity` (LINE 7), a hypernym of several more specialized types identified in an earlier iteration. The `cause` argument is marked as optional (denoted by the `?` symbol).

label is `Phosphorylation`, and the argument labels are `theme` & `cause`) are dispatched to a labeling action. By default, these actions simply create an `EventMention` Scala object with the corresponding event label, and the extracted named arguments. Example 5 summarizes the `EventMention` class. Custom actions may be defined as Scala code, and be attached to specific rules. For example, a custom action may trigger coreference resolution when a rule matches a common noun, e.g., *the protein*, instead of the expected named entity.

The second rule, shown in Example 2, captures the recursive event in Figure 1. Importantly, this rule takes other events as arguments, e.g., the `controlled` argument must be an event mention, here generated by the rule in Example 1. To guarantee correct execution, the runtime repeatedly applies the given EE grammar on each sentence until no rule matches. For example, here the rule in Example 2 would not match in the first

[6]https://github.com/allenai/taggers

[7]https://github.com/sistanlp/processors

[8]after the initial text processing pipeline

[9]Though the discussion focuses on event extraction, our framework can also be applied to the task of entity recognition.

```
- name: Positive_regulation_1
  label: [Positive_regulation, Event]
  priority: 3
  pattern: |
    trigger =
        [lemma=/promot|induc|increas
        |stimul|lead|enhanc|up-regulat/
        & tag=/^V|RB/]
    controller:PhysicalEntity = nsubj
        nn*
    controlled:Event = dobj nn*
```

Example 2: An example of a rule designed to capture a recursive event. The rule detects a relevant verbal or adverbial trigger and expects its arguments to be in a SUBJECT ↔ DIRECT OBJECT relationship. The `controlled` argument must be the mention of another event.

```
- name: Phosphorylation_surface_1
  priority: 2
  type: token
  label: [Phosphorylation, Event]
  pattern: |
    (?<trigger>
    [lemma="phosphorylation"]) of []*?
    @theme:PhysicalEntity []*?
    (by @cause:PhysicalEntity)?
```

Example 3: An alternative rule to Example 1 that uses a surface pattern. Surface patterns match event triggers and arguments over sequences of tokens and other mentions (e.g., the `theme` matches over an entire named entity of type `PhysicalEntity`). Event triggers (`trigger`) match the whole sequence of tokens encompassed in parentheses. Argument names preceded by the `@` symbol, e.g., `@theme`, require the specification of an event type (denoted by `:type`). This pattern is shorthand for matching the span of an entire named entity with the specified `type`.

iteration because no event mentions have been created yet, but would match in the second iteration. This process can optionally be optimized with rule priorities (as shown in the figure). For example, the priorities assigned to Examples 1 and 2 enforce that the second rule is executed only in an iteration following the first rule. Utilizing rule priorities allows for a derivational construction of complex events or complete grammars from their components.

Once the grammar has been defined, the entire system can be run in less than 10 lines of code, as shown in Example 4. The output of this code is a collection of event mentions, i.e., instances of the `EventMention` class outlined in Example 5.

3 Visualization

We accompany the above EE system with an interactive web-based tool for event grammar development and re-

```
1  class SimpleExample extends App {
2    // read rules from file
3    val rules = Source.fromFile(
4      "rules.yml").mkString
5    // make extractor engine
6    val engine = new ExtractorEngine(rules)
7    // create text processor for biomedical
8    // domain: POS, NER, and syntax
9    val processor = new BioNLPProcessor
10   // make document from free text;
11   // the document includes POS, NER, and
12   // syntactic annotations
13   val text = "TopBP1 promotes the
         phosphorylation of cyclin-D1 by ATR."
14   val doc = processor.annotate(text)
15   // run the actual EE grammar
16   val mentions = engine.extractFrom(doc)
17 }
```

Example 4: The minimal Scala code required to run the system. The input (LINE 13) is raw text. The output is a list of event mentions of the type `EventMention`. Here we show the use of a text processor specific to the biomedical domain. The framework also includes an open-domain text processor that includes POS tagging, named entity recognition, syntactic parsing, and coreference resolution. Additional processors for domain-specific tasks can easily be added.

sults visualization. Figure 2 shows the input fields for the user interface. The UI accepts free text to match against, and can be configured to run either a predefined domain grammar or one provided on-the-fly through a text box, allowing for the rapid development and tuning of rules.

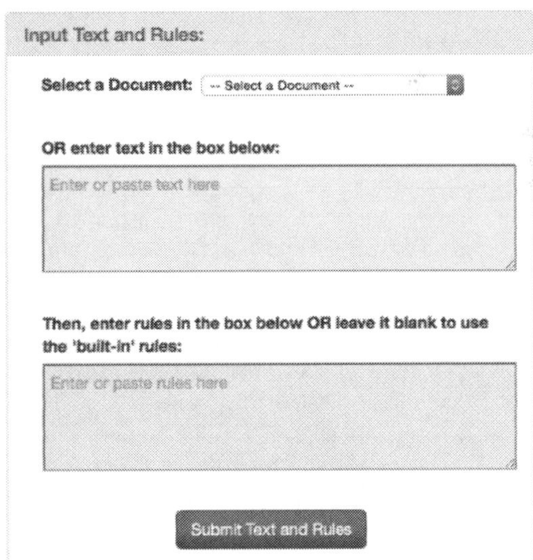

Figure 2: Our interactive environment for rapid development of event grammars.The UI supports the input of rules and free text.

Figure 3 shows the output of the visualization tool on the example sentence from Figure 1 using the gram-

```
class EventMention(
  /** The ontological labels associated with
    * the event (specified in the rule) */
  val label: Seq[String],
  /** The starting point of our pattern */
  val trigger: TextBoundMention,
  /** A mapping of argument names to the
    * Mentions that contain them */
  val arguments: Map[String, Seq[Mention]],
  /** The name of the corresponding rule */
  val foundBy: String
  /** The span of the Mention
    * in the original document*/
  val tokenInterval: Interval)
```

Example 5: Example 4 produces a set of mentions. Here we focus on mentions of events (`EventMention`). This code block shows relevant fields in the `EventMention` class, which stores each event mention detected and assembled by the system. The `arguments` field captures the fact that the mapping from names to arguments is one-to-many (e.g., there may be multiple `theme` arguments). `Interval` stores a token span in the input text. `TextBoundMention` stores a simple mention, minimally a label and a token span.

mar discussed in the previous section. The web interface is implemented as a client-server Grails[10] web application which runs the EE system on the server and displays the results on the client side. The application's client-side code displays both entity and event mentions, as well as the output of the text preprocessor (to help with debugging) using Brat (Stenetorp et al., 2012).

4 Results

We extended the grammar introduced previously to capture 10 different biochemical events, with an average of 11 rules per event type. Using this grammar we participated in a recent evaluation by DARPA's Big Mechanism program[11], where systems had to perform deep reading of two research papers on cancer biology. Table 1 summarizes our results.

Our system was ranked above the median, with respect to overall F1 score. We find these results encouraging for two reasons. First, inter-annotator agreement on the task was below 60%, which indicates that our system roughly approaches human performance, especially for precision. Second, the lower recall is partially explained by the fact that annotators marked also indirect biological relations (e.g., *A activates B*), which do not correspond to actual biochemical reactions but, instead, summarize sequences of biochemical reactions. Our grammar currently recognizes only direct biochemical reactions.

System	Precision	Recall	F1
Submitted run	54%	29%	37.3%
Ceiling system	82.1%	81.8%	82%

Table 1: Results from the January 2015 DARPA Big Mechanism Dry Run evaluation on reading biomedical papers, against a known biochemical model. In addition to event extraction, this evaluation required participants to identify if the extracted information corroborates, contradicts, or extends the given model. Here, extending the model means proposing a biochemical reaction that is not contained in the model, but it involves at least a biochemical entity from the model. The ceiling system indicates idealized performance of the rule-based framework, after a *post-hoc* analysis.

More importantly, this evaluation offers a good platform to analyze the potential of the proposed rule-based framework, by estimating the ceiling performance of our EE system, when all addressable issues are fixed. We performed this analysis after the evaluation deadline, and we manually:

1. Removed the keys that do not encode direct biochemical reactions.

2. Corrected three rules, to better model one event and one entity type.

3. Fixed system bugs, including XML parsing errors, which caused some meta data to appear in text and be misinterpreted as biological entities, and a syntax error in one rule, which caused several false positives.

The results of this ceiling system are listed in the second row in Table 1. This analysis highlights an encouraging finding: the current rule framework is expressive: it can capture approximately 80% of the events in this complex domain. The remaining 20% require coreference resolution and complex syntactic patterns, which were not correctly captured by the parser.

5 Related Work

Despite the dominant focus on machine learning models for IE in the literature, previous work includes several notable rule-based efforts. For example, GATE (Cunningham et al., 2011), and the Common Pattern Specification Language (Appelt and Onyshkevych, 1998) introduce a rule-based framework for IE, implemented as a cascade of grammars defined using surface patterns. The ICE system offers an active-learning system that learns named entity and binary relation patterns built on top of syntactic dependencies (He and Grishman, 2011). Stanford's Semgrex[12] and Tregex (Levy and Andrew, 2006) model syntactic patterns,

[10] `https://grails.org`

[11] `http://www.darpa.mil/Our_Work/I2O/Programs/Big_Mechanism.aspx`

[12] `http://nlp.stanford.edu/software/tregex.shtml`

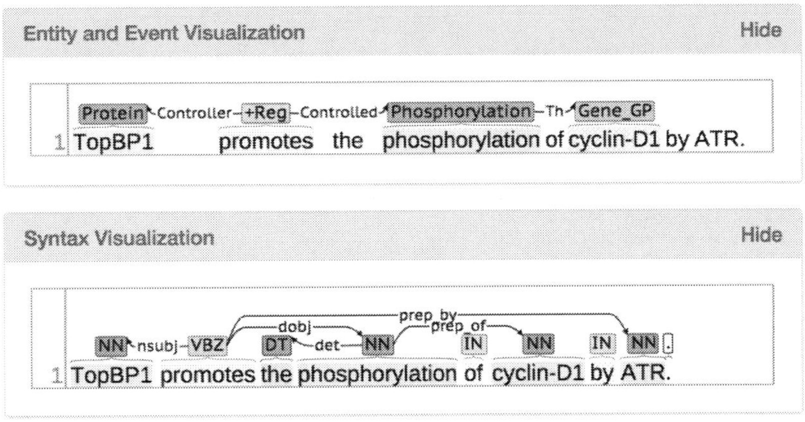

Figure 3: A Brat-based visualization of the event mentions created from the example sentence in Figure 1. Not shown but included in the visualization: a table with token information (lemmas, PoS tags, NE labels, and character spans).

while a separate tool from the same group, TokensRegex (Chang and Manning, 2014), defines surface patterns over token sequences. Chiticariu et al. (2011) demonstrated that a rule-based NER system can match or outperform results achieved with machine learning approaches, but also showed that rule-writing is a labor intensive process even with a language specifically designed for the task.

In addition to the above domain-independent frameworks, multiple previous works focused on rule-based systems built around specific domains. For example, in bioinformatics, several dedicated rule-based systems obtained state-of-the-art performance in the extraction of protein-protein interactions (PPI) (Hunter et al., 2008; Huang et al., 2004).

Our work complements and extends the above efforts with a relatively simple EE platform that: (a) hybridizes syntactic dependency patterns with surface patterns, (b) offers support for the extraction of recursive events; (c) is coupled with a fast runtime environment; and (d) is easily customizable to new domains.

6 Conclusion

We have described a domain-independent, rule-based event extraction framework and rapid development environment that is simple, fast, powerful, and robust. It is our hope that this framework reduces the entry cost in the development of rule-based event extraction systems.

We demonstrated how to build a biomedical domain from scratch, including rule examples and simple Scala code sufficient to run the domain grammar over free text. We recently extended this grammar to participate in the DARPA Big Mechanism evaluation, in which our system achieved an F1 of 37%. By modeling the underlying syntactic representation of events, our grammar for this task used an average of only 11 rules per event; this indicates that the syntactic structures of events are largely generalizable to a small set of predicate frames and that domain grammars can be constructed with relatively low effort. Our *post-hoc* analysis demonstrated that the system's true ceiling is 82%. This important result demonstrates that the proposed event extraction framework is expressive enough to capture most complex events annotated by domain experts.

Finally, to improve the user experience by aiding in the construction of event grammars, our framework is accompanied by a web-based interface for testing rules and visualizing matched events.

This whole effort is available as open-source code at: `https://github.com/sistanlp/processors`. See also: `https://github.com/sistanlp/processors/wiki/ODIN-(Open-Domain-INformer)`, for ODIN documentation.

Acknowledgments

This work was funded by the DARPA Big Mechanism program under ARO contract W911NF-14-1-0395.

References

Appelt, Douglas E and Boyan Onyshkevych. 1998. The common pattern specification language. In *Proc. of the TIPSTER Workshop*. pages 23–30.

Bui, Quoc-Chinh, Erik M Van Mulligen, David Campos, and Jan A Kors. 2013. A fast rule-based approach for biomedical event extraction. *Proc. of ACL* page 104.

Chang, Angel X. and Christopher D. Manning. 2014. TokensRegex: Defining cascaded regular expressions over tokens. Technical Report CSTR 2014-02, Computer Science, Stanford.

Chiticariu, Laura, R. Krishnamurthy, Y. Li, F. R. Reiss, and S. Vaithyanathan. 2011. Domain adaptation of rule-based annotators for named-entity recognition tasks. In *Proc. of EMNLP*.

Chiticariu, Laura, Yunyao Li, and Frederick R Reiss. 2013. Rule-based information extraction is dead! long live rule-based information extraction systems! In *Proc. of EMNLP*.

Cunningham, Hamish, Diana Maynard, Kalina Bontcheva, Valentin Tablan, Niraj Aswani, Ian Roberts, Genevieve Gorrell, Adam Funk, Angus Roberts, Danica Damljanovic, Thomas Heitz, Mark A. Greenwood, Horacio Saggion, Johann Petrak, Yaoyong Li, and Wim Peters. 2011. *Developing Language Processing Components with GATE (Version 6)*. University of Sheffield.

de Marneffe, Marie-Catherine and Christopher D. Manning. 2008. The Stanford typed dependencies representation. In *Proc. of COLING Workshop on Cross-framework and Cross-domain Parser Evaluation*.

He, Yifan and Ralph Grishman. 2011. Ice: Rapid information extraction customization for nlp novices. In *Proc. of NAACL*.

Huang, Minlie, Xiaoyan Zhu, Yu Hao, Donald G. Payan, Kunbin Qu, and Ming Li. 2004. Discovering patterns to extract proteinprotein interactions from full texts. *Bioinformatics* 20(18):3604–3612.

Hunter, Lawrence, Zhiyong Lu, James Firby, William A Baumgartner, Helen L Johnson, Philip V Ogren, and K Bretonnel Cohen. 2008. Opendmap: an open source, ontology-driven concept analysis engine, with applications to capturing knowledge regarding protein transport, protein interactions and cell-type-specific gene expression. *BMC bioinformatics* 9(1):78.

Levy, Roger and Galen Andrew. 2006. Tregex and Tsurgeon: tools for querying and manipulating tree data structures. In *Proc. of LREC*.

Manning, C. D., M. Surdeanu, J. Bauer, J. Finkel, S. J. Bethard, and D. McClosky. 2014. The Stanford CoreNLP natural language processing toolkit. In *Proc. of ACL*.

Ohta, Tomoko, Sampo Pyysalo, Rafal Rak, Andrew Rowley, Hong-Woo Chun, Sung-Jae Jung, Sung-Pil Choi, Sophia Ananiadou, and Junichi Tsujii. 2013. Overview of the pathway curation (pc) task of bionlp shared task 2013. In *Proc. of the BioNLP-ST Workshop*.

Peng, Yifan, Manabu Torii, Cathy H Wu, and K Vijay-Shanker. 2014. A generalizable NLP framework for fast development of pattern-based biomedical relation extraction systems. *BMC bioinformatics* 15(1):285.

Stenetorp, Pontus, Sampo Pyysalo, Goran Topić, Tomoko Ohta, Sophia Ananiadou, and Jun'ichi Tsujii. 2012. Brat: a web-based tool for nlp-assisted text annotation. In *Proc. of the Demonstrations at EACL*.

Storybase: Towards Building a Knowledge Base for News Events

Zhaohui Wu[†], **Chen Liang**[‡], **C. Lee Giles**[‡†]
[†]Computer Science and Engineering, [‡]Information Sciences and Technology
The Pennsylvania State University
University Park, PA 16802, USA
zzw109@psu.edu, {cul226,giles}@ist.psu.edu

Abstract

To better organize and understand online news information, we propose Storybase[1], a knowledge base for news events that builds upon Wikipedia current events and daily Web news. It first constructs stories and their timelines based on Wikipedia current events and then detects and links daily news to enrich those Wikipedia stories with more comprehensive events. We encode events and develop efficient event clustering and chaining techniques in an event space. We demonstrate Storybase with a news events search engine that helps find historical and ongoing news stories and inspect their dynamic timelines.

1 Introduction

Users are often overwhelmed by the flood of information, especially frequently daily updated news. Search engines effectively find news snippets and related Web pages, or group similar pages in clusters. However, it remains difficult to coherently connect isolated information nuggets to form the big picture, or to accurately track the flow of information to show the evolution of events. For example, current news search engines or aggregation sites, such as Google or Yahoo news, show only isolated daily news events, without linking them to historical events or show storylines.

Most existing knowledge bases such as DBpedia and Freebase are designed for managing general named entities or concepts and often lack coverage or representation for temporally evolving news events. For example, as of this writing, Freebase has not treated "2014 Ferguson unrest" as an "event", let alone show its sub events or timelines. As such, we propose building a knowledge base, namely Storybase, that stores news events in a semantic coherent schema that could explicitly display their evolving timelines. We define a *story* as a set of topically or causally related and temporally ordered news events, usually corresponding to a Wikipedia article such as "Malaysia Airlines Flight 370". An event is defined as something important happening at some time in some place, reported by a set of news articles, which is encoded by named entities, actors and actions used as the main points in a plot.

Building an event knowledge base from scratch is challenging, since it is difficult to obtain a gold standard for events and their timelines. We found that Wikipedia current events[2] provide high-quality manually edited news events. To scale up, we link daily news sources and fit them into existing stories or create new stories, by efficient event detection and storyline construction techniques in a semantic space which is encoded with news events' entities, actors, and actions. From April 1, 2013 to March 1, 2015, we have collected 1,256 stories consisting of 35,362 news events from Wikipedia current events, and 35,166,735 daily news articles. Experimental evaluation compares our methods for event clustering and chaining with multiple baselines. We build a news event search engine based on Storybase to show news stories and their event chains.

Our main contributions include:

- A news event knowledge base, Storybase, with a search interface for news storylines;
- The introduction of Wikipedia current events as resources for building event knowledge bases and as datasets for event detection and storyline construction;
- New approaches for event clustering and chaining with experimental comparisons to other baselines.

[1]http://breckenridge.ist.psu.edu:8000/storybase

[2]http://en.wikipedia.org/wiki/Portal:Current_events

Proceedings of ACL-IJCNLP 2015 System Demonstrations, pages 133–138,
Beijing, China, July 26-31, 2015.

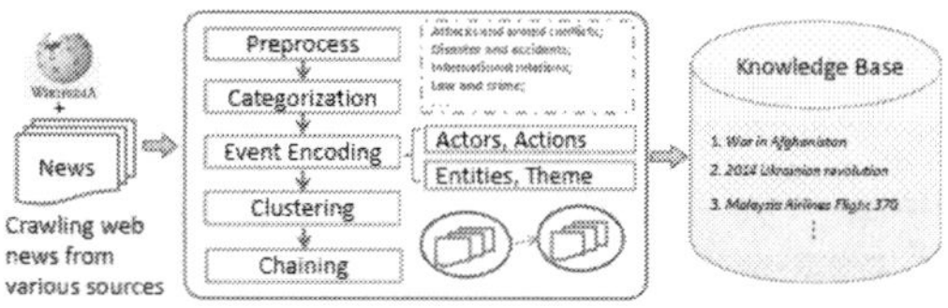

Figure 1: Overall process of building Storybase

Figure 2: Examples of Wikipedia current events

2 Overview and Definitions

Figure 1 shows the overall process for building S-torybase. Input is daily crawled web news articles and Wikipedia current events. This generates the storylines and builds the Storybase using five steps system: preprocessing, categorization, event encoding, clustering, and chaining. Details are in Section 4. A news event search engine is built to provide a query based interface to search and visualize the Storybase, which is shown in Section 5.

We now define concepts that will be frequently referred to.

- A *event* identifies something (non-trivial) happening in a certain place at a certain time (Yang et al., 1999); it is a set of news articles on the same news report.
- A *story* is a set of topical related news events.
- A *storyline* is a series of temporally ordered events of the same story.
- *Actors* in an event are named entities that make or receive actions.
- *Actions* are verbs that connect actors.

For example, as shown in Figure 2, "Pro-Russian militants seize the regional prosecutor's office in the eastern Ukrainian city of Donetsk" is an even-t reported by a set of articles from different news sites. "2014 pro-Russian unrest in Ukraine" represents a story that consists of temporally evolving events, which forms a storyline. "Pro-Russian militants" and "the regional prosecutor's office" are actors while "seize" is the action.

3 Data Collection

Wikipedia current events list manually edited daily news events since 1998, which provide rich semantics and structure for news stories and events such as story names, event categories (*not* Wikipedia categories), and links to Wikipedia concepts, as shown by Figure 2. For example, we can observe that the event "Pro-Russian militants seize the regional prosecutor's office in the eastern Ukrainian city of Donetsk" belongs to the story "2014 pro-Russian unrest in Ukraine" and the category "Armed conflicts and attacks", containing links to Wikipedia concepts "Eastern Ukrainian" and "Donetsk". Thus, we construct a storyline for "2014 pro-Russian unrest in Ukraine" by connecting all events under it.

The category labels provide a natural way to classify news events. However, since the Wikipedia events are edited by various users, the category labels are not always consistent. For example, one may use "Armed conflicts and attack-s" while others might use "Attack and conflict". After canonicalization using Levenshtein distance and grouping similar labels using word based Jaccard similarity, we manually clean all the labels into 12 categories, as shown in Table 1.

Although Wikipedia provides high quality manually edited news events, it covers only a smal-l number of events every day, usually less than 30. Thus, to scale up Storybase and make the stories more comprehensive, starting from April 1, 2013, we crawl daily news articles from a large number of sources from various news publishers, provided by GDELT[3] project (Leetaru and Schrodt, 2013).

4 Building Storybase

4.1 Preprocess and Categorization

To extract and parse Wikipedia current events, we implement two template based extractors for events between January 2003 and April 2006 and those events after April 2006 respectively due to their difference in templates. The news articles linked at the end of each event description are also crawled. We use boilerpipe[4] to extract the title and main text content of each news article. We extrac-t the first three sentences in the main content for summarization.

[3]http://www.gdeltproject.org/data.html

[4]https://code.google.com/p/boilerpipe/

ID	Category
1	conflict, attack
2	disaster, accident
3	international relations
4	politics and elections
5	law and crime
6	business and economy
7	science and technology
8	sports
9	arts and culture
10	health, medicine, environment
11	education
12	deaths

Table 1: Categories of events in Storybase

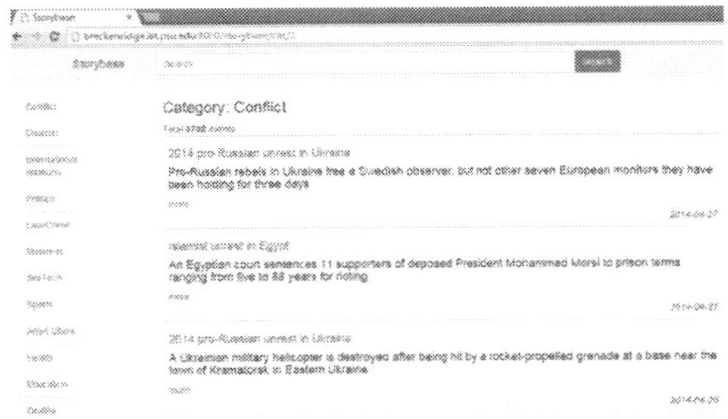

Figure 3: Screenshot of category "Conflict"

We maintain an N-to-1 mapping for each category listed in Table 1. For example, any category label in {"Armed conflicts and attacks", "conflicts and attacks", "Armed conflicts", "Attacks and conflicts", "Attacks and armed conflicts"} will be mapped to Category 1. For an event not belonging to existing stories, we label its category using the majority of their k-nearest (k=10) neighbors based on the cosine similarity of event descriptions.

4.2 Event Encoding

We encode an event as a vector containing named entities, actors and actions. Named entities such as people and locations in news reports contain important information of the event. Core entities that play important roles in an event are called actors, which are usually people or organizations that make or receive actions. We use the Stanford CoreNLP (Manning et al., 2014) for the named entity recognition and extract all Wikipedia concepts appearing in news content. Entities that are subjects or objects in the title and description are treated as actors. If no entities are found, we then use the CAMEO dictionaries[5] for actor and action extraction.

4.3 Event Clustering and Chaining

Event clustering groups together news on the same event. Locality-Sensitive Hashing (LSH) (Van Durme and Lall, 2010) is used for fast similarity comparison. We first do deduplication on all articles on the same date using 84 bits sim-Hashing (Charikar, 2002). We then use modified sim-Hashing on the vector space of event described in Section 4.2, rather than shingling or bag-of-words (Paulev et al., 2010). A new article is encoded into the event space with the content of its title and description. Its LSH key k (84 bits binary code) is computed and compared to keys of other articles. Articles whose keys have hamming distances smaller than a threshold θ among each other will be clustered as an event. We then check all events of the previous date and merge two events into one if their distance (average hamming distances of key pairs) is smaller than θ and their categories are the same.

Event chaining links an event to an existing story or determines if it is the starting event of a new story. While LSH could give high-purity event clusters, it might not be able to determine whether two events with distance larger than θ are topically related, or belong to the same story. Intuitively, an event should bring some novelty and preserve some common information compared with the previous ones in the story, causing a tradeoff between relevance and novelty, which could be measured by some textual similarity. Adding an event should also keep the storyline coherent. To model coherence, we investigate two features, the Connecting-Dots coherence score (Shahaf and Guestrin, 2010) and KL-divergence. We use the gradient boosting tree (Friedman, 2001) to learn if an event belongs to a story by using the above features of relevance/novelty and coherence, all based on storylines constructed from Wikipedia current events. For a story $\{e_1,...,e_m\}$, $(e_i, \{e_1, ..., e_{i-1}\})$ are positive pairs; $(e_-, \{e_1, ..., e_{i-1}\})$ are negative pairs, $i = 2, ..., m$, where e_- is an event randomly sampled from other stories in the same date of e_i.

For all GDELT news on date t, we first detect all events using event clustering. For an event that has not been merged into events of the previous date, we use the model to decide which story it belongs to. If none, the event will be served as the first event of a new story with an empty story name.

[5]http://eventdata.parusanalytics.com/data.dir/cameo.html

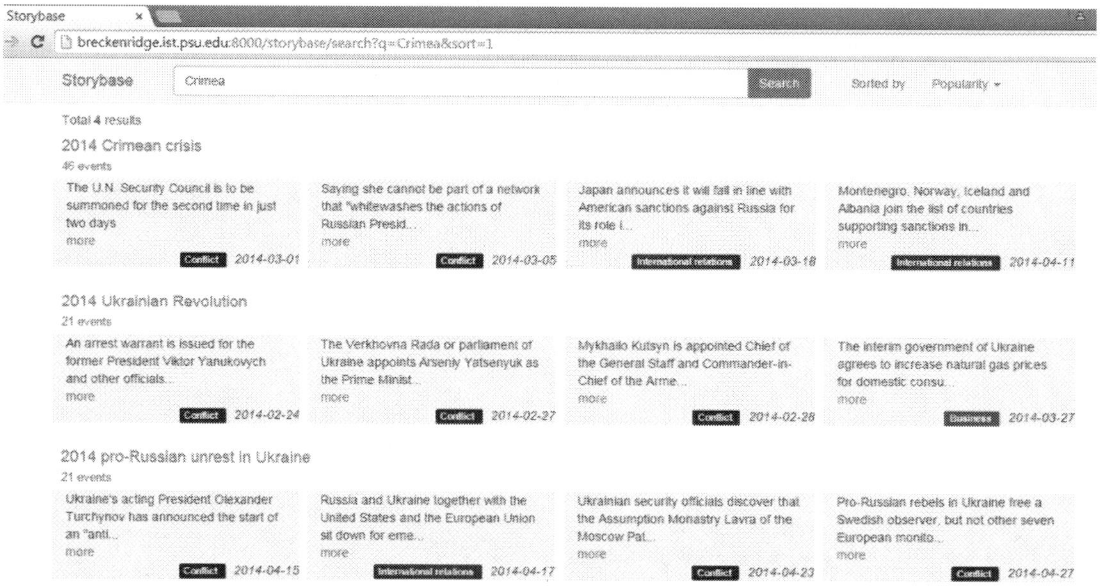

Figure 4: Screenshot results for the query "Crimea"

5 Storybase Demonstration

We demonstrate Storybase by building a news event search engine that can retrieve and visualize the stories. In the backend, we implemented various facilities, such as ranking functions (BM25, cosine similarity, and inner product) and refining metrics (popularity and recency). The ranking functions compute relevance between queries and stories while a story is represented by the story name and all event descriptions. *Popularity* measures the impact of stories on Web. For simplicity, we implement popularity as the accumulative number of unique news reports for all events of a story. *Recency* measures the timeliness or freshness, which is an important and helpful feature for sorting and filtering news stories, and is implemented by simply sorting stories based on the date of their latest event.

The front page gives a category navigation list in the left, a search box in the middle, and the recent stories behind the box. A category links to the recent events from the category, as shown by Figure 3. The demo contains three views: storyline, story, and event. Figure 4 shows a screenshot of the storyline view returned by querying "Crimea". The results are organized at the story level, where we show a thumbnail of the event chain for each story. The description, category, and date of an event are presented in the event box. By clicking the story name, it will direct to a story view page that chronologically lists all its events where the story name links to the corresponding Wikipedia article. Clicking "more" for each event links to the event view page that lists all the news articles of the event. At the upper right corner there is dropdown menu which allow users to set the ranking functions and refine metrics.

6 Experiments

We evaluate the event clustering and chaining in an experimental dataset constructed using Wikipedia current events from 01/01/2013 to 01/31/2015, which contains 652 stories covering 9004 events with 8,944 news articles.

We first explore whether our event clustering can effectively and efficiently cluster news articles of the same event. To construct the dataset, we select the events that link to more than 4 news articles, which in total gives us 55 events from 229 news articles. We then compare our method with the state-of-art clustering algorithms including K-means (Hartigan and Wong, 1979) and DBSCAN (Ester et al., 1996), and the state-of-art LSH methods including min-Hashing (Broder, 1997) and sim-Hashing (Charikar, 2002). We use the cluster module provided by *sklearn*[6]. For both K-means and DBSCAN, we use TFIDF based Euclidean distance in bag-of-word space. For K-means, we set the number of clusters to 55. For

[6] http://scikit-learn.org/stable/modules/clustering.html

Methods	Precision	Recall	F1
K-means	76.2%	73.1%	74.6%
DBSCAN	77.9%	74.6%	76.2%
Min-Hashing	**82.1%**	51.2%	63.1%
Sim-Hashing	80.1%	50.2%	61.7%
Event-Hashing	79.6%	**76.8%**	**78.2%**

Table 2: Event clustering comparisons

Methods	Avg. Accuracy
Cosine	66.7%
Connecting-Dots Coherence	45.2%
KL Coherence	43.3%
Learning based Model	**71.5%**

Table 3: Comparisons of event chaining

DBSCAN, we set the neighborhood size (the minimum number of points required to form a dense region) as 1. Both min-Hashing and sim-Hashing generate an 84 bits binary code to represent an event. We set θ as 5.

Table 2 shows the average precision, recall, and F1 scores over all clusters. Our method (Event-Hashing) outperforms both distance-based and LSH based clustering algorithms in terms of effectiveness, suggesting that our event representation using entities, actors, and actions is a more promising approach than bag-of-word ones. Our method is somewhat slower than min-Hashing and sim-Hashing because of the extra computing on the event space. It is worth noting that min-Hashing and sim-Hashing have higher precisions than ours, but at the cost of a big loss in recall.

We then evaluate the effectiveness of the event chaining for constructing storylines. We use the 458 stories starting in range [01/01/2013, 02/28/2014] for training and the other 194 stories for testing. We define *accuracy* of a constructed storyline as the fraction of the correctly linked events. For testing, each story is initialized by its first event. Thresholds of the three baseline measures are tuned in the training set. As shown by Table 3, our learning based model combining the three features significantly outperforms the baselines in average accuracy over the testing stories.

A small scale evaluation on the effectiveness and efficiency of the news event search engine is also performed. First, we evaluate the ranking performance for different ranking functions on a test query set including 10 different queries using precision at k (P@k). The query set contains "United States", "Russia", "China", "Barack Obama", "European Union", "President of the United States", "Car bomb", "North Korea", "South Korea", "President of Russia". We choose these queries because they appear frequently in the news articles and are very likely to be searched by users. Table 4 shows the performance of three ranking functions. The P@k scores for BM25 and cosine similarity is higher than inner product. This happens because the inner product does not do normalization thus favors the longer documents which should be less relevant in our setting.

Method	P@3	P@5	P@10	AvgTimePerQuery
Inn. Pro.	57	66	69	133ms
BM25	100	94	92	104ms
Cosine	100	94	96	136ms

Table 4: Performance comparisons of ranking methods on event search

7 Related Work

Little work has been reported on the building of event knowledge bases with the exception of EVIN (Kuzey and Weikum, 2014). However, their main focus is on extracting named events from news articles in an offline setting for knowledge base population (Ji and Grishman, 2011), but not building storylines for new events from large scale daily news streams.

Topic detection and tracking (TDT) that addresses event-based organization of news has been widely studied (Yang et al., 1999; Allan, 2002; Petrović et al., 2012). Furthermore, there is a rich literature on bursty event detection (Kleinberg, 2002; Fung et al., 2005; He et al., 2007), where an "event" is a set of word features that co-occur in certain time windows in text streams. There is also an emerging interest in building news timelines (Li and Li, 2013; Yan et al., 2011), event chains (Chambers and Jurafsky, 2008; Shahaf and Guestrin, 2010; Tannier and Moriceau, 2013), or topic model based storylines (Ahmed et al., 2011). It is worth noting that some work uses similar event encoding based on actors and actions for political events (O'Connor et al., 2013). Our work is different from existing work in both the representation of an "event" and event detection techniques. We use a three-layer (story-event-article) representation to organize the storylines and develop efficient clustering and chaining methods on the event space.

8 Conclusion and Future Work

We presented Storybase, an event knowledge base for news stories containing rich temporal and semantic information and described a storyline based news event search engine. Experimental results demonstrated that our proposed methods are effective and efficient for event detection and storyline based search. Future work could include enriching properties of a story using Wikipedia infobox and better summarizing events and stories.

9 Acknowledgements

We acknowledge partial support from Raytheon and the National Science Foundation, useful discussions with B.J. Simpson, Robert Cole, Philip A. Schrodt, and Muhammed Y. Idris, and technical support from Jian Wu, Kyle Williams, and the CiteseerX team.

References

Amr Ahmed, Qirong Ho, Jacob Eisenstein, Eric Xing, Alexander J Smola, and Choon Hui Teo. 2011. Unified analysis of streaming news. In *WWW*, pages 267–276.

James Allan. 2002. Introduction to topic detection and tracking. In James Allan, editor, *Topic Detection and Tracking*, volume 12 of *The Information Retrieval Series*, pages 1–16.

Andrei Z Broder. 1997. On the resemblance and containment of documents. In *Compression and Complexity of Sequences 1997.*, pages 21–29. IEEE.

Nathanael Chambers and Daniel Jurafsky. 2008. Unsupervised learning of narrative event chains. In *ACL*, pages 789–797.

Moses S Charikar. 2002. Similarity estimation techniques from rounding algorithms. In *STOC*, pages 380–388.

Martin Ester, Hans-Peter Kriegel, Jörg Sander, and Xiaowei Xu. 1996. A density-based algorithm for discovering clusters in large spatial databases with noise. In *KDD*, volume 96, pages 226–231.

Jerome H Friedman. 2001. Greedy function approximation: a gradient boosting machine. *Annals of statistics*, pages 1189–1232.

Gabriel Pui Cheong Fung, Jeffrey Xu Yu, Philip S. Yu, and Hongjun Lu. 2005. Parameter free bursty events detection in text streams. In *VLDB*, pages 181–192.

J. A. Hartigan and M. A. Wong. 1979. A k-means clustering algorithm. *JSTOR: Applied Statistics*, 28(1):100–108.

Qi He, Kuiyu Chang, and Ee-Peng Lim. 2007. Analyzing feature trajectories for event detection. In *SIGIR*, pages 207–214.

Heng Ji and Ralph Grishman. 2011. Knowledge base population: Successful approaches and challenges. In *ACL*, pages 1148–1158.

Jon Kleinberg. 2002. Bursty and hierarchical structure in streams. In *KDD*, pages 91–101.

Erdal Kuzey and Gerhard Weikum. 2014. Evin: building a knowledge base of events. In *WWW companion*, pages 103–106.

Kalev Leetaru and Philip A Schrodt. 2013. Gdelt: Global data on events, location, and tone, 1979–2012. In *Paper presented at the ISA Annual Convention*, volume 2, page 4.

Jiwei Li and Sujian Li. 2013. Evolutionary hierarchical dirichlet process for timeline summarization. In *ACL*, pages 556–560.

Christopher D. Manning, Mihai Surdeanu, John Bauer, Jenny Finkel, Steven J. Bethard, and David McClosky. 2014. The Stanford CoreNLP natural language processing toolkit. In *ACL*, pages 55–60.

Brendan O'Connor, Brandon M Stewart, and Noah A Smith. 2013. Learning to extract international relations from political context. In *ACL (1)*, pages 1094–1104.

Loc Paulev, Herv Jgou, and Laurent Amsaleg. 2010. Locality sensitive hashing: A comparison of hash function types and querying mechanisms. *Pattern Recognition Letters*, 31(11):1348 – 1358.

Saša Petrović, Miles Osborne, and Victor Lavrenko. 2012. Using paraphrases for improving first story detection in news and twitter. In *NAACL*, pages 338–346.

Dafna Shahaf and Carlos Guestrin. 2010. Connecting the dots between news articles. In *KDD*, pages 623–632.

Xavier Tannier and Véronique Moriceau. 2013. Building event threads out of multiple news articles. In *EMNLP*, pages 958–967.

Benjamin Van Durme and Ashwin Lall. 2010. Online generation of locality sensitive hash signatures. In *ACL*, pages 231–235.

Rui Yan, Liang Kong, Congrui Huang, Xiaojun Wan, Xiaoming Li, and Yan Zhang. 2011. Timeline generation through evolutionary trans-temporal summarization. In *EMNLP*, pages 433–443.

Yiming Yang, Jaime G Carbonell, Ralf D Brown, Thomas Pierce, Brian T Archibald, and Xin Liu. 1999. Learning approaches for detecting and tracking news events. *IEEE Intelligent Systems*, 14(4):32–43.

WriteAhead: Mining Grammar Patterns in Corpora for Assisted Writing

Tzu-Hsi Yen, Jian-Cheng Wu+ Joanne Boisson, Jim Chang, Jason Chang
Department of Computer Science +National Academy for Educational Research
National Tsing Hua University Minstry of Education
Hsinchu, Taiwan, R.O.C. 30013 Taipei, Taiwan, R.O.C. 30013
{joe, jiancheng}@nlplab.cc {joanne, jim, jason}@nlplab.cc

Abstract

This paper describes *WriteAhead*, a resource-rich, Interactive Writing Environment that provides L2 learners with writing prompts, as well as "get it right" advice, to helps them write fluently and accurately. The method involves automatically analyzing reference and learner corpora, extracting grammar patterns with example phrases, and computing dubious, overused patterns. At run-time, as the user types (or mouses over) a word, the system automatically retrieves and displays grammar patterns and examples, most relevant to the word. The user can opt for patterns from a general corpus, academic corpus, learner corpus, or commonly overused dubious patterns found in a learner corpus. *WriteAhead* proactively engages the user with steady, timely, and spot-on information for effective assisted writing. Preliminary experiments show that *WriteAhead* fulfills the design goal of fostering learner independence and encouraging self-editing, and is likely to induce better writing, and improve writing skills in the long run.

1 Introduction

The British Council has estimated that roughly a billion people are learning and using English around the world (British Council 1997), mostly as a second language, and the numbers are growing. Clearly, many of L2 speakers of English feel themselves to be at a disadvantage in work that requires communication in English. For example, Flowerdew (1999) reports that a third of Hong Kong academics feel disadvantged in publishing a paper internationally, as compared to native speakers.

These L2 speakers and learners provide motivation for research and development of computer assisted language learning, in particular tools that help identify and correct learners' writing errors. Much work has been done on developing technologies for automated gramatical error correction (GEC) to assist language learners (Leacock, Chodorow, Gamon, and Tetreault 2010). However, such efforts have not led to the development of a production system (Wampler, 2002).

However, Milton (2010) pointed out that focusing on fully-automatic, high quality GEC solutions has overlooked the long-term pedagogical needs of L2 learner writers. Learners could be more effectively assisted in an interactive writring environment (IWE) that constantly provides context-sensitive writing suggestions, right in the process of writing or self-editing.

Consider an online writer who starts a sentence with *"This paper discusses ...."* The best way the system can help is probably displaying the patterns related to the last word *discuss* such as **discuss something** and **discusses with someone**, that help the user to write accurately and fluently. If the user somehow writes or pastes in some incorrect sentence, *"This paper discusses about the influence of interference and reflection of light."* The best way the system can help is probably displaying the erroneous or overused pattern, **discuss about something**, that prompts the user to change the sentence to *"This paper discusses the influence of interference and reflection of light."*

Intuitively, by extracting and displaying such patterns and examples, distilled from a very large corpus, we can guide the user towards writing flu-

Proceedings of ACL-IJCNLP 2015 System Demonstrations, pages 139–144,
Beijing, China, July 26-31, 2015.

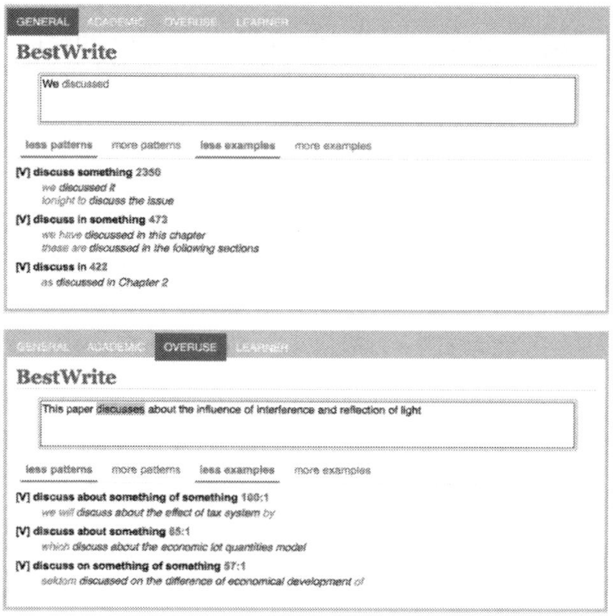

Figure 1: Example *WriteAhead* session where an user typed "This paper present method".

ently, and free of grammatical errors.

We present a new system, *WriteAhead*, that proactively provides just-in-time writing suggestions to assist student writers, while they type away. Example *WriteAhead* suggestions for "*We discussed ...*" are shown in Figure 1. *WriteAhead* has determined the best patterns and examples extracted from the underlying corpus. *WriteAhead* learns these patterns and examples automatically during training by analyzing annotated dictionary examples and automatically tagged sentences in a corpus. As will be described in Section 4, we used the information on collocation and syntax (ICS) for example sentences from online *Macmillan English Dictionary*, as well as in the *Citeseer x* corpus, to develop *WriteAhead*.

At run-time, *WriteAhead* activates itself as the user types in yet another word (e.g., "*discussed*" in the prefix "*We discussed ...*"). *WriteAhead* then retrieves patterns related to the last word. *WriteAhead* goes one step further and re-ranks the suggestions, in an attempt to move most relevant suggestions to the top. *WriteAhead* can be accessed at `http://writehead.nlpweb.org/`.

In our prototype, *WriteAhead* returns the suggestions to the user directly (see Figure 1); alternatively, the suggestions returned by *WriteAhead* can be used as input to an automatic grammar checker or an essay rater.

The rest of this paper is organized as follows. We review the related work in the next section. Then we present our method for automatically learning normal and overused grammar patterns and examples for use in an interactive writing environment (Section 3). Section 5 gives a demonstration script of the interactive writing environment.

2 Related Work

Much work described in a recent survey (Leacock, Chodorow, Gamon, and Tetreault 2010) show that the elusive goal of fully-automatic and high-quality grammatical error correction is far from a reality. Moreover, Milton (2010) pointed out that we should shift the focus and responsibility to the learner, since no conclusive evidence shows explicit correction by a teacher or machine is leads to improved writing skills (Truscott, 1996; Ferris and Hedgcock, 2005). In this paper, we develop an interactive writing environment (IWE) that constantly provides context-sensitive writing suggestions, right in the process of writing or self-editing.

Autocompletion has been widely used in many language production tasks (e.g., search query and translation). Examples include *Google Suggest* and *TransType*, which pioneered the interactive user interface for statistical machine translation (Langlais et al., 2002; Casacuberta et al. 2009). However, previous work focuses exclusively on

Procedure ExtractPatterns(*Sent, Keywords, Corpus*)

(1) Learning phrase templates for grammar patterns of content words (Section 3.1.1)

(2) Extracting grammar patterns for all keywords in the given corpus based on phrase templates (Section 3.1.2)

(3) Extracting exemplary instances for all patterns of all keywords (Section 3.1.3)

Figure 2: Outline of the pattern extraction process

providing surface suggestions lacking in generality to be truely effective for all users in different writing situation. In contrast, we provide suggestions in the form of theoretical and pedagogically sound language representation, in the form of Pattern Grammar (Hunston and Francis 2000). We also provide concise examples much like concordance advocated by Sinclair (1991).

Much work has been done in deriving context-free grammar from a corpus, while very little work has been done in deriving pattern grammar. Mason and Hunston (2004) reports on a pilot study to automatically recognize grammar patterns for verbs, using only limited linguistic knowledge. It is unclear whether their method can scale up and extend to other parts of speech. In contrast, we show it is feasible to extract grammar patterns for nouns, verbs, and adjectives on a large scale using a corpus with hundreds of million words.

Researchers have been extracting error patterns in the form of word or part of speech (POS) sequencesto detect real-word spelling errors (e.g., Golding and Schabes, 1996; Verberne, 2002). For example, the sequence of **det. det. n.** definitely indicate an error, while **v. prep. adv.** might or might not indicate an error. For this reason, function words (e.g., prepositions) are not necessarily reduced to POS tags (e.g., **v. to adv.**). Sometimes, even lexicalized patterns are necessary (e.g., **go to adv.**) Sun et al. (2007) extend n-grams to non-continuous sequential patterns allowing arbitrary gaps between words. In a recent study closer to our work, Gamon (2011) use high-order part-of-speech ngram to model and detect learner errors on the sentence level.

In contrast to the previous research in developing computer assisted writing environment, we present a system that automatically learns grammar patterns and examples from an academic written corpus as well as learner corpus, with the goal of providing relevant, in-context suggestions.

3 Method

Non-native speakers often make grammatically error, particularly in using some common words in writing (e.g., *discuss* vs. *discuss *about*). In addition, using dictionaries or mere lexical suggestions to assist learner in writing is often not sufficient, and the information could be irrelevant at times. In this section, we address such a problem. Given various corpora (e.g., *BNC* or *CiteseerX*) in a specific genre/domain and a unfinished or completed sentence, we intend to assist the user by retrieving and displaying a set of suggestions extracted from each corpus. For this, by a simple and intuitional method, we extract grammatical error patterns and correction such that the top ranked suggestions are likely to contain a pattern that fits well with the context of the unfinished sentence. We describe the stage of our solution to this problem in the subsections that followed.

3.1 Extracting Grammar Patterns

We attempt to extract grammatical error patterns and correction for keywords in a given corpus to provide writing suggestions, in order to assist ESL learners in an online writing session. Our extraction process is shown in Figure 2.

3.1.1 *Learning Extraction Templates* In the first stage of the extraction process (Step (1) in Figure 2), we generate a set of phrase templates for identifying grammar patterns based on information on Collocation and Syntax (ICS) in an online dictionary.

For example, the dictionary entry of *difficulty* may provide examples with ICS pattern, such as **have difficulty/problem (in) doing something**: *Six months after the accident, he still has difficulty walking*. This complicated pattern with parenthetical and alternative parts can be expanded to yield patterns such as **have difficulty in doing something**. By generalizing such a pattern into templates with PoS and phrase tags (e.g., **v. np prep. v np**, we can identify instances of such a pattern in tagged and chunked sentences. For this, we expand the parentheticals (e.g., **(in)**) and alternatives (e.g., **difficulty/problem**) in ICS.

Then, we replace (non-entry) words in ICS with the most frequent part of speech tags or phrase tags, resulting in sequences of POS and phrase labels (e.g., **v. difficulty prep. v. np**). Then, we take only the complementation part (e.g., **prep. v. np**). Finally, we convert each complementation into a regular expression for a *RegExp* chunk parser.

Subsequently, we convert each template into a regular expression of chunk labels, intended to match instances of potential patterns in tagged sentences. The chunk labels typically are represented using B-I-O symbols followed by phrase type, with each symbol denoting **B**eginning, **I**nside, and **O**utside of the phrase. Note that in order to identify the head of a phrase, we change the B-I-O representation to I-H-O, with H signifying the **H**ead.

3.1.2 *Extracting Patterns* In the second stage of the extraction process (Step (2) in Figure 2), we identify instances of potential patterns for all keywords. These instances are generated for each tagged and chunked sentence in the given corpus and for each chunk templates obtained in the previous stage.

We adopt the *MapReduce* framework to extract salient patterns. At the start of the *Map Procedure*, we perform part of speech, lemmatization, and base phrase tagging on the sentences. We then find all pattern instances anchoring at a keyword and matching templates obtained in the first stage. Then, from each matched instance, we extract the tuple, (*grammar pattern*, *collocation*, and *ngrams*). Finally, we emit all tuples extracted from the tagged sentence. The map procedure is applied to every tagged sentence in the given corpus.

In the *reduce* part, the *ReducePattern Procedure* receives a batch of tuples, locally sorted and grouped by keyword, as is usually done in the *MapReduce* paradigm. At the start of the *ReducePattern Procedure*, we further group the tuple by pattern. Then we count the number of tuples of each pattern as well as within-group average and standard deviation of the counts. Finally, with these statistics, we filter and identify patterns more frequent than average by 1 standard deviation. The *ReducePattern Procedure* is applied to all tuples generated in the *Map Procedure*. Sample output of this stage is shown in Table 1.

3.1.3 *Extracting Exemplary Phrases* In the third and final stage of extraction, we generate exemplary phrases for all patterns of all keywords of interest using the *ReduceCollExm Procedure*, which is done after the Map procedure, and essentially the same as the *ReducePattern Procedure* in the second stage (Section 3.1.2).

In the spirit of the GDEX method (Kilgarriff et al. 2008) of selecting good dictionary examples for a headword via collocations, we propose a method for selection good example for a pattern. For this, we count and select salient collocations (e.g., the heads of phrases, *difficulty in process* in pattern instance *difficulty in the optimization process*). For each selected collocation, we choose the most frequent instance (augmented with context) to show the user the typical situation of using the collocation.

Table 1: Example *difficulty* patterns extracted.

Pattern	Count	Example
difficulty of something	2169	*of the problem*
difficulty in doing something	1790	*in solving the problems*
difficulty of doing something	1264	*of solving this problem*
difficulty in something	1219	*in the previous analyses*
difficulty with something	755	*with this approach*
difficulty doing something	718	*using it*

Note: There are 11200 instances of potential *difficulty* patterns with average count of 215 and a standard deviation of 318

These examples also facilitate the system in ranking patterns (as will be described in Section 3.2). For that, we add one chunk before, and one chunk after the collocational instance. For example, the collocation, **method for solution of equation** is exemplified using the authentic corpus example, "*method for exact solution of homogeneous linear differential equation*" in the context of "*report a new analytical ... with.*" We use a similar procedure as describe in Section 3.1.2 to extract examples.

After the grammar patterns are extracted from a reference corpus and a learner corpus, we normalize and compared the counts of the same pattern in the two corpora and compuate an overuse ratio for all patterns and retain patterns with a high overuse ratio.

3.2 Retrieving and Ranking Suggestions

Once the patterns and examples are automatically extracted for each keyword in the given corpus, they are stored and indexed by keyword. At run-time in a writing session, *WriteAway* constantly probes and gets the last keyword of the unfinished sentence *Sent* in the text box (or the word under the mouse when in editing mode). With the keyword as a query, *WriteAway* retrieves and ranks all relevant patterns and examples (*Pat* and *Exm*) aiming to move the most relevant information toward the top. We compute the longest common subsequence (LCS) of *Sent* and an example, *Exm*. The examples and patterns are ranked by

$$\text{Score}(Exm) = |\ LCS(Exm, Sent)\ | \times \text{Count}(Exm).$$

$$\text{Score}(Pat) = \sum \text{Score}(E), \text{ where } E \text{ is an example of } Pat$$

To improve ranking, we also try to find the longest similar subsequence (LSS) between the user input, *Sent* and retrieved example, *Exm* based on distributional word similarity using the word2vec (Mikolov et al., 2013) cosine distance. The new score function is:

$$\text{Score}(Exm) = LSS(Exm, Sent) \times \text{Count}(Exm),$$
$$LSS(Exm, Sent) = \max sim(Exm_{sub}, Sent_{sub}),$$
$$\text{sim}(A, B) = 0, \qquad \text{if } |A| \neq |B|.$$
$$\text{sim}(A, B) = \sum word\text{-}sim(A_i, B_i), \quad \text{otherwise.}$$

4 Experiments and Results

For training, we used a collection of approximately 3,000 examples for 700 headwords obtained from online Macmillan English Dictionary (Rundel 2007), to develop the templates of patterns. The headwords include nouns, verbs, adjectives, and adverbs. We then proceeded to extract writing grammar patterns and examples from the British National Corpus (BNC, with 100 million words), *CiteseerX* corpus (with 460 million words) and Taiwan Degree Thesis Corpus (with 10 million words). First, we used Tsujii POS Tagger (Tsuruoka and Tsujii 2005) to generate tagged sentences. We applied the proposed method to generate suggestions for each of the 700 content keywords in Academic Keyword List.

4.1 Technical Architecture

WriteAhead was implemented in Python and Flask Web framework. We stored the suggestions in JSON format using PostgreSQL for faster access. *WriteAhead* server obtains client input from a popular browser (Safari, Chrome, or Firefox) dynamically with AJAX techniques. For uninterrupted service and ease of scaling up, we chose to host *WriteAhead* on Heroku, a cloud-platform-as-a-service (PaaS) site.

4.2 Evaluating *WriteAhead*

To evaluate the performance of *WriteAhead*, we randomly sampled 100 sentences from a learner corpus with complementation errors. For each sentence, we identify the keyword related to the error and checked whether we have identify an overused pattern relevant to the error, and if positive the rank of this pattern. We then use the Mean Reciprocate Rank (MRR) to measure performance. Evaluation of *WriteAhead* showed a MMR rate of .30 and a recall rate of 24%. The Top 1, 2, 3 recall rates are 31%, 35%, and 38% respectively

5 Demo script

In this demo, we will present a new writing assistance system, *WriteAhead*, which makes it easy to obtain writing tips as you type away. *WriteAhead* does two things really well.

First, it examines the unfinished sentence you just typed in and then automatically gives you tips in the form of grammar patterns (accompanied with examples similar to those found in a good dictionary) for continuing your sentence.

Second, WriteAhead automatically ranks suggestions relevant to your writing, so you spend less time looking at tips, and focus more on writing your text.

You might type in *The paper present method* and you are not sure about how to continue. You will instantly receive tips on grammar as well as content as shown in Figure 1. At a quick glance, you might find a relevant pattern, *method for doing something* with examples such as *This paper presents/describes a method* for generating solutions. That could tip you off as to change the sentence into *This paper presents a method*, thus getting rid of tense and article errors, and help you continue to write something like *method for extracting information*.

Using *WriteAhead* this way, you could at once speed up writing and avoid making common writing errors. This writing and tip-taking process repeats until you finish writing a sentence. And as you start writing a new, the process starts all over again.

Most autocompletion systems such as Google Suggest and TransType offer word-level suggestions, while *WriteAhead* organizes, summarizes, and ranks suggestions, so you can, at a glance, grasp complex linguistic information and make quick decision. Our philosophy is that it is important to show information from general to specific to reduce the cognitive load, so while minding the form, you can still focus on the content of writing.

WriteAhead makes writing easy and fun, and it also turns writing into a continuous learning process by combining problem solving and information seeking together to create a satisfying user experience. *WriteAhead* can even help you beat Writers Block. *WriteAhead* can be accessed at `http://writeahead.nlpweb.org/`.

6 Conclusion

Many avenues exist for future research and improvement of *WriteAhead*. For example, corpora for different language levels, genres (e.g., emails, news) could be used to make the suggestions more relevant to users with diverse proficiency levels and interests. NLP, IR, and machine learning techniques could be used to provide more relevant ranking, to pin-point grammatical errors, or to generate finer-grained semantic patterns (e.g., **assist someone in something** or **attend activity/institution**) Additionally, an interesting direction is identifying grammar patterns using a CRF sequence labeller.

In summary, in an attempt to assist learner writers, we have proposed a method for providing writing suggestion as a user is typewriting. The method involves extracting, retrieving, and ranking grammar patterns and examples. We have implemented and evaluated the proposed method as applied to a scholarly corpus with promising results.

References

Casacuberta, Francisco, et al. "Human interaction for high-quality machine translation." Communications of the ACM 52.10 (2009): 135-138.

Dagneaux, Estelle, Sharon Denness, and Sylviane Granger. "Computer-aided error analysis." System 26.2 (1998): 163-174.

Flowerdew, John. "Problems in writing for scholarly publication in English: The case of Hong Kong." Journal of Second Language Writing 8.3 (1999): 243-264.

Ferris, Dana, and J. S. Hedgcock. "Teacher response to student writing: Issues in oral and written feedback." Teaching ESL composition: Purpose, process and practice (2005): 184-222.

Graddol, David. "The future of English?: A guide to forecasting the popularity of the English language in the 21st century." (1997).

Granger, Sylviane, and Paul Rayson. Automatic profiling of learner texts." Learner English on computer (1998): 119-131.

Granger, Sylviane, and Stephanie Tyson. "Connector usage in the English essay writing of native and non-native EFL speakers of English." World Englishes 15.1 (1996): 17-27.

Golding, Andrew R., and Yves Schabes. "Combining trigram-based and feature-based methods for context-sensitive spelling correction." Proceedings of the 34th annual meeting on Association for Computational Linguistics. Association for Computational Linguistics, 1996.

Gamon, Michael. "High-order sequence modeling for language learner error detection." Proceedings of the 6th Workshop on Innovative Use of NLP for Building Educational Applications. Association for Computational Linguistics, 2011.

Hunston, Susan, and Gill Francis. Pattern grammar: A corpus-driven approach to the lexical grammar of English. Amsterdam: John Benjamins, 2000.

Leacock, Claudia, et al. "Automated grammatical error detection for language learners." Synthesis lectures on human language technologies 3.1 (2010): 1-134.

Milton, John, and Vivying SY Cheng. "A toolkit to assist L2 learners become independent writers." Proceedings of the NAACL HLT 2010 Workshop on Computational Linguistics and Writing: Writing Processes and Authoring Aids. Association for Computational Linguistics, 2010.

Mason, Oliver, and Susan Hunston. "The automatic recognition of verb patterns: A feasibility study." International journal of corpus linguistics 9.2 (2004): 253-270.

Mikolov, Tomas, et al. "Distributed representations of words and phrases and their compositionality." Advances in Neural Information Processing Systems. 2013.

Sun, Guihua, et al. "Detecting erroneous sentences using automatically mined sequential patterns." Annual Meeting-Association for Computational Linguistics. Vol. 45. No. 1. 2007.

Truscott, John. "The case against grammar correction in L2 writing classes." Language learning 46.2 (1996): 327-369.

Tsuruoka, Yoshimasa, and Jun'ichi Tsujii. "Chunk parsing revisited." Proceedings of the Ninth International Workshop on Parsing Technology. Association for Computational Linguistics, 2005.

Verberne, Suzan. "Context-sensitive spell checking based on word trigram probabilities." Unpublished masters thesis, University of Nijmegen (2002).

Sinclair J. (1991) Corpus, Concordance, Collocation. Oxford University Press, Hong Kong.

P. Langlais, G. Foster, and G. Lapalme. 2000. TransType: a computer-aided translation typing system. In Workshop on Embedded Machine Translation Systems.

Caragea, Cornelia, et al. "CiteSeer x: A Scholarly Big Dataset." Advances in Information Retrieval. Springer International Publishing, 2014. 311-322.

NiuParser: A Chinese Syntactic and Semantic Parsing Toolkit

Jingbo Zhu Muhua Zhu * Qiang Wang Tong Xiao

Natural Language Processing Lab.
Northeastern University

zhujingbo@mail.neu.edu.cn zhumuhua@gmail.com
wangqiangneu@gmail.com xiaotong@mail.neu.edu.cn

Abstract

We present a new toolkit - NiuParser - for Chinese syntactic and semantic analysis. It can handle a wide range of Natural Language Processing (NLP) tasks in Chinese, including word segmentation, part-of-speech tagging, named entity recognition, chunking, constituent parsing, dependency parsing, and semantic role labeling. The NiuParser system runs fast and shows state-of-the-art performance on several benchmarks. Moreover, it is very easy to use for both research and industrial purposes. Advanced features include the Software Development Kit (SDK) interfaces and a multi-thread implementation for system speed-up.

1 Introduction

Chinese has been one of the most popular world languages for years. Due to its complexity and diverse underlying structures, processing this language is a challenging issue and has been clearly an important part of Natural Language Processing (NLP). Many tasks are proposed to analyze and understand Chinese, ranging from word segmentation to syntactic and/or semantic parsing, which can benefit a wide range of natural language applications. To date, several systems have been developed for Chinese word segmentation, part-of-speech tagging and syntactic parsing (examples include Stanford CoreNLP[1], FudanNLP[2], LTP[3] and etc.) though some of them are not optimized for Chinese.

In this paper we present a new toolkit for Chinese syntactic and semantic analysis (call it *NiuParser*[4]). Unlike previous systems, the NiuParser toolkit can handle most of Chinese parsing-related tasks, including word segmentation, part-of-speech tagging, named entity recognition, chunking, constituent parsing, dependency parsing, and semantic role labeling. To the best of our knowledge we are the first to report that all seven of these functions are supported in a single NLP package.

All subsystems in NiuParser are based on statistical models and are learned automatically from data. Also, we optimize these systems for Chinese in several ways, including handcrafted rules used in pre/post-processing, heuristics used in various algorithms, and a number of tuned features. The systems are implemented with C++ and run fast. On several benchmarks, we demonstrate state-of-the-art performance in both accuracy/F1 score and speed.

In addition, NiuParser can be fit into large-scale tasks which are common in both research-oriented experiments and industrial applications. Several useful utilities are distributed with NiuParser, such as the Software Development Kit (SDK) interfaces and a multi-thread implementation for system speed-up.

The rest of the demonstration is organized as follows. Section 2 describes the implementation details of each subsystem, including statistical approaches and some enhancements with handcrafted rules and dictionaries. Section 3 represents the ways to use the toolkit. We also show the performance of the system in Section 4 and finally we conclude the demonstration and point out the future work of NiuParser in Section 5.

* This work was done during his Ph.D. study in Northeastern University.

[1] http://nlp.stanford.edu/software/corenlp.shtml

[2] http://fudannlp.googlecode.com

[3] http://www.ltp-cloud.com/intro/en/

[4] http://www.niuparser.com/index.en.html

Proceedings of ACL-IJCNLP 2015 System Demonstrations, pages 145–150,
Beijing, China, July 26-31, 2015.

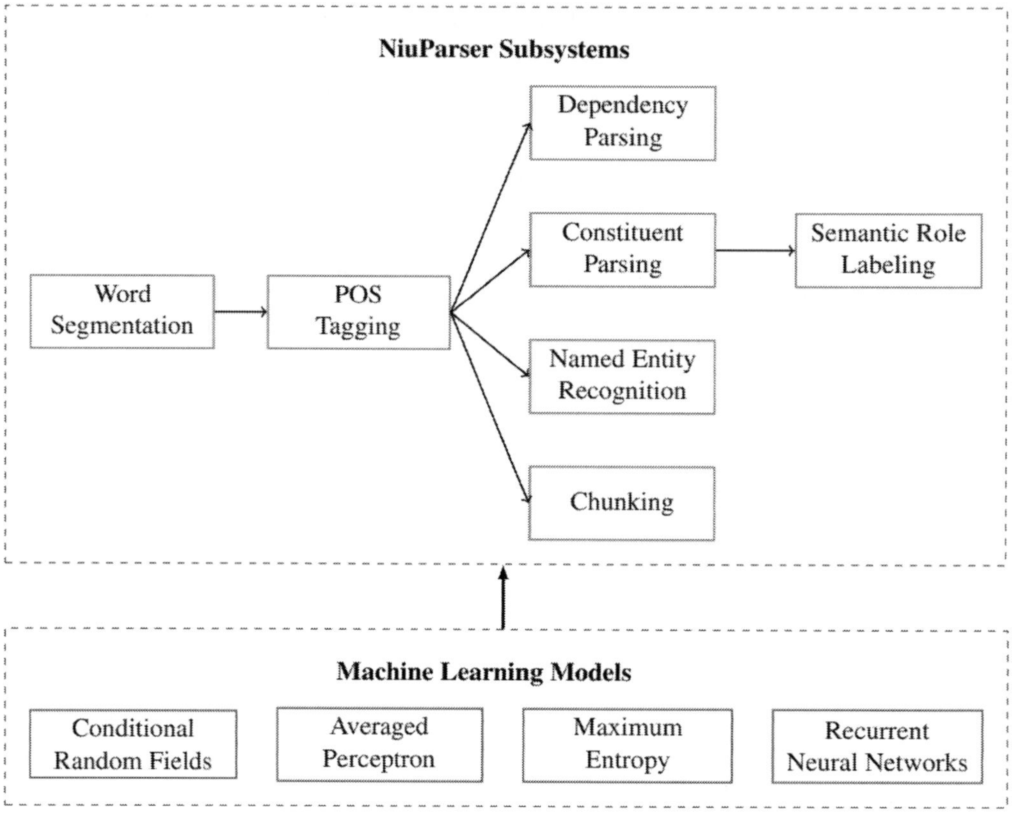

Figure 1: The system architecture of NiuParser.

2 The NiuParser System

2.1 What is NiuParser

The NiuParser system is a sentence-level syntactic and semantic parsing toolkit developed by Natural Language Processing Laboratory in Northeastern University of China. The system is designed specifically to process the Chinese language. Subsystems of NiuParser include word segmentation, POS tagging, named entity recognition, shallow syntactic parsing (chunking), constituent parsing, dependency parsing, and constituent parse-based semantic role labeling. Figure 1 shows the architecture of the NiuParser system. As we can see from the figure, subsystems in NiuParser are organized in a pipeline structure. A given sentence is first segmented into a word sequence, each word in which is assigned a POS tag by the POS tagging subsystem. Based on the POS tagging result, we can choose to do named entity recognition or syntactic parsing. Finally, shallow semantic structures are generated by semantic role labeling on the base of constituent parsing.

2.2 Statistical Approaches to Subsystems

2.2.1 Sequence Labeling

The subsystems of word segmentation, POS tagging, named entity recognition, and chunking in NiuParser are based on statistical sequence labeling models. Specifically, we adopt linear-chain Conditional Random Fields (CRF) (Lafferty et al., 2001) as the method for sequence labeling. Given an input sample $X = x_1, x_2, \ldots, x_L$ and its corresponding sequence $Y = y_1, y_2, \ldots, y_L$, Conditional Random Fields are defined as follows.

$$P_w(Y|X) = \frac{1}{Z_w(X)} exp(W^T \Phi(X, Y)) \qquad (1)$$

where $Z_w(X)$ denotes the normalization constant and $\Phi(X, Y)$ are manually defined feature functions. In the testing phase, the Viterbi algorithm is applied to find an optimal label sequence or a k-best list for a testing instance.

With Conditional Random Fields, **Chinese word segmentation** is regarded as a character-based sequence labeling problem. We adopt the scheme of six tags (*B, B2, B3, I, E, O*) to translate between a segmented sentence and its corresponding label sequence (Zhao et al., 2005). Specifically, *B, B2, B3* denotes the first, the second, and the third character in a word, respectively. *I* means that the character is inside in a word, and *E* means that the character is at the end of a word. Finally, *O* denotes a single-character word. Features include the characters (and their combinations) in a sliding window.

As mentioned above, the NiuParser system utilizes the pipeline method to integrate all the subsystems. That is, **POS tagging**, **named entity recognition**, and **chunking** take the output of the preceding subsystem as input. For POS tagging, we obtain training data from Penn Chinese Treebank (CTB) (Xue et al., 2005), which has 32 POS tags. The named entity recognition subsystem takes the guideline of OntoNotes (Pradhan et al., 2007). Named entities annotated in OntoNotes have 18 entity types in total, including *person names*, *organization names*, and *events*, etc. Table 1 presents a complete list of the entity types in OntoNotes. Chunking uses training data derived from constituent parse trees in CTB. In NiuParser, we consider phrase types including *noun phrase (NP)*, *verbal phrase (VP)*, *quantifier phrase (QP)*, *prepositional phrase (PP)*, *adjective phrase (ADJP)*, and *classifier phrase (CLP)*, etc. Features for the three subsystems are words (and their combinations) in a sliding window. Prefix and suffix of words are also used as features for better system generalization.

2.2.2 Transition-based Parsing

Syntactic parsers can be grouped into two categories according to decoding algorithms: dynamic programming-based and transition-based. For the purpose of efficiency, we implement the constituent and two versions of dependency parsers in the NiuParser system with transition-based methods (Zhu et al., 2013; Zhang and Nivre, 2011; Chen and Manning, 2014). Specifically, parsers are variants of shift-reduce parsers, which start from an initial state and reach a final state by performing an action in each stage transition. Figure 2 and Figure 3 present an example parse of the two parsers, respectively.

One version of the dependency parsers follows the work in (Chen and Manning, 2014), regarding the state transition process as a sequence of classification decisions. In each transition, a best action is chosen by a Neural Network classifier. The other parses (the constituent parser and the other version of dependency parser) utilize exactly the same framework, where both training and decoding phases are formalized as a beam search process. In the decoding phase, the candidate parse with the highest score in the beam will be picked as the parsing result once the beam search process terminates. In the training phase, a beam search-based global online training method is adopted. The training process iterates through the whole training data by decoding the sentences sequently. On each sentence, parameters will be updated immediately once the gold parse is pruned off the beam. In the NiuParser system, we utilize averaged perceptron to learn parameters.

2.2.3 Two-Stage Classification

Researchers in semantic role labeling have explored diverse syntactic structures (chunks, constituent parses, and dependency parses) as input. The semantic role labeling subsystem in NiuParser considers constituent parse trees as input. The subsystem can recognize constituents in a parse tree as arguments with respect to a specified predicate (See Figure 4). Here, semantic role labeling is formalized as a two-stage classification problem. The first stage (called *identification*) conducts a binary classification to decide whether a constituent in a parse tree is an argument. After the first stage, a set of constituents is fed to the second stage (called *classification*) classifier which is a multi-class classifier, used for assigning each argument an appropriate semantic label.

The statistical model used in the semantic role labeling subsystem is Maximum Entropy (Berger et al., 1996), which provides classification decisions with corresponding probabilities. With such probabilities, the identification stage applies the algorithm of enforcing non-overlapping arguments (Jiang and Ng, 2006) to maximize the log-probability of the entire labeled parse tree. In the classification stage, the classifier assigns labels to arguments independently.

2.3 Improvements and Advanced Features

2.3.1 Word Segmentation

In Chinese sentences, words like dates, email addresses, and web page URLs are pervasive but training data for statistical methods is limited in size to cover enough such words. A purely statistical approach often fails to recognize such words once the words do not appear in the training

PERSON	peopel, including fictional	NORP	nationalities or religious or political groups
FACILITY	building, airports, highways, etc.	ORGANIZATION	companies, agencies, etc.
GPE	countries, cities, states	LOCATION	non-GPE, mountain ranges, bodies of water
PRODUCT	vehicles, weapons, foods, etc.	EVENT	named hurricanes, battles, wars, sports events
WORD OF ART	titles or books, songs, etc.	LAW	named documents made into laws
LANGUAGE	named language	DATE	absolute or relative dates or periods
TIME	times smaller than a day	PERCENT	percentage *including ”%”
MONEY	monetary values, including unit	QUANTITY	measurements, as of weight or distances
ORDINAL	”first”, ”second”	CARDINAL	numerals that do not fall under another type

Table 1: Named entity types in OntoNotes

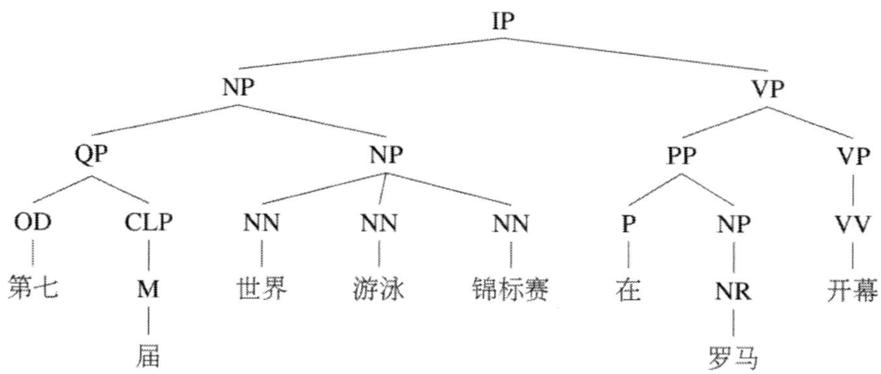

Figure 2: Example of constituent parsing in NiuParser.

data. Fortunately, such words generally have some regular patterns and can be recognized by regular expressions. The NiuParser system provides a regular expression engine to do preprocessing for the CRF-based segmenter.

Post-processing: Besides the word types handled in the preprocessing step, a CRF-based segmenter has a low accuracy in recognizing out-of-vocabulary words. The NiuParser system implements a double-array trie for post-processing. Users can add entries (each entry is a string of characters and its corresponding segments) into a dictionary. String of characters in the dictionary will be assured to be segmented according to its corresponding segments.

2.3.2 Named Entity Recognition

In academics, named entity recognition often suffers from limited training data. In contrast, practitioners generally seek to mine a large-vocabulary entity dictionary from the Web, and then use the entity dictionary to recognize entities as a maximum matching problem. This approach, however, fails to resolve ambiguities. The improvement here is to combine dictionary-based methods and statistical methods.

We first use the forward maximum matching approach to recognize entities in an input sentence by using an entity dictionary. The recognition result is then sent to a CRF-based recognizer. Here each word is assigned a label (start of an entity, inside an entity, or end of an entity) according to the maximum matching result. The labels are used as additional features in the CRF-based recognizer. This approach is similar to the stacking method.

2.3.3 System Speed-up

In addition to fast algorithms (e.g., shift-reduce parsing), NiuParser also supports a multithreading mode to make full advantage of computers with more than one CPU or core. In general, the speed can be improved when multiple threads are involved. However, it does not run faster when too many threads are used (e.g., run with more than 8 threads) due to the increased cost of scheduling.

2.4 Usage

The NiuParser system supports three ways to use the functionalities in the toolkit.

First, users can use the toolkit as an executable file in the command lines. Model files and configuration of the system are specified in a configuration file. Input-output files and the functionality to

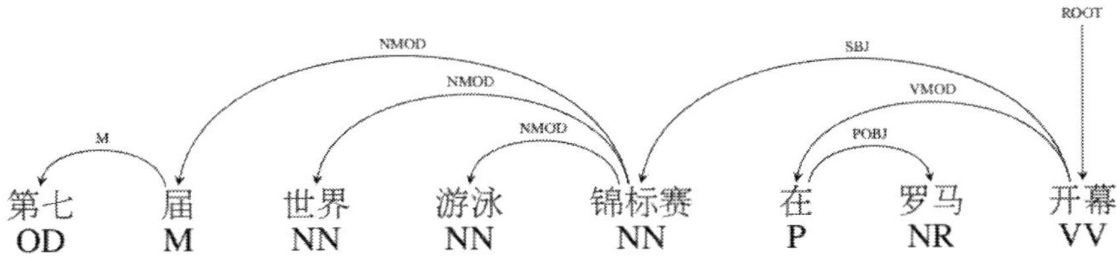

Figure 3: Example of dependency parsing in NiuParser.

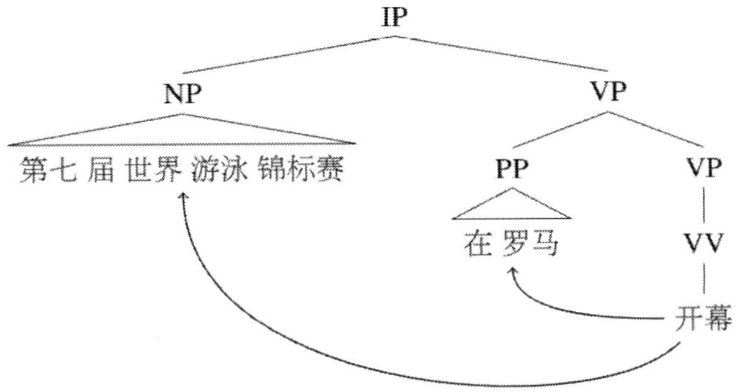

Figure 4: Example of semantic role labeling in NiuParser.

be used are specified as command line arguments.

Second, all the functionalities in NiuParser can be integrated into users' own applications or business process by using the toolkit's SDK interfaces. The SDK supports both Windows and Linux platforms. In contrast to web services, SDK is more suitable to be deployed in the server side.

Third, a demo web page is provided for users to view the analysis results intuitively.[5] All the analysis results are presented graphically.

3 Experiments

We ran our system on several benchmarks. Specifically, we trained and tested word segmentation, POS tagging, chunking, and constituent parsing on CTB5.1: articles 001-270 and 440-1151 were used for training and articles 271-300 were used for testing. The performance of named entity recognition was reported on OntoNotes, where 49,011 sentences were used for training and 1,340 sentences were used for testing. For semantic role labeling, we adopted the same data set and splitting as in (Xue, 2008). Finally, the data set and splitting in (Zhang and Clark, 2011) were used to evaluate the performance of dependency parsing.

All results were reported on a machine with a 800MHz CPU and 4GB memory. See Table 2 for results of acurracy/F1 scores, memory use, model sizes and speed. Note that we evaluated the speed with a single thread and the accuracies were achieved with statistical models only.

From the results we can see that most of the subsystems achieve state-of-the-art performance, (the chunking subsystem is an exception, whose accuracy still have some room left for further improvements.). In addition, the memory use of dependency parsing is extremely heavy. We will optimize the implementation of dependency parsing in our future work.

4 Conclusions and Future Work

We have presented the NiuParser Chinese syntactic and semantic analysis toolkit. It can handle several parsing tasks for Chinese, including word segmentation, part-of-speech tagging, named entity recognition, chunking, constituent parsing, dependency parsing, and constituent parser-based semantic role labeling. The NiuParser system is fast and shows state-of-the-art performance on several benchmarks. Moreover, it supports several advanced features, such as the Software Development Kit (SDK) interfaces and the multi-thread implementation for system speed-up.

In our future work, we will add more function-

[5] http://demo.niuparser.com/index.en.html

Task	Acurrary/F1	Memory Used	Model Size	Speed[⋆]
word segmentation	97.3%	68M	57M	45K
POS tagging	93.5%	93M	185M	38.8K
named entity recognition	88.1%	687M	708M	1.87K
chunking	81.1%	71.9MG	90M	18.8K
constituent parsing	83.2%	0.98G	243M	583.3
dependency parsing[†]	82.4%	2.9G	116M	402.4
dependency parsing[‡]	82.1%	597M	22M	13.5K
semantic role labeling	68.4%	1.2M/0.9M	30M	494*

Table 2: Evaluation of NiuParser on various tasks. [†]beam search-based global training method. [‡]classification-based method with Neural Networks. [⋆]characters per second. * predicates per second.

alities to NiuParser. First of all, we will integrate a new subsystem which conducts dependency-based semantic role labeling. In addition, we will develop a faster constituent parsers by using Recurrent Neural Network. According to the previous work (Chen and Manning, 2014) (and its clone in the NiuParser system), this method reduces the cost of feature extraction and thus shows the advantage in speed. We expect the same approach can be adapted to constituent parsing.

Acknowledges

This work was supported in part by the National Science Foundation of China (Grants 61272376, 61300097, and 61432013).

References

Adam L. Berger, Stephen A. Della Pietra, and Vincent J. Dealla Pietra. 1996. A maximum entropy approach to natural language processing. *Computational Linguics*, 22:39–71.

Danqi Chen and Christopher D. Manning. 2014. A fast and accurate dependency parser using neural networks. *Proc. of EMNLP 2014*, pages 740–750.

Zheng Ping Jiang and Hwee Tou Ng. 2006. Semantic role labeling of nombank: a maximum entropy approach. *Proc. of EMNLP 2006*, pages 138–145.

John D. Lafferty, Andrew McCallum, and Fernando C. N. Pereira. 2001. Conditional random fields: Probabilistic models for segmenting and labeling sequence data. *Proc. of ICML 2001*.

Sameer S. Pradhan, Hovy Eduard, Mitch Marcus, Martha Palmer, Lance Ramshaw, and Ralph Weischedel. 2007. Ontonotes: A unified relational semantic representation. *Proc. of ICSC 2007*.

Nianwen Xue, Fei Xia, Chiou Fu-Dong, and Palmer Martha. 2005. The penn chinese treebank: Phrase structure annotation of a large corpus. *Natural Language Engineering*, 11:207–238.

Nianwen Xue. 2008. Labeling chinese predicates with semantic roles. *Computational Linguistics*, 32:225–255.

Yue Zhang and Stephen Clark. 2011. Syntactic processing using the generalized perceptron and beam search. *Computational Linguistics*, 37:105–151.

Yue Zhang and Joakim Nivre. 2011. Transition-based dependency parsing with rich non-local features. *Proc. of ACL 2011*, pages 188–193.

Hai. Zhao, Chang-Ning Huang, and Mu Li. 2005. An improved chinese word segmentation system with conditional randome fileds. *Proc. of SIGHAN 2006*, pages 162–165.

Muhua Zhu, Yue Zhang, Wenliang Chen, Min Zhang, and Jingbo Zhu. 2013. A fast and accurate constituent parsing. *Proc. of ACL 2013*.

Author Index

Association for Computational Linguistics
209 N. Eighth Street
Stroudsburg, Pennsylvania 18360

ISBN 978-1-5108-0847-8
9 781510 808478